BOOKS BY ELMER A. LESLIE

THE PROPHETS TELL THEIR OWN STORY
OLD TESTAMENT RELIGION
THE COMRADESHIP HOUR
ACQUAINTING YOUTH WITH CHRIST

The Prophets Tell Their Own Story

ELMER A. LESLIE

Professor of Hebrew and Old Testament Literature
in Boston University School of Theology

THE ABINGDON PRESS

NEW YORK   CINCINNATI   CHICAGO

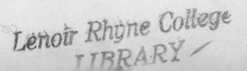

LESLIE
THE PROPHETS TELL THEIR OWN STORY

Copyright, 1939, by
ELMER A. LESLIE

Printed in the United States of America

CONTENTS

PREFACE

*T*HIS volume had its inception at a meeting of the Boston Clerical Club, November 17, 1932. The author had been assigned the subject, "The Life and Message of Jeremiah," to be presented in a twenty-five minute paper. It occurred to him to make the experiment of letting Jeremiah tell his own story. The response to this experiment was genuinely appreciative. During the discussion period one of the members made the suggestion that a series of "prophetic autobiographies" similarly treated would meet a great need on the part of ministers and Bible students in general. The author then determined to carry out the suggestion. He began to share his work in its early stages as it developed with his students in his course in Old Testament Prophets. Their immediate response encouraged him to feel the value of the venture.

In this volume he has limited himself to the prophets from Amos to Jeremiah, as the pre-exilic prophets lend themselves to biographical treatment to a greater degree than is the case with the post-exilic sections of prophecy. And he shares the judgment of the late Professor John Skinner that the prophetic religion of the Old Testament reaches its climax in Jeremiah.

The author has tried to make each of the eight chapters complete in itself. This has necessitated some slight repetition in certain instances where particular prophets date from approximately the same period. In each case a connected account of the material gleaned from the historical books of the Old Testament, from the Assyrian, Babylonian, and Egyptian records, from Palestinian and Syrian archaeology, and from the pertinent prophetic book has been woven together and presented in the first person. This, he believes, is justified, for the prophets knew the history and politics of their own times with remarkable fullness. He has tried to be true to the historical situation and background as he understands it and has refrained from modernizing. His aim has been to let each prophet speak largely in the words of his own book, and to arrive at the exact meaning he had for his times. To present a living picture of each prophet in his day, dealing with the social, political, religious, and personal issues as they developed, and always as the interpreter of Yahweh's mind and will—this has been his sole purpose.

He has made his own translations of the prophetic material, using as the basis the best critical edition of the Hebrew text available, the third edition of R. Kittel's *Biblia Hebraica*. He has gratefully availed himself discriminatingly of the judgment of the textual authorities concentrated in the critical notes which embody the sifted results of recent textual and interpretive study. He has confined himself in each particular prophetic book to those passages which at the bar of a judicious criticism may be justified as authentic utterances of the prophet's soul. A brief chronological table has been appended which serves as a guide to the history of the times. Here he has followed the findings of the most thoroughgoing recent treatment of Old Testament chronology, that of Joachim Begrich. A selected bibliography, arranged according to the individual prophetic books dealt with, and including only such works as have proved helpful in the preparation of this volume, is presented for the sake of students who wish to pursue these studies further and may welcome such guidance.

The author makes grateful acknowledgment to Miss Gertrude M. Allison, librarian of the Boston University School of Theology, for her co-operation in putting the resources of our own library at his disposal. And he is particularly indebted to the authorities of Widener Library of Harvard University and the Andover-Harvard Library, without whose richly furnished resources these studies could scarcely have been undertaken.

He feels deeply grateful also to his assistant and typist, the Rev. Otis R. Fischer, A.M., S.T.B., Ph.D., who has read the manuscript with critical thoroughness and whose many suggestions have greatly strengthened the work. And he is greatly indebted to the hearty co-operation of his wife, for her many helpful suggestions and for her unfailing encouragement.

The book is dedicated to one whose creative teaching first introduced the author to the prophets, and whose generous friendship has been and remains one of life's most inspiring privileges.

The author is deeply convinced of the living power of prophetic thought for our own times. Yet the Old Testament prophets crucially need to be brought near the non-technical reader, for the prophetic books, which bear the deepest thought of Israel, abound in difficulties. This volume is no substitute for patient, detailed study of each prophetic book. But it offers a living guide through the maze of prophetic thought and recovers something of that rich humanity which underlies prophetic experience. It is sent out in the hope that for ministers, college and theological students, young people, and Bible students generally it may make the prophets live in their individuality and greatness and thus open the way for them to influence our times afresh with their peculiarly pertinent religious message.

CHAPTER I
AMOS OF TEKOA

I WAS born at Tekoa, a sparsely inhabited town on the edge of the wilderness of Judah. From my home six miles away to the north I can see the town of Bethlehem, from among whose shepherds King David had come. Sometimes, on one of a range of limestone hills, I can just barely make out the dim gray outlines of the towers of Jerusalem. To the west, far off in the distance I can see the rolling hills yet higher than my home, which cut off the view of western Judah. In the spring and early summer I can always see the black bedouin tents of the near-by nomads whom I have come to know very well. The very name of my town means "to pitch a tent" and indicates that it was founded by nomads. To the south likewise rolling hills bar any further sight of Judah.

All my life I have loved this rugged hill country. These heights, a thousand yards above the sea level, haunt me with their stern grandeur, and in the face of the wide horizons thus open before me I have shepherded my flocks and passed my days. I have grown to feel a kinship of spirit with the rugged wilds that face me as I look toward the east. There, only eighteen miles away, I can see the deep-blue waters of the Dead Sea lying over a thousand yards below me, a welcome contrast to the waste land—"desolation" my people call it—formed by the ragged crests and shuddering flanks which lie between. The austerity of this rugged country has shaped

13

my very soul. The sternness of this desert wilderness is
in my blood.

I was a shepherd, as were my nomadic ancestors, and
raised a breed of sheep small and stunted in stature,
famous for the fineness of their wool. I was likewise a
herdsman of larger cattle. And, as the shepherds between Judaea and the desert have always done, I tended
a few sycamore trees down below on the oases of the coast
of the Dead Sea. I would nip the small watery figs to
hasten their ripening and fit them for eating.

The Judaean markets for wool and figs were in
Hebron, Beer-sheba, Bethlehem, and Jerusalem. But
the greater Hebrew centers for trade were in the kingdom
of Israel—at Bethel, just over the boundary of Judah, at
Gilgal, seven miles to the north, and, yet twenty miles
further off, at Samaria, the capital city of the Northern
Kingdom. To all of these markets I have often gone, and
occasionally I have even been in Damascus. But the
luxury and high life of these cities appall and irritate
me. Whenever I visit them, I long for the plainness of
Tekoa with its quiet and its freedom from sham.

In my early days I shared the religious views held generally by the rank and file of my people. I knew the
stories of the great Israelite ancestor, Jacob, and am accustomed to call the people of Israel after his name.
When I was still following the flock, I constantly brooded
over the living conditions of my people. And when I
went upon journeys to Jerusalem, Beer-sheba, Gilgal,
Samaria, and Bethel, I was never deceived by the political pomp or by the seeming brilliancy of Hebrew society.
For I could see that the leadership of the Hebrew people,
beneath that surface display, was rotten at the heart.

Twice in strange, deeply moving inner experiences I was led to feel the displeasure of Yahweh against his people.

One spring day after the king's tax of herbage for his horses had been mowed off the fields, and the aftermath, the first green herbage of the latter growth, the people's crop, was beginning to appear, I had the first such experience. I saw in a vision a destructive invasion of locusts yet more terrible than I had ever witnessed in conscious experience, although I knew all too well the blight such pests periodically bring to my country. As I watched in tense anxiety, I felt that Yahweh had sent them as a punishment. But when the locusts appeared to be just at the point of utterly wiping out the growing crop, I cried passionately unto Yahweh:

> O Lord Yahweh, pray forgive,
> How can Jacob stand (it)?
> For he is small.[1]

And Yahweh heeded my intercession, and revoked his destructive purpose.

> It shall not be, he said (7. 1-3).

In the summer of the same year I experienced a second such vision. Our land had been suffering from a terrible drought. The burning heat of the sun had been so fierce that it had dried up the springs of the ground and the very life of crops, animals, and men was threatened. While anxiously brooding over all this I was again seized by an overwhelming experience. I saw in a vision a terrible fire licking up as in awful thirst the underground fountains. Just when it was at the point of turning in its unearthly fury to consume the corn harvest, I cried out in yet greater alarm to Him whose destructive agent it was:

> O Lord Yahweh, pray cease,
> How can Jacob stand (it)?
> For he is small.

And again he relented.

> It also shall not be, he said (7. 4-6).

I was not yet prepared at that time for the visions of unrelieved darkness that were yet to shadow my soul. In those days I felt that Yahweh would not permit Israel to be destroyed. Uniquely he had known and cared for his people. I was sure he could still be appealed to and his mercy implored for them. But the terror of those two visions had left its abiding deposit in my heart, as I was soon to realize.

For one day considerably later I had another similar experience. I now see that with it the distinctly prophetic phase of my life began. It was an experience which forever set me in opposition to the nationalistic presumption which then characterized the religion of my people. I saw lying on a wall an ordinary plummet left there by a builder who had been using it as a guide to correct construction. Suddenly this familiar sight achieved astonishing significance. I felt the majestic presence of Yahweh with a plumbline in his hand and he was causing me to see in that ordinary instrument a solemn meaning for Israel. A shadow came over my spirit which has never left it. "The Lord was also constructing something," that plummet seemed to tell me. And Yahweh said,

16

Behold, I am placing a plummet
In the midst of my people Israel;
I will not yet again forgive him;
But the High Places of Jacob shall be devastated,
And the sanctuaries of Israel shall be desolated;
And I will rise up against the House of Jeroboam
    with a sword (7. 7-9).

Yahweh with his plummet was laying plans for a destruction of Israel, and it would take place while the reigning dynasty was still in power. This awful sight marked the turning point in my life.

It was one autumn day when an experience of similar solemnizing import came to me. I was looking at a basket of summer fruit, a joyous sight to one who pruned the sycamores. My people call such a *qāyiç*. But while I was gazing upon this *qāyiç*, there came to my mind with awful vividness a word of similar sound but of contrasted meaning, *qēç*, signifying "end," and I was indubitably conscious that Yahweh was saying to me, even as my eyes rested on the *qāyiç*,

There has come
The *end* to my people Israel;
I will not again forgive him.
And the songs of the temple shall become wailings
    in that day, saith the Lord Yahweh:
The corpses shall be many;
In every place I will cast you forth (8. 1-3).

I had now begun to see how, in these moving experiences, Yahweh was drawing me away from the shallow religious confidence popularly held, in his protection of his people. No longer now could I consistently pray as I had earlier done for Yahweh to desist. Being what he was, his judgment could not be withheld. Now I could

17

see that only inescapable destruction and inexpressible suffering were in store for Israel.

The climax of these psychological experiences came one day when I had gone into the Temple at Jerusalem to worship. There I had a vision of Yahweh. He stood towering over the altar and with his mighty fist struck the capitals of the pillars so that the threshold trembled. Then I heard his voice revealing to me the meaning of the vision, the destruction of all Israel:

> By earthquake[2] I will destroy them all;
> And what is left of them I will slay with the sword:
> No refugee of them will flee,
> And no fugitive will slip through (9. 1).

With such certainty as I had never before felt, I now knew that this divine judgment being wrought out by Yahweh could neither be frustrated nor escaped by any Israelites however confidently they might presume upon his protection. For Yahweh was saying:

> If they dig to Sheol,
> From there my hand will take them;
> Or if they ascend to heaven,
> From there I shall bring them down.
> And if they hide themselves on the peak of Carmel,
> I shall search and take them from there;
> Or if they screen themselves from before my eyes on
> the floor of the sea,
> I shall command the serpent and it will bite them.
> And although they should go into captivity before
> their enemies,
> I would command the sword and it would kill them
> (9. 2-4).

The conviction that Yahweh wanted me to be his prophet only gradually fastened itself upon my soul. These intensely stirring psychological experiences had shaken me to the depths of my inner being. They had given me an utterly new conception of Yahweh which clashed sharply with the existing views held by my countrymen who worshiped him. I now saw that no one nation was Yahweh's exclusive concern. He towered over them all and no territorial limits could be set to his might. He was the absolute transcendent Being. From now on this conception was central to me: I saw all life in Israel, Judah, and the nations from the standpoint of Yahweh's will. Therefore I could be sure of only one thing—the judgment which Yahweh must bring upon all the nations. The necessary consequence of these personal experiences of Yahweh's reality was a soul-shaking conviction that his judgment was coming. In these decisive hours I was irresistibly seized by a new God-consciousness. The culmination came in a terrifying storm. Amid the roar of thunder that seemed to emerge from the dim gray heights of the Temple hill in Jerusalem, I knew that Yahweh was speaking to me:

> Yahweh from Zion is roaring,
> Yes, from Jerusalem he gives forth his voice (1. 2).

I had always loved the crash and the roar of a storm, for such seemed akin to my own nature. But this storm had far deeper significance, for in its din and roar I was conscious of a personal summons from Yahweh:

> Go, prophesy unto my people Israel! (7. 15b.)

I cannot explain this call to be a proclaimer of Yahweh's word. There was nothing of the prophet in my background, and I had felt content to work among my sheep, cattle, and sycamores. Yet that moment I knew that I stood at the parting of the ways, for the experience shook my innermost soul. I can only explain God's seizure of my life by saying,

Yahweh took me from following the flock (7. 15a).

Of one thing I was certain, he had laid his hand upon me, and in spite of my limited background he had commissioned me to be a prophetic spokesman of his will.

All that which I had abominated in the market places and in the temples and shrines of Judaean and Israelite cities now took on deepened meaning. All that I had learned in my journeyings about Syrians, Philistines, Ammonites, and Moabites, the report of whose ruthless barbarities had filled my soul with horror, I now viewed in the light of Yahweh's will.

I first journeyed northward to Samaria, the capital of Judah's brother kingdom, Israel, to fulfill my prophetic commission. Long and earnestly had I brooded over what I should say to Yahweh's people of the Northern Kingdom, and his message lay clear in my mind. But how could I make them heed it? The Israelite nation had felt the thrill of power. It was now the ruling nation between the Nile and the Euphrates. Its vigorous king, Jeroboam II, had then been on the throne twenty-six years.[3] He had just brought the hundred years' war against the Aramaeans of Damascus to a victorious close. He had also dominated Moab and had extended the limits of Israel from Hamath in Syria to the brook of the Arabah, south of the Dead Sea (6. 14). Israel was proud of its proven strength which had recently accomplished the recapture of Lodebar and Karnaim in Transjordan (6. 13). How could I open the eyes of the nation to the tragic fate which awaited it?

I decided to begin where they would gladly listen, with the judgment Yahweh had purposed upon the nations surrounding Israel—Syria, Philistia, Ammon, and Moab.[4] I chose but one typical national sin of each nation, already well known to my hearers, and set it in a solemn poetic framework fashioned after the pattern of nationalistic prophecy. It pointed out the transgression, the consequent unthwartable judgment of Yahweh upon the guilty nation, and the instruments by which such judgment would be executed—war, invasion, exile, and national annihilation.

How they did listen as in solemn words I began my condemnation of their enemies! The oracle against Moab was due to the reckless and vengeful King Mesha, who had outraged the tomb of his old adversary, the king of Edom, burning the corpse and strewing its ashes to the winds, thus arousing to horror our instinctive Hebrew reverence for the dead. The oracle of Yahweh directed against the notoriously cruel Ammonites was due to their unutterable barbarity toward pregnant women of Gilead during their bedouin raids, expeditions which they justified solely on the plea that they needed more land. The oracle against the Philistines concentrated upon Gaza, the chief of the four remaining city centers of the remnant of that once powerful people. Gaza was the Damascus of the south, the natural outpost across the desert from Egypt, and the door of Asia. Aided by Ashdod, Ashkelon, and Ekron, it had become an emporium for an organized slave-raiding traffic, carried on along the old caravan route from Gaza to Petra and Elath in Edom, the victims being the entire population of villages from southern Judah.

21

But it was Syria whom Israel had cause to hate the most, for the nation was still suffering from fresh Syrian wounds. True to the fears of Elisha, Hazael, the ruthless usurper on the throne of Syria, had decimated Gilead and harassed all the Israelites of Transjordan (2 Kings 10. 32f.). His son, Benhadad III, had reduced the fighting forces of Israel which King Jehoahaz, son of Jehu, could muster, to about fifty horsemen, ten chariots, and ten thousand footmen, leaving Israel like the dust from the threshing (2 Kings 13. 7). The Syrians had devastated Northern Israel even as an iron-pronged threshing instrument breaks up the grain on the threshing floor. The capital of Hazael's Syrian kingdom was proud and beautiful Damascus, ancient, well-fortified, and rich. But the Syrian domain embraced also the inhabitants of the fertile "valley of On" which lay between the Lebanons, with Baalbek at its head. It also included the free citizens of Beth Eden,[5] a little kingdom situated on both sides of the Euphrates.

So with the oracle against Damascus I began,

Thus Yahweh says:
Because of three transgressions of Damascus,
Yes, for four, I will not turn it back;
Because they have threshed Gilead with sharp instruments of iron.
But I will send a fire into the house of Hazael,
And it shall devour the palaces of Benhadad.
Yes, I will break the bar of Damascus.
And I will destroy the inhabitant from the valley of On,
And the free citizen from Beth Eden;
And the Syrian people shall go in captivity to Qir
    (1. 3-5).

To Qir, west of the Caspian Sea, whence the Syrians had

entered Canaan, the hand of Yahweh, which had brought
their migration to pass, would forcibly return them, thus
reversing and nullifying it.

These solemn words of judgment upon Israel's most
feared and hated enemy gripped their attention at once.
The old God of Israel still lives! thought they. He will
take vengeance upon our enemies! Fascinated, they
hung upon every word, and as I went on pronouncing
Yahweh's judgment upon the slave-trading Philistines,
the brutal Ammonites, and the ruthless, irreverent Moabites, their enthusiasm for my words grew with leaps and
bounds. Then came my crashing close. I can still see
the sudden, surprised indignation and resentment which
flushed the faces of the proud Israelite leaders as my solemn words continued:

> Because of three transgressions of Israel,
> Yes, for four, I will not turn it back.
> Because they have sold the righteous for silver,
> And the needy for a pair of sandals—
> They who keep trampling upon the head of the weak,
> And thrust aside the way of the humble:
> Garments taken in pledge they stretch out
> Beside every altar.
> Yes, the wine of those fined they drink
> In the house of their God.
> And, a man and his father
> Go in to the same damsel,
> So as to profane my holy name (2. 6, 7a, 8a, 8b, 7b).

As I saw it, Yahweh's judgment upon Israel was based
upon certain root sins.[6] The most universal and basic
sin among the leaders of the nation was that of greed.
The righteous poor, because of debt, were sold into
slavery by the rich and powerful worshipers of Yahweh,
sometimes indeed for a paltry sum, no more than the

cost of a pair of sandals. They imposed upon the peasant tillers of the soil exorbitant taxes of grain. They ruthlessly trampled upon the personalities of the common people who were not powerful enough to defend their rights, harshly oppressing them. Their greed led to another major sin—dishonesty. They gave short weight in commercial transactions and overcharged the dependent needy, deceitfully mixing in refuse with the good wheat which they sold to them. They made a mockery of the courts, accepting bribes and defrauding the poor, loathing the man who exposed their wrongdoing. Another sin of the Israelites was their irreverence. The sacred days as New Moon and Sabbath were to Israelite merchants but irritating interruptions of their scheming commercial transactions. They had the effrontery to spread out beside the altars at the high-places, as a gesture of cultic homage, garments which they had ruthlessly seized from the poor man for security because of his debt. According to law, at sundown these garments were to be restored to the poor whose sole protection they were from the cold of the Palestinian nights (Exodus 22. 26f.). And they piously poured and drank at the sanctuary wine which they had purchased with money received from excessive fines. Most horrible of all to me was the sin of sacred immorality, plain prostitution as I viewed it, whereby, in the name of worship, sexual intercourse was held with sacred harlots. A father and his son might engage in this cultic act with the same harlot! How I abhorred it! What a profanation it was of the character of Yahweh! So with sharp directness I pointed out in detail these reasons for the approaching judgment Yahweh was sending.

Here was indeed a jarring note in the nationalistic religion of the Northern Kingdom, and the Israelite leaders challenged my authority to speak as the representative of Yahweh. It was their attitude that led me to give my defense of appearing before them as a prophet. For of this I was sure. My message to Israel had in it nothing haphazard or accidental. And it was of no merely human impulse. Behind it there was an adequate cause. So in illustrations of cause and effect familiar to all, I gave my defense:

> You see two people walking together:
> You know they have come together for a common
>   purpose.
> You hear a lion roaring in the forest:
> You know he has leaped upon prey.
> You hear the young lion growl:
> You know it has taken something.
> You see a bird fall upon the ground:
> You know a bait has been set for it.
> You see a trap spring up from the ground:
> You know something has been caught.
> You hear a trumpet blown in the gate:
> You know it gives alarm that an enemy is approach-
>   ing.
> You learn of disaster in a city:
> You know you hold Yahweh as its cause (3. 3-7).

I paused for a moment—for he, who, by their own admission, had caused disaster in many a city, was to bring a yet greater one which stood just at the door. Then I came to the climax of my defense:

> The lion has roared;
> Who would not fear!
> The Lord Yahweh has spoken;
> Who would not prophesy! (3. 8.)

Yahweh had spoken to my very soul. I could not keep

silent. My prophetic word to Israel was itself but the
result of a divine cause.

It was not because Israel did not know better that the
nation stood condemned. It was Yahweh's hand that
had brought Israel out of Egypt into Canaan, dispossess-
ing the Amorites. His hand had raised up prophets for
Israel's guidance. The long-haired Nazirites under the
vow of abstinence from the fruit of the vine—nomadic
protestors against the self-indulgent civilization of
Canaan—had been of his provision. But these agents of
Yahweh, the Israelites had humiliated and had throttled
their message (2. 9-12). So in Yahweh's name I pronounced judgment upon Israel:

> Behold, I will make it crack under you,
> Like a threshing instrument crackles (2. 13).

Well did they know that noise—the earthquake! What
war, captivity, and exile was to be in bringing Yahweh's
judgment upon nations generally, earthquake was to be
in bringing his judgment upon Israel, and the Israelites,
even the bravest and fleetest of them, could not
escape it.

They would not believe me. Yahweh knows *us*. Out
of all the families of the earth he cares for *us*. Therefore
he will forgive us all our sins—thus they spoke in their
superficial nationalism. I took the very words out of
their mouths:

> Hear this word which Yahweh has spoken
>   concerning you:
> You only have I known
> Out of all the families of the earth;
> Therefore will I visit upon you
> All your iniquities (3. 1-2).

26

Yahweh's "Therefore" was like a bolt from the blue to them. I saw clearly that his relationship to his people was not by nature but had a moral basis. The closer his relationship had been to Israel, just so much the greater was Israel's moral accountability. Such teaching was new and startling to the Israelites.

To the proud leaders of the Northern Kingdom I suggested in irony that they invite the pagan Assyrians and Egyptians of rank to their great city, to behold the moral collapse of Israel:

> Make proclamation to the castles in Assyria,
> And to the palaces in the land of Egypt.
> Gather upon the mountains of Samaria,
> And see the great commotion in its midst,
> And the oppression within it (3. 9).

But as I saw them, those brilliant palaces of Samaria, the luxurious homes of the first-citizens of Israel, were made possible only by their violence and robbery—deeds that had so dulled their moral sense that now,

> They did not know how to do right (3. 10).

So I uttered against them Yahweh's oracle:

> Therefore, thus the Lord Yahweh says,
> An enemy will surround your land;
> And your strength will be stripped from you,
> And your palaces will be plundered (3. 11).

Since King Ahab's victory over Benhadad II of Damascus, a century ago, it has become fashionable for the rich Israelite merchant, in addition to his house in Samaria, to have a house in the Israelite quarters of Damascus (I Kings 20. 34). One he would occupy during the business season in Samaria, the other when this was over. They were richly furnished with brilliantly carved ivory and ebony trimmings.[7]   But these luxurious houses too were doomed.   So I cried to the rich merchants of the capital:

> You who sit in Samaria on the border of a divan,
> And in Damascus on the bed of a place of rest,
> Hear and bear witness in the house of Jacob,
> (It is an) oracle of the Lord Yahweh of hosts:
> In the day when I punish Israel for his transgressions,
> I will strike the autumn house in addition to the
>   summer house;
> And the houses of ivory shall come to an end,
> And many houses shall perish,
> Oracle of Yahweh (3. 12c, 13-15).

These distinguished citizens of Samaria felt all too secure and self-confident in their capital.   They lived in careless luxury and idleness.   They thought themselves to be the distinguished ones of the first of the nations, to whom the whole Israelite people looked up (6. 1).   Careless of any day of reckoning, and with no deep national concern,

> They lay upon their couches of ivory,
> And sprawled upon their beds,
> Eating the rams from the flock,
> And the fat stall-fed calves;
> They improvise in accord with the lyre;
> They think themselves skillful as was David in song.
> They drink refined wine,
> They anoint themselves with the best of oils;
> But they are not sick (at heart) at the break-up of
>   Joseph.
> At the head of their nation they are,
> And at the head of the captives will they march into
>   exile;
> No longer will the streets of Samaria hear the shouts
>   of their revelry (6. 4-7).

With all the solemnity I could muster I uttered Yahweh's invective against such self-indulgence:

> The Lord Yahweh has sworn by himself:
> I loathe the pride of Jacob,
> And its palaces I hate;
> And I will deliver up the city and its contents (6. 8).

Yet more responsible for the social corruption of Israel than these lords of Samaria were the pleasure-mad ladies. They were the blue bloods of Israelite aristocracy, but they were utterly indifferent to the desperate condition of the poor. Their sleek, well-fed appearance was in awful contrast to the desperate circumstances of the poor and needy. They reminded me of the thoroughbred cows of the rich pasture land of Bashan in north Transjordan I had occasionally watched as they were being driven round and round stolidly breaking up the grain on the threshing floor. But in the light of Yahweh's judgment upon them and their city I pictured these proud, shallow women in the near future, being driven out toward Mount Hermon by their captors, one after the other, like cattle driven out of their "pasture land." Their magnificence did not awe Yahweh's prophet, and what I dubbed them arrested their attention:

> Hear this word, you cows of Bashan,
> Who are in the mountain of Samaria,
> Who are oppressing the poor,
> Who are crushing the needy,
> Who keep saying to their lords,
> "Bring, and let us drink!" (4. 1.)

In accents of solemn prophetic certainty I pictured their captivity, designating Mount Hermon as the first stage

of the exile that was to take them beyond Damascus
(5. 27):

> The Lord Yahweh has sworn by his holiness,
> That days are coming upon you,
> When you shall be taken off with pricks,
> And those left of you with prods.
> And by force you shall be driven out,
> One in front of the other, and you shall be cast out
>   to Hermon (4. 2-3).

I finished the deliverance of Yahweh's judgment upon
Samaria by the most definite, though still veiled, reference that I ever gave to the ruthless nation which was to
execute it:

> For behold, I am raising against you, House of Israel,
> It is an oracle of Yahweh God of hosts; a nation,
> And they shall oppress you
> From where Hamath begins,
> Down to the brook of the Arabah (6. 14).

Then some said: "Even should our *nation* be destroyed, Yahweh would rescue us, his *people. We* would
escape destruction." But my answer was final and to
them hopeless:

> Thus Yahweh says:
> As a shepherd snatches from the mouth of a lion,
> Two legs or a fragment of an ear,
> Just so shall the Israelites be rescued! (3. 12a.)

The religious center of the kingdom of Israel was
Bethel. It was a royal residency, where the chief sanctuary of the nation had been established by Jeroboam I,
the first Israelite king after Israel separated from Judah.
He had given authoritative recognition there to the
worship of Yahweh under the image of the golden bull
(1 Kings 12. 28ff.). In its rootage that worship center

30

reached back into the early Canaanite era, long before
our Hebrew Fathers had entered Canaan. Since the migration there of the Hebrews, that famous sanctuary had
come to be associated with the memories of our Fathers
Abraham and Jacob. In my day it was the king's sanctuary. There the public worship was carried on with
the most elaborate rites of all the sanctuaries in Israel.

It was at the festival of ingathering, held in Israel, by
decree of Jeroboam I, on the 15th day of the eighth month
(1 Kings 12. 32), when throngs of Israelite pilgrims were
in Bethel, that I journeyed there to get the ear of the
nation for Yahweh's message. My words must have
seemed strange to those Israelites, for to all outward appearances their nation was then in its heyday of glory.
Taking my stand in the Bethel sanctuary where all could
hear, I chanted a death lament over the proud nation:

> Fallen, not again to rise;
> Is the virgin of Israel:
> She lies forsaken upon her land;
> None lifting her up (5. 2).

Then I uttered Yahweh's solemn oracle, stating with
certainty, as though it had already taken place, the collapse of the nation:

> For thus says the Lord Yahweh:
> The city which marched out a thousand,
> But a hundred is left,
> And the city which marched out a hundred,
> But ten are left (5. 3).

I kept watching the groups of pilgrims to the sanctuary
at Bethel, as on the first morning after arrival they
brought the prescribed offering, and at the three days'
festival (Exodus 19. 10f.) gave their tithe. Thank offer-

ings of leavened bread such as was used by the Canaanites were customary, and they brought free-will offerings in which, by public announcement, friends of the offerer and the poor were invited to participate. These festivals were occasions of hilarious joy to the participants, as one could easily see. But Yahweh did not enjoy them. For what the Israelites thought was the only way to draw near to him, I saw to be in reality sacrilege, and the Israelite practice of making pilgrimages to one famous sanctuary after another, only increased the offense. In the style of familiar hymns of pilgrimage, but in ironical temper, I cried out to the worshiping pilgrims:

> Come to Bethel, and—rebel!
> To Gilgal and increase transgression,
> Yes, bring on the next morning your sacrifices,
> And on the third day your tithes;
> For so you love (to do), sons of Israel,
> Oracle of the Lord Yahweh (4. 4-5).

Yahweh who had revealed himself to me was an utterly different kind of a Being from what these pilgrims considered him to be. They thought that by such gifts they could bend him to their own desires, coercing his good will on their behalf. But I saw that the thing which should have been of supreme concern was not what they wanted from Yahweh but what *he* wanted from *them*. He wanted them truly and rightly to seek *him*. Their very existence as a people depended upon it.

And Yahweh caused me to see how through the bitter experiences the Israelites had suffered, of hunger and thirst, blight, locust invasions, pestilence, misfortune in war, and destruction by earthquake, he had ever been seeking to get the ear of Israel that he might appeal to the reason of the people and turn the nation in repentance back to himself. I reasoned in his name:

> I gave you teeth untouched by food in all your cities,
> And want of bread in all your places;
>> Yet you did not return unto me, oracle of Yahweh.
>
> And as for me, I withheld from you the rain
> While there were still three months until harvest;
> And two, three cities staggered to one city to drink,
> To drink water.
>> Yet you did not return unto me.
>
> I smote you with blight and with mildew:
> I laid waste your gardens;
> And your vineyards, and your fig trees and your
> olive trees,
> The locusts frequently ate.
>> Yet you did not return unto me, oracle of Yahweh.
>
> I sent among you the Egyptian pestilence:
> I hewed down with the sword the choice youth of
> the nation,
> And I set your camps afire.
>> Yet you did not return unto me, oracle of Yahweh.
>
> I overthrew you like God's overturning of Sodom
> and Gomorrah;
> And you were as a fire brand plucked from the
> burning.
>> Yet you did not return unto me, oracle of Yahweh.
>
> Therefore thus will I do to you, Israel . . . !
> As a consequence of the fact that I shall do thus
> to you,
> Prepare to meet your God, O Israel (4. 6-12).

They thought they were already on good terms with Yahweh. Were they not faithful in the performance of the pilgrimages to the famous sanctuaries? Did they not bring the requisite offerings? So I uttered Yahweh's

oracle with conceptions new to them and which went
directly counter to their deeply entrenched ways of seeking him:

> Thus says Yahweh to the house of Israel:
> Seek me, and live;
> But seek not Bethel,
> And enter not Gilgal,
> And unto Beer-sheba cross not over.
> For Gilgal will surely go to the gallows;
> And Bethel will go to the devil.[8]
> Seek Yahweh, and live;
> Lest he set on fire the house of Joseph,
> And consume, no one extinguishing it, the house
> of Israel (5. 4-6).

They had not heard words like these before. They
presumptuously thought themselves the people of Yahweh. When "the day of Yahweh" came, he would surely
destroy the enemy nations of Israel, but he would just
as surely glorify his people—so they longed for that day.
But I said to them:

> Woe unto you who long for the day of Yahweh!
> Why would you have the day of Yahweh?
> Darkness it is, and not light! (5. 18.)

I knew that this day would bring a judgment upon
Israel that could not be escaped. To try to flee from it
would be like escaping from a lion only to encounter
a bear; like resting one's weary hand upon a wall in a
house only to be bitten by a serpent hiding in a crevice
of it (5. 19). So I concluded:

> Shall not the day of Yahweh be gloom and not light?
> Pitch dark, no brightness in it? (5. 20.)

How the solemnity of these words shadowed my own
soul even while I spoke! Yet it seemed impossible for

me to break through their shallow complacency. "Whatever comes, Yahweh will be with us," so they insisted. But their confidence I could not share in the least. Even though there were within the nation "a repentant and purified few," a remnant I called it, I could not be sure even then that they would be saved. But of one thing I was certain—unless they sought Yahweh by means of ethical living in terms of goodness and justice, there could be no hope whatever for Israel. So in still more specific concepts than I had thus far used in my summons to the nation, I cried:

> Seek good and not evil,
> In order that you may live, that it may be so (that)
> Yahweh God of hosts
> Will be with you, as you have said.
> Hate evil and love good,
> And set up justice in the gates;
> Perhaps he will be gracious, even
> Yahweh of hosts,
> To the remnant of Joseph (5. 14-15).

But the Israelites to whom I was speaking could not think of any other way to seek Yahweh than through the great pilgrimage feasts with their sacred assemblies, and their sacrifices, such as whole-burnt offerings, meal offerings, and peace offerings of fat beasts, in the feasting upon which the worshipers shared. And all this was accompanied by boisterous songs to the music of the harp. It took courage to criticize these practices at the very time and place where they were being performed. But I could only see all this as a tragic mistake and an utter misconception of the true way to seek him. So I felt myself to be Yahweh's very mouthpiece as I said in utter solemnity, weighing every word:

I hate, I reject your feasts,
And delight not in your sacred assemblies.
When you offer up to me burnt offerings,
And your meal offerings, I am not pleased;
And to the peace offerings of your fatlings I pay no
    attention.
Take away from me the sound of your songs;
And the melody of your lyres let me not hear.
But let justice roll along like waters,
And righteousness as a perpetual torrent (5. 21-24).

These worshipers at the Bethel sanctuary had been substituting for such justice and righteousness in daily life impressive religious ceremonials. They were accustomed to carry in dignified processionals images of Sakkuth and Kaiwan, manifestations of the Babylonian vegetation deity, Ninurta (Ninib), the god of spring and of the morning sun. But such images made by their own hands were powerless to help them. Those dignified carriers of them will themselves be carried into exile (5. 27). I saw a sharp contrast and an impassable gulf between the way the Israelites were seeking Yahweh and the only way wherein he could be found. But when I so criticized the time-honored and universally accepted practice of sacrifice as a way to him, I was on dangerous ground, for my words now aroused the ire of Amaziah, the high priest of the Bethel sanctuary, the custodian of the requisite sacrifices. When I had first uttered my message at Bethel which predicted disaster to the reigning dynasty and its greatest king and exile for the entire nation, Amaziah had reported my "seditious" utterances to his king, Jeroboam, at Samaria (7. 10-11). But when I touched upon the sacrificial worship at Bethel over which Amaziah himself was director and sponsor, it cut *him* to

36

the quick. In all his priestly dignity, clothed in the brilliant emblems of his office, his face white with anger, and his voice quivering with suppressed indignation, he confronted me. I can still feel the sneering insult of his manner, and his sense of priestly superiority as he addressed me:

> O seer, flee to the land of Judah,
> And there eat bread, and there play the prophet;
> But at Bethel, do not ever prophesy again,
> For the sanctuary of our king is it, and it is a royal
>   house (7. 12).

But his haughty superiority did not awe me in the least. When he had the presumption to imply that I was a professional prophet, concerned chiefly with getting something to eat by playing the part, I felt impelled to give my solemn defense of my divine call to be a prophet. Said I:

> No prophet was I,
> Nor the son of a prophet was I;
> But a shepherd was I,
> And a ripener of sycamore figs:
> Then Yahweh took me
> From behind the flock,
> And Yahweh said unto me,
> Go, prophesy
> To my people Israel (7. 14-15).

Then, with solemn certainty of the hostile capture of Israel in mind, I delivered unto Amaziah Yahweh's oracle as it concerned him:

> You are saying,
> "Do not prophesy against Israel,
> And do not drip (speech) against the house of Isaac."
> Therefore, thus Yahweh says:
> Your wife shall be a harlot in the city,

And your sons and your daughters
Shall fall by the sword,
And your land shall be divided up by measuring line,
And you, upon land
Unclean, shall die,
For Israel shall certainly go into captivity (7. 16-17).

You can well imagine the bitter anger of Amaziah. The Temple servants at his nod surrounded me, forcibly ejected me, and conducted me across the Israelite border to Judah.

My active ministry is over. From bitter experience I now know how true it is that the Israelites,

Command the prophets, saying
"Prophesy not" (2. 12b).

Yet I would take back no single word of what Yahweh revealed to my soul. If a man is greatly concerned with what happens to him himself, he had better not heed the call to be a prophet in these days.

He that is prudent should keep silent in such a time,
For it is an evil time (5. 13).

Just two years after I had preached Yahweh's message of judgment upon his people, the earthquake I had anticipated as his primary agent of destruction came.[9] We Palestinians will never be able to erase from our minds the awful memories of it, with its moving scenes of terror-stricken people fleeing for safety to the valleys as great fissures opened up in the earth (Zechariah 14. 5). It occurred at the New Year's festival, when King Uzziah had clashed with Azariah and the entrenched priests of the Temple over the question of our monarch's sacrificial prerogatives. Then the leprosy which laid him low first broke out upon him, making it necessary for Jotham, his son, to rule as regent. Many an Israelite then remembered my solemn words which I had preached two full years before. But now that order has reappeared in Palestine and life has become normal again, word has come to me that many Israelites, in their superficial presumption, are thinking that Yahweh's judgment has now come and that they need have no further fear. But Yahweh has made me see that this is but the beginning of calamity to Israel. In the face of the popular tide of unbelief and superficial national self-confidence, I have been conscious of a deep-seated urge to make a permanent record of my message to Israel, of how it grew upon my soul and of the experiences I had in delivering it. It may be that my words will rebuke Yahweh's people in their perilous complacency and yet win Israel to repentance. At heart I am still Yahweh's prophet. So now, here at my home in Tekoa, I am setting down, in Yahweh's name, the stern words he caused me to hear and to speak.

CHAPTER II

HOSEA OF EPHRAIM

ONE day I was aware, in the deepest depths of my soul, that Yahweh was speaking to me his summons to be his prophet.

> To your mouth your trumpet,
> O watchman over the house of Yahweh!
> Because they have transgressed my covenant,
> And against my teaching have they sinned (8. 1).

A watchman over my beloved nation to warn my presumptuous fellow-Israelites against their transgression and rejection of Yahweh's will—so from the first I conceived my prophetic task. This summons which made me his prophet came while the dynasty of Jehu was still the ruling house in Israel.

It was toward the end of King Jeroboam II's reign that in moments of ecstatic seizure (9. 7) I became aware of Yahweh's intimate, yet strange, dealings with me. An irresistible incentive, which I now believe came from him, led me to take as my wife Gomer, "the maiden with the fig cakes,"[1] an Israelite sanctuary maiden, one of the sacred harlots such as had thronged Canaanite High Places as votaries of the goddess Ashtart. Due to the stubborn influence of the fertility cult of Baal upon the religion of my people, the practice of cultic prostitution was still countenanced at Israelite sanctuaries and was indeed just taken for granted by the majority of my people. To us was born our first child, a son.

40

In a state of ecstasy I became aware that Yahweh was speaking:

> Call his name Jezreel (God-sows);
> For yet a little time,
> And I will requite the blood of Jezreel
> From the house of Jehu;
> And I will bring to an end the kingdom of the house
>   of Israel.
> And it shall come to pass in that day,
> That I will shatter the bow of Israel,
> In the valley of Jezreel (1. 2-5).

The Lord thus revealed to me that my child's name was to preach his message of threat to the nation. The very word "Jezreel" would bring vividly to the conscience of Israel and the kings of Jehu's line the ruthless scenes of the bloody horror which had occurred a hundred years before in that beautiful valley, and the awful baptism of blood by which the revolution of Jehu had secured the throne for his dynasty. For on the plain of Jezreel, the eastern sector of Israel's famous battle-plain of Esdraelon, the prowess of my people would come to an ignominious end.

When a second child, a daughter, was born, Yahweh, again in ecstatic revelation, spoke to me:

> Call her name Lo-ruhamah (she-hath-not-been-pitied);
> For no longer will I continue
> To show pity to the house of Israel,
> But I will fully charge (it) to their account[2] (1. 6).

Yahweh would warn Israel through my daughter's name that his pity toward his presumptuous and wayward people was at an end. Punishment was now certain and imminent.

After Lo-ruhamah had been weaned, Gomer again

41

became pregnant, and in due time a third child came, a second son. Once more in ecstasy I heard Yahweh's voice saying:

> Call his name Lo-ammi (not-my-people);
> For you are not my people,
> And I am not your God (1. 8-9).

The name of our third child was to be Yahweh's solemn and climactic message to his nation that he had abandoned them. Their disloyalty had canceled their right any longer to be called his people.

The tone of my preaching to my people during the first years of my prophetic ministry is well expressed in these symbolic names. It was sharp, unrelieved denunciation in the name of Yahweh. Yet in my family life I was happy with Gomer and the children. My love to my wife absorbed me to the roots of my being. I glorified in the conviction that our marriage was of the very will of Yahweh and I gave myself utterly to her in conjugal devotion. But the happiness of our home was soon to be ruthlessly interrupted. I began to detect that something was wrong. Night after night I was left alone with the children to shift for myself. My heart was eating itself out in bitter suspicion and awful loneliness.[3] Never can I drive from my memory the bitter pain of my spirit when the tragic revelation forced itself upon me. My wife had backslidden into the old life she had formerly followed as a votary of the sanctuary. I had given her my heart's love and protection, but this had not permanently satisfied her. She had no exclusive devotion for me but still hankered after the gifts, "harlot's hire,"[4] which, as representing Ashtart

to the Israelite worshipers, she had received in the
sanctuary at her "lovers'" hands.

> For she said, Let me go
> After my lovers,
> Who gave me my bread and my water,
> My wool and my flax,
> My oil and my drink (2. 5b).

My heart was well-nigh breaking as in mingled anguish, disillusionment, rage, and shame, I poured out
the bitterness of my soul in the presence of the children:

> Dispute with your mother, dispute,
> For she is not my wife,
> And I am not her husband.
> Yes, let her thrust her harlotry from before her,
> And her adultery from between her breasts;
> Lest I strip her naked,
> And exhibit her as in the day when she was born
> (2. 2-3).

Could it be that even the children of my home whom
I had claimed as legitimate were the issue of such disloyalty? The very possibility filled my sensitive soul
with revulsion:

> Yes, upon her children I will not show compassion,
> For children of adultery are they.
> For their mother has played the harlot,
> Conceiving them in shame (2. 4-5a).

I could only put my faithless wife away, for although
she had borne the protection of my name, she had in
disloyalty given herself to others. I tried to forget her,
to uproot my affection for her, to drive the thought of
her out of my mind, but I could not. There was something about her which, in the very face of her unworthi-
ness, again and again drew my heart to her.[5] In spite

of her inconstancy and disloyalty to me, I began to
scheme how I might save her from herself, how I might
"hedge up her way" to her former partners as though
with a "barrier of thorns," how I might erect high pro-
hibiting walls across her paths so that at length she might
be brought back to her senses and to her better self and
eventually say:

> I will go
> And return to my first husband,
> For it was better with me then than now (2. 7).

I was almost wholly absorbed in such thoughts when
one day, in a luminous ecstatic moment, Yahweh showed
me the momentous step I should take. I seemed to be
conscious of him saying:

> Go, still love[6] such a woman
> Who is in love with an intimate,
> Yes, who commits adultery (3. 1).

I was to love Gomer still, in spite of her treachery. It
meant buying her back again from the sanctuary life to
which she had backslidden, but depriving her of her
conjugal rights until she would be justly disciplined and
her loyalty to me would return.

> So I traded for her with fifteen (shekels) of silver
> And a homer of barley and a skin of wine.
> Then I said to her:
> "Many days
> You shall dwell with me, you shall not play the harlot,
> And you shall not have relations with a man;
> Neither will I have with you" (3. 2-3).

During those six years, ever since my prophetic ministry began, I had proclaimed Yahweh's rejection of
Israel. But one could not travel the way of anguish my

feet had trod and one's message remain unchanged. I began to see that the tragedy of my heart had meaning for *Israel*. Now I dimly understood how Yahweh's hand had been in the whole affair from the first. The tragic experience of my personal suffering had led me to comprehend Yahweh's feeling for Israel. Through my love for Gomer, which, in spite of her unfaithfulness, would not let me give her up, I was taught the intensity and persistency of Yahweh's redemptive passion. So I began to interpret Yahweh's relationship to Israel through the symbol of the marriage bond, now so poignantly familiar to me. As I was to Gomer, so is he to Israel. Yahweh is the husband of Israel. Israel is the wife of Yahweh. As Gomer forsook me for her "lovers" who gave her, as "harlot's hire," bread and water, wool and flax, oil and drink, so Israel had forsaken Yahweh. Like a shallow flirt lured by gifts showered upon her by her immoral lovers, decking herself with rings and jewelry, Israel had pursued the Baals whom she thought held the fertility of the soil in their control. For she did not know that it was Yahweh, and not the Baals,

> That gave her
> The grain and the new wine and the fresh oil (2. 8).

Even as I had put Gomer away and thus had thrust her from the protection of my home, so I now began to see how Yahweh would withhold from his people her crops and by removing her through exile from the lure of the Canaanized cult of Palestine with its agricultural festivals and sensual hilarity, would reduce her to wilderness status (2. 11). Surely Yahweh *"sows" judgment* for Israel! Aye, Israel will indeed be *"unpitied"!*

45

Its desperate plight will then make all too manifest to Israel and to the world that my nation can *no longer* be called *Yahweh's people!*

Yahweh's strange dealings with me had assured me of the imminent fall of the dynasty of Jehu. Even sooner than I had expected, his word came to pass. King Jeroboam's long forty-year reign, which had brought Israel to a peak of material prosperity equaled only by the pomp of King Solomon, came to an end. Jeroboam's son, Zechariah, had been king but six months when a ruthless usurper, Shallum, plotted his death and killed him at Ibleam (2 Kings 15. 10 LXX, Lucian) at the edge of the valley of Jezreel, then took the reins of government into his own hands. This marked the beginning of the downfall of my people. A period of political chaos ensued. Shallum had held the throne but one month when Menahem, the son of Gadi, went up from Tirzah, the ancient capital of Israel, to Samaria, defeated and killed King Shallum and usurped the throne (2 Kings 15. 14). Tappuah, a town east of Shechem and not far from my home, was held by partisans of the murdered king and would not acknowledge the new usurper's authority. Thereupon by the bloody murder of its entire population and with unmentionable cruelty (2 Kings 15. 16) King Menahem compelled recognition, and for six years held the reins of Israel's rapidly decaying power. The whole nation was in moral and political collapse, and I cried to my fellow countrymen:

> Hear the word of Yahweh, sons of Israel,
> For Yahweh has a dispute with the dwellers in the land;
> For there is no faithfulness and no piety,
> And no knowledge of God in the land.

Swearing and deception,
And murder and stealing,
And committing adultery have broken out,
And murder follows hard upon murder (4. 1-2).

The primary cause of the collapse of Israel, as Yahweh had caused me to perceive, was religious. And I was deeply convinced that upon the priesthood as it operated at the various sanctuaries of the nation lay the heaviest responsibility for the prevailing religious corruption. Wherever there was a permanent altar or shrine there was at least one priest. They constituted the most continuous and recognized religious teachers in my country. They were custodians of the law and were charged with moral instruction. They spoke out of the accumulated wisdom and social experience of their class. They had the responsibility of maintaining an abiding ethical and religious tradition. They kept the record of God's dealings with the Fathers. Knowledge of Yahweh was their province, and this the people as a whole had the right to expect from them.[7]

So from one sanctuary to another in Israel I went, but especially to Gilgal, Bethel, and Samaria, and striving for the ear of the priesthood, I spoke to them Yahweh's word:

My people has been destroyed
From lack of knowledge.
Since you have lightly esteemed knowledge,
I will reject you from being my priest;
Since you have forgotten the teaching of your God
I will forget your sons, even I (4. 6).

During the unprecedentedly prosperous reign of Jeroboam II, the priests had increased in numbers and in prestige, but, I lamented in Yahweh's name,

> In proportion to their increase they have sinned against me;
> Their prestige I will change into disgrace (4. 7).

The priests had turned aside from their primary duty of declaring the directions of Yahweh, substituting for it their own professional performance of the debased popular cult:

> The sin of my people they eat;
> And on their iniquity they direct their desires (4. 8).

Instead of reproving and correcting the sins of the people, the priests had surrendered to the prevailing self-indulgence and the people, in turn, excused themselves by pointing to the example set by their leaders. I uttered upon them Yahweh's indictment:

> So it will be "like people like priest,"
> And I will requite unto them their ways,
> And their practices will I pay back to them (4. 9).

The priests were parties to the Canaanized worship as practiced at the Israelite High Places. I charged them, along with the civic and political leaders, with the guilt of ensnaring the people at certain famous sanctuaries which were centers of Canaanite immoral rites:

> Hear this, O priests,
> Because it is yours to administer judgment.
> For a trap you have been at Mizpah (Gilead),
> And a net spread out upon Tabor;
> And the pit of Shittim you have made deep.
> But I am a discipline unto all of you (5. 1-2).

It was at Shittim, a center of the cult of Baal Peor, that

the Israelites had first encountered the immoral rites of
Canaan. There

> They came to Baal Peor;
> And devoted themselves to the shameful thing,
> And they became detested ones,
> Like what Ephraim loved (9. 10b).

The shameful thing to which I referred was sacred
prostitution. To me it was the most abhorrent among
the rites of worship practiced at the High Places. My
tragic experience with Gomer had made it all the more
obnoxious to me and had showed it up sharply in its
insidious peril to Israel. It demanded all the courage
that I could muster to grapple with these deeply rooted
practices at the sanctuaries, rites which now were
weighted with the authority of age-old custom and popular acquiescence. I condemned first the consultation of
idol oracles and the priestly magical manipulation of
the oracular response. Then I passed on to "the spirit
of harlotry" which the repulsive practice of sacred prostitution had called forth in my people, and in which
priests and people were implicated:

> At their wood (Asherah) they (my people) inquire,
> And their (divining) rod declares to them.
> For the spirit of harlotry has misled them,
> They go off whoring, not being in subjection to their
>   God.
> Upon the tops of the mountains they sacrifice,
> And upon the hills they burn incense,
> Under oak, and poplar,
> And terebinth, for its shadow is good.
> Therefore your daughters play the harlot,
> And your young brides commit adultery.
> I will not punish your daughters because they play the
>   harlot,

Or your young brides because they commit adultery;
For the men themselves go apart with the harlots,
And they sacrifice with the sacred prostitutes;
And a people which does not understand shall be thrown
down.
Wine and new wine take possession of the mind of my
people (4. 12-15, 11b).

The Israelite male leadership in general was to blame
as well as the priests, for when they thus consorted with
cultic prostitutes and sacrificed with sacred harlots, you
could not greatly blame the innocent Israelite daughters
and daughters-in-law for participating in such practices.
I dared to dub this time-sanctioned pagan practice plain
harlotry and adultery.

These rites had a degenerating and devastating grip
upon the whole nation. Designating Israel by the name
of her chief tribe, the name I loved best for my people,
I cried:

I know Ephraim,
And Israel is not hidden from me.
For you have played the harlot, O Ephraim;
Israel has defiled itself.
Their deeds will not allow them
To return to their God.
For the spirit of whoredom is within them,
And they know not Yahweh (5. 3-4).

Such degenerating practices vetoed any possible repentance. At Bethel my own eyes had witnessed the nature
of these disgusting rites and their defiling effect. So I
reported:

In Bethel I have seen a thing of horror;
There is the harlotry of Ephraim,
Israel has defiled herself (6. 10).

I understood the magical purpose of these rituals. They were intended to coerce, by acts of sympathetic magic, the blessings of fertility for fields and vineyards, flocks, herds, and homes. But I saw their utter futility, for Yahweh alone was the giver of all such increase and these immoral rites could not coerce his *gifts*. I cried:

> Be not glad, Israel!
> Rejoice not like the nations!
> For you have played the harlot from adhesion to your
>   God.
> You have loved "harlot's hire,"
> Upon every threshing floor for grain.
> (But) threshing floor and vat
> Will not know them,
> And new wine will deny them (9. 1-2).

These blessings of the soil, the herd, and the family must be sought from Yahweh in other ways.

I was always instinctively interested in the international politics of Israel and followed with ever-deepening concern the emergence of different political parties in my nation. Yahweh led me to see these political movements and international alignments from the standpoint of his will for Israel and Judah. Almost at the very same time that I became Yahweh's prophet, a usurper, one Pulu (Pul), who assumed the throne name, Tiglath-pileser III, ascended the Assyrian throne. He was one of the most powerful of the Assyrian kings. Early in his reign he made an expedition into the Westland, and after a three years' campaign mastered Arvad, which had become the focal center of reorganization for the small states of northern Syria. On his second military expedition into Syria two years later, which brought the first decisive interference of Assyria in the internal affairs of my people, King Menahem, in order to secure his throne against a rival (anti-Assyrian) party that was already developing in Israel, paid a vast tribute of one thousand silver talents to Tiglath-pileser III, exacting it from wealthy Israelite citizens.[8]

I clearly saw the folly of this alliance of my people with Assyria, and I condemned the stubborn policy of King Menahem in buying, at such a terrific Israelite cost, Assyria's very questionable support. There was sure to be a disastrous harvest from such political seed-sowing, and Assyria—most certainly not Israel—would reap the benefits of it. So I said:

> For the wind they sow;
> But the storm wind they shall reap.
> As for standing grain, there will be no sprouting of it;
> It will not make meal.
> If peradventure it should make it,
> Foreigners will swallow it up.
> For they (the Israelites) have gone up to Assyria
> Like a wild ass going alone by itself.
> Israel has been swallowed up.
> Now are they among the nations
> Like a vessel in which there is no delight.

Such tribute to Assyria I compared to the service of her person Gomer had given her paramours for their gifts to her:

> Ephraim has given love gifts.
> Yes, though they hire among the nations,
> Now I will scatter them.
> And they shall cease for a little to anoint
> Kings and princes (8. 7, 9ab, 8, 9c, 10).

Exiled to Assyria, my countrymen would have neither king nor royal court!

Contrary to the trend of the times toward anarchy, King Menahem's reign was not ended by murder. He died a normal death. His son, King Pekahiah, had been on the throne of Israel but two years when a new factor was introduced into Israel under the ruthless and vigorous leadership of his third officer, Pekah, son of Remaliah, a Gileadite from Transjordan. It is likely that he already had the backing of Syria, when at the head of a bodyguard of fifty fellow Gileadites he entered the royal castle at Samaria, murdered King Pekahiah, and usurped his throne.

I had no confidence in this ruthless usurper from Gilead. Ever since the reign of Jeroboam II, one unstable and transient phantom king had been succeeded by another in Israel, until the throne of my people had become a plaything, at the mercy of ambition, plot, and intrigue. Within my lifetime three Israelite monarchs had met their death by dastardly, murderous plots. And now another such murderer was upon the throne. These rulers were utterly lacking in character or statesmanship; they were voluptuous and dissipated, controlled by fires of passion rather than by the fear of Yahweh. In Yahweh's name I condemned both these irresponsible monarchs and my people who had enthroned them:

They have set up kings, but not by me;
They have made princes, but I did not know it (8. 4a).
In their evil they anoint kings,
And in their falsity princes.
All of them are committers of adultery (7. 3-4a).

These kings were the godless leaders of a godless people.

I compared the inflamed plotting hearts of these corrupt politicians of my people to burning fire pots such as we used in baking bread. While the leaven is invisibly spreading throughout the mass of dough, the baker does not stir up the fire but allows it to smolder. Then when the dough is thoroughly leavened, he stirs the fire into blazing heat for baking. So the corrupt leaders of my people quiet down after one outrageous outburst of evil passion only to flare forth in another iniquitous plot, for which under cover of secrecy they have been preparing. What the baker is to the fire, which he now stirs and now lets smolder, the unbridled passion is in the hearts of those scheming politicians who fear neither men nor God. So I cried:

> Like a burning fire pot are they;
> The baker ceases from stirring (i. e., the fire),
> From kneading the dough until it is leavened.

> For their inward parts are like a furnace;
> Their heart burns within them;[9]
> Their anger smolders all night.
> In the morning it flames forth like a blazing fire (7. 4b-6).

When the political policies of Israel are at the mercy of godless officials dominated by unchecked and undisciplined passions, there can be no stable throne ruling over my people:

> All of them grow hot like an oven,
> And they devour their rulers.
> And their kings have fallen;
> None of them, saith Yahweh, calls unto me (7. 7).

Our king was no check to such anarchy but, rather, took his own share in all this political corruption, participating in the very excesses and intrigues which in turn led to his own downfall. Our New Year's day festival, during which our king was annually re-enthroned with

pompous ceremony,[10] was a standing disgrace to my
people, an annual shameful exhibition of dissipation and
treachery:

> On the day of our king they show sickness,
> Do the princes, (from) the fever of wine.
> He stretches out his hand with the scoffers! (7. 5.)

The other political alignment in my nation, which
now rapidly gained headway under King Pekah, was
the Syrian party, which looked to King Rezon of Syria
for help. It was solidly set against any kind of alliance
with Assyria. The campaigns of Tiglath-pileser into
the Westland and his domination of the small states, of
which ours was one, had aroused these smaller powers
to attempt a new political combination, designed to unite
their strength for a common stand against Assyrian control. The center of initiative in this program was Rezon
of Damascus, king of Syria. United with him were the
princes of the Philistine cities, the chief among them
being Hanno, king of Gaza, and the king of Edom, and
especially King Pekah of Israel, who was the soul of the
Syrian party among our people. It was the purpose of
this union of western nations to dethrone Ahaz, king of
Judah, and put a Syrian puppet, the son of Tabeel, in his
place, and so control Judah, forcing her to stand with
them against Assyria.

So began the Syrian-Ephraimite war, which was destined to have serious consequences for all participants.
The united forces of King Rezon and of the Israelites
under our king, Pekah, besieged King Ahaz of Judah
but could not defeat him. The king of Edom, who was
an ally of Syria and Israel at that time, recovered the

great commercial port of Elath (2 Kings 16. 6, LXX), situated at the head of the Gulf of Akaba, the eastern arm of the Red Sea, a commercial center which King Azariah of Judah had taken early in his reign (2 Kings 14. 22). The Edomite king then exiled all the Jews who dwelt there. King Ahaz, although strong enough to hold out against Syria and our nation, yet in order to maintain his throne, now followed the shortsighted policy which our late King Menahem had pursued, and appealed for the protection of Tiglath-pileser III of Assyria. At the price of heavy tribute, which emptied the Judaean treasuries of the royal palace and of the Temple, he bought the help of the Assyrian monarch and, for the time being, secured his throne from molestation (2 Kings 16. 5-9).

I was deeply interested in all this and watched every movement of the nations with keenest concern. Certain cities on the border between our kingdom and that of Judah, such as Gibeah, Ramah, and Bethel, had for over two centuries been claimed by Judah.[11] Originally they had belonged to us, for they were in the tribal district of Benjamin. But King Asa of Judah, with Syrian aid, had wrested them from our King Baasha (1 Kings 15. 17-22). At the beginning of the Syrian-Ephraimite war Judah lost this territory to King Pekah of Israel. It was clear to me that before long Tiglath-pileser would be in the west to protect his new Judaean ally and to punish Rezon and Pekah for their ambitious, rebellious designs against Assyrian dominion in the Westland. When this should occur, Rezon and Pekah would be forced to withdraw from Judah to protect their northern borders. I anticipated that then Judah, protected by Assyria, would take

advantage of the forced withdrawal of Syrian and Israelite troops to make a counter thrust which would not
content itself with merely regaining the contested border
cities of Gibeah, Ramah, and Bethel, but would, in addition, seize and wrest from our hands uncontested Israelite territory.   Accordingly, I warned my people Israel
that Judah would come to wreak vengeance upon her
and would concentrate her wrath upon the mountains
of Ephraim.   I viewed this counter thrust against Israel
as a judgment of Yahweh upon my people, for I was certain that Yahweh was opposed to the policies of King
Pekah which had leagued our nation with the schemes
of Syria.   Only national disaster could result from it
for us.   Thus I lifted my voice to Israel:

> Blow the cornet in Gibeah,
> And the trumpet in Ramah;
> Sound an alarm at Bethel;
> Bring Benjamin into terror.
> The district of Ephraim will become a desolation,
> Among the tribes of Israel.
> In the day of rebuke (i.e., Yahweh's chastening or
>   correction),
> I have made known what will surely happen
>   (5. 8-9).

This Judaean counter thrust succeeded.   Judah's military and political leaders took quick advantage of the
withdrawal of Israel.   Not only did they regain the
border territory to which they had some semblance of
claim, but in addition they seized and annexed a strip of
undisputed Israelite territory and thus violated the
ancient territorial rights of my people.   Yahweh was
opposed to such annexation politics and in his name I

condemned the Judaean officials who had advocated and accomplished it:

> There were officials of Judah
> Like removers of boundaries.
> Against them I will pour out,
> Like water my wrath (5. 10).

At length, on the pretext of King Ahaz's appeal, Tiglath-pileser appeared in the Westland. After looting Gaza, he turned back to punish my country for its share in the rebellion. He terribly decreased the territory of my people, taking city after city, among them being Ijon, Abel-beth-maacah, Janoah, Kedesh, and Hazor. From these cities he took many captives to Assyria. He took Gilead, King Pekah's native country, and wrested all Transjordan from Israel (2 Kings 15. 29). An Assyrian province was created out of the mastered territory to be ruled from Megiddo. He narrowed down the Israelite territory to a few square miles around Samaria. Finally he turned against Damascus, King Rezon's capital. Its sixteen provinces were taken and the king was shut up in the city. Damascus itself was captured, King Rezon was put to death, and the city's inhabitants were deported to Qir (2 Kings 16. 9).

Only a torso of my nation was left. My countrymen sharply resented this inhuman devastation of our territory and the contracting of its boundaries to the mountains of Ephraim. Tragic it was indeed for us in those hours to recall the glorious ancient hopes my people had once held for the Joseph tribes of Ephraim and Manasseh,[12] and compare them with the poor fragment that now remained. Upon every side I heard fellow Israelites saying in anger, humiliation, and despair,

> Crushed is Ephraim,
> Oppressed as to (his) right (5. 11a).

They bitterly lamented the cruel dessication of their land at the hand of that barbarous world power which had put might for right. But, in the name of Yahweh, I placed the responsibility for Israel's desperate plight squarely upon the shoulders of my fellow countrymen, who had allowed themselves to be duped by Syrian schemes. All this had happened, I told them,

> Because he (Ephraim) persisted to walk
> After his enemy (Syria) (5. 11b).

For King Rezon of Damascus had been a snare to Pekah and to my people, and his relationship worse than enmity.

By this time mighty currents of antagonism had set in among my fellow countrymen against our king and his Syrian alliance. Our nation accordingly disowned and overthrew him.

> The king of Samaria has been cut off,
> Like a splinter upon the face of the water (10. 7)

—such was my comment upon this popular tide of antagonism against our vanquished and helpless monarch. At the instigation of the rival Assyrian party in Israel and with Assyrian support, King Pekah was plotted against and murdered by Hoshea, the son of Elah (2 Kings 15. 30). Tiglath-pileser then established Hoshea upon the throne of my desolated people as his loyal vassal, demanding a heavy annual tribute as tangible evidence of Assyrian overlordship.

The disastrous Syrian-Ephraimite war was at an end, and now, for the first time in history, both my nation and

Judah were tributary to Assyria. Within both sections of the Hebrew people the Assyrian party had finally prevailed. Judah was paying tribute to Assyria in order to ward off its dissolution as an independent state. And Israel was now following the same course, hoping against hope that the strong arm of Assyria would ward off the disastrous fate which her erstwhile ally had suffered in the total destruction of the Syrian nation.

Yahweh had clearly revealed to me that both Israel and Judah were following a policy of desperation. The two nations were incurably sick, yet each had deceived itself into thinking that the one way to sound health lay in such political alliance. But it was perfectly plain to me that such was not Yahweh's way to national security. So I spoke to Israel:

> Then saw Ephraim his sickness,
> And the house of Judah its abscess,
> So Ephraim went to Assyria,
> And the house of Judah to the great king.
> But he is not able to heal,
> And he cannot cure the abscess (5. 13).

Clearer than any of my fellow countrymen I saw that the sickness of both Israel and Judah was a spiritual sickness. It was a new religious loyalty, not political alliance, that was needed. I saw with incisive clarity that the one effective power in history is Yahweh. He is at once the creator of national well-being, and—what was ever hard for my people to understand—the bringer of national misfortune, the *destroyer* as well as the only saviour, of Israel. It was Yahweh's moral judgment, his inevitable retribution upon our disobedience, that like a moth was eating the garment of Israel, that like dry rot was spreading decay in Judah. As a lion carries off his prey and no one can hinder, so must the righteous Yahweh destroy his people. How weak a force is mere political alliance before so majestic and righteous a judge of nations and men! (5. 12, 14.)

As long as Tiglath-pileser III lived, King Hoshea remained loyal to his Assyrian overlord. When Shalmaneser V, his successor, ascended the throne of Assyria, one of the petty kings of the Egyptian[13] delta, So (Sibu) by name, was arousing the spirit of revolt among us Palestinian-Syrian states, evidently with the intent of creating a protecting fringe of buffer states between Egypt and Assyria. At this time there had developed in my country a strong trend toward alliance with Egypt. Our King Hoshea gave such sufficient evidence of a transfer of loyalty from Assyria to Egypt as to lead Shalmaneser of Assyria to come up against him and force him to pay tribute (2 Kings 17. 3). But soon King Hoshea, desperately trying to shake off the Assyrian yoke, definitely broke with Shalmaneser, withholding his annual tribute, and through his ambassadors began to make overtures to So of Egypt (2 Kings 17. 4).

Once again there were two parties within the remnant of my people, one favoring continued alliance with Assyria, the other urging resort to Egypt for aid in casting off the heavy Assyrian yoke. The will of Yahweh concerning all this was clear to me. This policy of alliance with foreign powers had brought my people into the international stream and had introduced into Israel foreign customs and ideals, which were harmful to our national character. For Yahweh's people had not a political but a spiritual and a moral mission. In her flirting now with Egypt and then with Assyria, my nation had become skilled in worldly political intrigue. But Israel was utterly undeveloped in that spiritual responsiveness to Yahweh and to his will which alone could make my people great. Thus the payment of heavy tribute to hire the help either of Egypt or Assyria seemed to me like Gomer offering her person to her paramours in return for the gifts which they were only too eager to provide. Israel in so doing was forsaking Yahweh her true "husband." And the resultant drafts upon her economic resources were bringing my nation to premature decay for,

> A covenant they make with Assyria,
> And oil is carried to Egypt (12. 1).

So I warned my people:

> Ephraim among the peoples
> Is mingling himself.
> Ephraim has become a cake,
> Not turned.
> Foreigners have eaten up his strength,
> And he does not know it.
> Yes, gray hair is profuse upon him,
> But he does not know it.
> And the haughtiness of Israel testifies in his
> countenance,
> Yet they have not returned to Yahweh,
> Nor have they sought him in all this (7. 8-10).

Moreover, our nation was too naïve to see the treachery which lay in the heart of her helpers:

> Ephraim has been like a dove,
> Simple, with no intelligence.
> Yes, to Egypt they have called;
> To Assyria they have gone.
> When they go I will spread

Upon them my net;
Like birds of the heavens,
I will bring them down.
I will chasten them,
When is heard the clamour of their as-
    semblage.
Woe to them for they have fled from me! (after
    capture in the foreign net)
Violence to them for they have transgressed
    against me! (7. 11-13.)

In these last words I hinted at a thought which I now
clarified. I had come to understand how Yahweh would
use these very nations, upon whose help Israel now trusts,
to reduce and discipline my people by carrying the inhabitants of Israel into exile. And there my countrymen
would be subject to the domination of their foreign over-
lords and would be cut off from the familiar practices of
their worship. So I cried:

Ephraim will return to Egypt,
And as for Assyria, he shall be his (Ephraim's) king
    (11. 5).
They shall not dwell in the land of Yahweh,
But Ephraim shall return to Egypt,
And in Assyria they shall eat unclean food.
They shall not pour out wine to Yahweh,
And they shall not set in order their sacrifices for him.
Like the bread of mourning will be their bread,
Everyone eating it will be unclean.
For their bread is for themselves;
It will not come into the house of Yahweh.
What will you do in the days of festivals,
And in the day of the feast of Yahweh? (9. 3b-5.)

There, to Assyria and to Egypt, I was convinced Yahweh's judgment would pursue the exiled Israelites, and
the richly productive regions of the Tigris-Euphrates

and Nile valleys would yield them only thistles and briars:

> For behold, as for those going to Assyria,
> Thistles shall take possession of them (9. 6).

It was the Egyptian practice to bury with the Pharaohs, in their brilliant tombs, much treasure gathered from their subjected peoples.   So I pictured Israelite treasures as enriching the royal tombs at Memphis:

> Egypt shall gather them;
> Memphis shall bury the precious things of their silver;
> Briars (will be) in their tents (9. 6).

Such words were most distasteful to the responsible leaders of my people.   And never before in my career as a prophet had I been so conscious of their antagonism, yes, even of their fierce animosity, as I was at that time. One day during this period, at the temple of Bethel, I was stressing this threat of exile to Egypt or to Assyria as Yahweh's requital upon my people for their folly and disloyalty to him.   My heart was deeply serious as in slow, emphatic words that throbbed with the atmosphere of imminent crisis, I chanted in solemn, ominous tones:

> The days of reckoning have come,
> The days of requital have come;
> Israel shall know it! (9. 7a.)

My solemn words were interrupted by an indignant and sneering retort of my hearers,

> A fool is the prophet!
> Maddened is the man of the spirit! (9. 7b.)

Yes, I interrupted, "maddened,"

> On account of the great quantity of your iniquities,
> And because the animosity is great!

It is indeed a lonely life which the true prophet of God must live among the people whom he loves:

> A watchman of Ephraim,
> In the service of my God, is a prophet;
> A trap of a bait layer is upon all his words,
> (And) animosity in the house of his God! (9. 8.)

One of the gravest offenses to Yahweh which impressed me in the public cult of Israel was the worship of the golden bull as practiced especially at the royal temple in Bethel. In origin, this idol went back to the reign of Jeroboam I, our king after the north broke away from the monarchy, who had dignified by regal recognition a feature of the worship which by that time had already, through Canaanite influence, found entrance into the official Yahweh religion. This cult was furnished with its own degenerate priests who carried it on. The stately bull image of Yahweh at Bethel, in a derogatory aspersion and with biting sarcasm, I dubbed Samaria's "calf"! Speaking in Yahweh's name and at the sanctuary in Bethel, in the very presence of the familiar and impressive image, I said:

> I have spurned your calf, O Samaria;
> My anger has been kindled against them (i.e., Israelites):
> How long (will it be that) they cannot be innocent,
> O house of Israel? (8. 5.)

I saw how the worship of the golden bull had introduced such corruption in Israel that Israel could never be purged of the havoc it had wrought. I hurled my scorn at this idol—a man-made god!

> For an artisan made it,
> And it is not a god;
> For the calf of Samaria will become splinters (8. 6).

I heaped ridicule upon it. It is the task of a God to care for and to bear up his people. Their God should help them in their hour of need. But the worshipers of the calf of Bethel—Beth-awen, "house of wickedness," I contemptuously called the seat of its worship—will fear for its capture! In ironical vein I continued:

> For the calf of Beth-awen they are agitated,
> Are the dwellers in Samaria;
> For its people shall lament over it,
> And its (idolatrous) priests (shall wail) for it.

This idol could not protect itself. It would be one of the first treasures the Assyrians would sack. I pictured the Assyrians bearing it along and the priests of the bull cult moaning their lamentations as they followed it into exile:

> They will wail over its glory,
> For it has gone from them into exile;
> Yes, to Assyria they will bear it along,
> As tribute to the great king.
> Shame shall Ephraim receive;
> Yes, Israel shall be ashamed of its idol (10. 5-6).

The attachment on the part of my people to this cult of the golden bull I viewed as a sensual love, for it was associated with immoral rites. Thus this idol had degraded the character of Yahweh and though viewed by my countrymen as a symbol of him, it had blinded Israel to his true significance.

My passionate hope for Israel was that the terrific blows being dealt her might open her eyes to see that the very disasters through which our nation was passing, and would yet be called upon to pass, represented the discipline of Yahweh. Through it Yahweh was speaking to her heart. I never completely lost confidence that ultimately Israel would turn from reliance upon Assyria and Egypt to Yahweh as the true source of her help. Speaking in Yahweh's name, I said,

> I will go and return to my place,
> Until they are appalled and seek my face:
> In their straits they will look earnestly for me (5. 15).

Yet my people could not understand me when I spoke such words. "Are we not now seeking Yahweh?" they asked. "Do not we Israelites regularly bring our lambs, our sheep, our goats, and our bullocks, and sacrifice them to Yahweh?" Yes, I said, as for the Israelites,

> With their flocks and with their herds they shall go
> To seek Yahweh but shall not find him;
> He has withdrawn from them (5. 6).
> Though Ephraim has multiplied altars,
> They have been unto him for sinning.
> On altars beloved they sacrifice,
> And flesh they eat.
> Yahweh has not been pleased with them (8. 11, 13).

I share with the Judaean shepherd prophet of Tekoa the conviction that the system of sacrifices and offerings, now in vogue in Israelite worship, does not offer a true way of approach to Yahweh.

It was the loved practice of the women of Israel during the spring time, the season of sowing seed, by planting in the Adonis gardens rapidly growing seeds and slips and carefully attending their growth, to seek the help of the deity, thus magically assuring from him the annual renewal of vegetation. But I was convinced that Yahweh could not be found nor his help evoked by such pagan rites. An entirely different type of sowing is required to find him. So I called to them:

> Sow to yourselves in righteousness,
> Harvest in proportion to piety;
> Freshly till your untilled ground;
> For it is time to seek Yahweh
> Until he come and rain righteousness upon you (10. 12).

Their seeking for Yahweh was at times passionately in earnest, but it was utterly misguided and mistook his true nature. Under the influence of Canaanite practices they sought the blessings of Yahweh's fertility-giving energy in orgiastic rites of lamentation and self-mutilation, just as the Baal prophets had done in Elijah's time. But, so Yahweh laments,

> They have not cried unto me with their heart,
> Though they wail upon their beds:
> For grain and for new wine they lacerate themselves;
> They rebel against me (7. 14).

And their seeking of Yahweh for his material blessings and in these magical ways was done with superficial presumption by my people which had no justification whatsoever. They had naïve confidence that their wailing rites, carried out in the Adonis cult, which continued for two days and then turned to rejoicing on the third day, would change Yahweh's hurting into healing, his punishment into restoration. These rituals, so they thought, would coerce his life-giving energy and bring him in refreshing and saving power to his people. So they sang:

> Come and let us return unto Yahweh;
> For he has torn, but he will heal us;
> Yahweh has smitten but he will bind us up.
> He will restore us to life after two days;
> On the third day he will raise us up,

And we shall live before him.
And let us know, let us pursue to know Yahweh:
His going forth is sure like dawn;
And he will come like the rain shower to us;
Like the spring rain, he will saturate the earth
 (6. 1-3).

Their words were a lovely but shallow song. Their
assertion of Yahweh's healing, fructifying, and quicken-
ing power was true, but unaccompanied by those acts
and attitudes that would assure it. Sick at heart over the
shallowness and ephemeral quality of such repentance I
broke out in lament:

What shall I do to you, Ephraim?
Yes, what shall I do to you, Judah?
For your piety is like the morning cloud,
And like the dew which early goes away (6. 4).

So, under the power of this insight granted to me by
Yahweh, I summoned my people to turn from their futile rituals to an utterly different kind of search for him:

Therefore turn to your God:
Keep piety and justice,
And wait for your God continually (12. 6).

Then in a single sentence, spoken in Yahweh's name, I
uttered the full ripe fruit of my heart searchings and
broodings as to how Israel must seek Yahweh. It crowns
my battle for Israel's soul in these years.

For piety I desire, and not sacrifice;
And the knowledge of God without burnt offering
 (6. 6).

Ever since King Hoshea had given open evidence of
rebellion against his overlord, Shalmaneser V of Assyria,
and had begun to make overtures to King So of Egypt, I

was sure that my nation was nearing its end. It meant final disaster and the tragic culmination was at hand. I felt then the awful sternness of Yahweh's wrath. Through pictures of wild animals enraged and just at the point of leaping with destructive violence upon their prey, I poured out upon my countrymen the wrath of Yahweh. Speaking of him in relation to his people, I said:

> My God will reject them,
> For they have not hearkened to him.
> And they will be wanderers among the nations (9. 17).

Then, speaking for Yahweh, I cried:

> And I will be to them as a lion;
> As a leopard on the way will I lie in wait;
> I will encounter them like a bear robbed of offspring;
> And I will tear the encasement of their heart;
> And dogs shall devour them there.
> I have destroyed you, O Israel,
> For you are against me, against your help (13. 7-9).

Israel had not taken its spiritual mission seriously. My people had wanted an earthly king when their sole king should have been Yahweh. They had set out to be "like all the nations," but Yahweh had "found" Israel (9. 10) and opened his very heart to her because he wanted her to be not the people of Ahab or Jeroboam, of Menahem or Hoshea, but the people of Yahweh, rich in knowledge of his nature and will, full of love and loyalty to him. The collapse of Israel I could only see as the unfolding in history of the consequences of Israel's fatal refusal. So I challenged my people:

> Where is your king then, that he may save you
> In all your cities?
> And where are your judges of whom you said,

"Give to me a king and princes"?
I kept giving you a king in my anger,
And I repeatedly took him away in my wrath (13. 10-11).

Then Yahweh's purpose toward Israel, as he caused
me to see it, reached a depth of sternness so awful that
only my deep heartache at Gomer's disloyalty when I
had thrust her out from my home, could make me understand it. For Yahweh was saying, as though counseling
with himself as to how to deal with his people:

> Shall I ransom them from the hand of Sheol?
> Shall I redeem them from death?
> Hither with your plagues, O death!
> Hither with your destruction, O Sheol!
> Repentance is hid from my eyes! (13. 14.)

My words of outraged love uttered in Yahweh's name
soon seemed justified to my countrymen and achieved
the greater credence from my people because of the de-
velopments that now ensued. Shalmaneser V discovered
that King Hoshea was carrying on negotiations with
Egypt, conspiring with the help of Pharaoh to throw off
the Assyrian yoke. The Assyrian monarch invaded the
west to punish such duplicity. He shut King Hoshea
up and bound him in prison (2 Kings 17. 5). It seemed
to me then that the fall of Israel was inescapable, and I
sensed with sharp pain of soul the awful days ahead for
my people. I was certain that Israel's sinful rebellion
against Yahweh was the ultimate cause of her collapse.
In such words as pained me to the very heart as I uttered
them I said:

> Samaria is guilty, for she has rebelled against her God:
> By the sword they shall fall;
> Their children shall be dashed into pieces;
> And their pregnant women shall be ripped up (13. 16).

71

As the fall of my nation became more and more certain and I could see nothing ahead save dark calamity, Yahweh again illumined my saddened mind with hope. I began to see that Israel's end as a nation was not to be Yahweh's end for Israel. Through the deepest impulses of my private life which had led me to long for Gomer, to love her in spite of her disloyalty, to redeem, purge, and restore her, Yahweh had unlocked for me the depth and persistence of his own saving love for his people. Now I began to live and to teach in the power of that love. The seeming destruction of the nation by exile would, to be sure, reduce Israel to wilderness status (2. 9-13). But Yahweh's purpose in thus disciplining his people is not merely punitive but redemptive. His wrath is only the reverse side of his passionate love. In those wilderness hours of my people's national collapse Yahweh will speak to Israel's heart, even as he did in the days of old in those earlier wilderness hours, when Moses was her teacher and leader.

Just as my love would not down but forced me to seek Gomer in her zero hour, so I now saw that the suffering and banishment of exile was Yahweh's plan to win back the heart of Israel in loyalty to himself. I seemed to hear him say concerning Israel:

> Therefore, behold me enticing her,
> And bringing her back to the wilderness;
> And I will speak to her heart (2. 14).

I now realized that if Israel would but understand and respond, Yahweh would turn her valley of troubling into a door of hope (2. 15). The memory of the fresh strong bonds that had been welded when I betrothed

Gomer to me in a renewed and deepened betrothal, now quickened my mind and heart as I became an evangelist to my people and held out to Israel the basis of Yahweh's new betrothal:

> I will betroth you to me forever;
> And I will betroth you to me in righteousness,
> And in justice and in lovingkindness;
> And I will betroth you unto me in faithfulness
>   (2. 19-20).

With all the tenderness of feeling with which my spirit was endowed and with all the enthusiasm of intense hope, I pleaded with my people. How could I arouse them to respond to Yahweh's stern but tender discipline? How could I get them to pass through his exacting yet challenging doorway of hope, thus making it the starting point of a new career of prosperity and success?

My teaching had made Israel familiar with the conception of Yahweh as her husband and Israel as his bride. Now I employed another figure which had its origin in my loving recall of the tender devotion which my own father, Beeri, had showered upon me, his son. Yahweh thus revealed to me a new avenue of appeal to my people: Yahweh is the father of Israel, Israel is Yahweh's son. Yet this new conception was shot through and through with the tenderness and passion of the earlier husband-wife relationship. I began Yahweh's lament in idyllic vein:

> When Israel was a child, then I loved him,
> And called my son from Egypt.
> According as I called them, (i.e., the Israelites)
> So they went from me;
> To the Baals they sacrificed,

> And they burned incense to graven images.
> Yet I taught Ephraim to walk;
> I took him (repeatedly) upon my arms;
> But they did not know that I healed them.
> With human cords I drew them,
> With ropes of love;
> And I was to them
> Like one lifting the yoke from upon their jaws;
> And I spread out their food and they ate (11. 1-4).

Could Yahweh allow Ephraim, his son of so great a love, to perish from the face of the earth, just as he had destroyed the cities of Admah and Zeboim along with Sodom and Gomorrah, according to the old Hebrew story, because of their desperate wickedness? Well did I recall the conflict of passions within my own soul over Gomer, as Yahweh now spoke his mighty redemptive words through me:

> How can I give you up, Ephraim?
> Can I reject you, Israel?
> How can I deliver you up like Admah?
> Can I make you like Zeboim?
> My heart is turned upon me.
> My compassions are kindled together.
> I will not perform the heat of my anger,
> I will not turn back to destroy Ephraim:
> For God am I, and not man;
> In the midst of you, the Holy One;
> And I will not come in wrath (11. 8-9).

I am convinced that the wrath of Yahweh does not sound the depths of his nature. My people is held in a love that will not let her go. Yahweh loves Israel of his own initiative and of his own volition. He will heal my people of their rebellious spirit. So in these days when I await the final blow I am continually calling my people to return to Yahweh:

74

> Return, Israel, unto Yahweh your God;
> For you have stumbled in your iniquity.
> Take with you words and return to Yahweh:
> Say to him:
> "You are able to forgive all iniquity;
> Accept in return for it good;
> In places of steers we will pay our lips" (14. 1-2).

Here and there now as I deal with my people I am beginning to hear expressions of opinion that awaken my hope. Some are turning in disillusionment from their confidence in the power of their revered idols, the golden bull, and the images of Anath, whom they have worshiped as mother goddess, and as giver of victory in war, and of Asherah, ancient mother of the gods, whose idol was the sacred tree or post of wood, and who was revered as creator of fountains and springs. I hear some say:

> What have I any more to do with idols? (14. 8a.)
> We shall not say any longer "Our God,"
> To the work of our hands (14. 3b).

And some of them are beginning to realize how futile it is for Israel to depend upon the protection of Assyria or upon the horses and military resources generally of Egypt. I hear some who were formerly of Assyrian or Egyptian leanings now declaring that

> Assyria will not save us;
> Upon horses (i.e., of Egypt) we will not ride (14. 3a).

Such evidence encourages me greatly. But most of all I base my hope for Israel in Yahweh's love for his people. In these days of Palestine's spring glory the new life in nature, which has ever thrilled my spirit, seems vocal with Yahweh's voice gently murmuring:

> I will be like the dew to Israel;
> He shall sprout like the lily,
> And he shall cast his roots like the poplar.
> His shoots shall spread,
> And his vigor shall be like the olive tree,
> And his scent like the (tree of) Lebanon (14. 5-6).

I have faith to believe that just as in the days of the exodus, when, at Yahweh's mighty act of deliverance, Miriam and her companions sang their song of triumph and thanksgiving, so in the experience of Israel's new deliverance, wrought in her by Yahweh's punitive and redemptive discipline,

> There will she (Israel) sing
> Even as the day when she went up
> From the land of Egypt (2. 15b).

And at last—of this my faith is sure—after bitter discipline and privation, Israel's eyes will be opened and her heart reached. She will repent and respond, thrillingly vibrant to the wonder of Yahweh's redemptive love. She will be astir with fresh new life, a prosperous and a productive people (2. 21-23). As though she were a naïve adolescent child conscious of great resources and aware of strange, new, yet wonderful powers, my people will then exclaim unto Yahweh:

> I am like a green cypress tree!
> From me is found fruit for thee! (14. 8b.)

CHAPTER III

ISAIAH OF JERUSALEM

I WAS born in Jerusalem, the capital city of Judah, which in deep affection I call "the daughter of Zion" (1. 8). King Uzziah was then on the throne of my nation, under whose statesmanship Judah's lost glory was restored. He recovered Elath, gateway to Arabia, the most important port on the Red Sea, upon which many caravan routes converged, thus giving fresh impetus to Judaean commerce (2 Kings 14. 22). He battered down the walls of the old Philistine cities of Gath, Jabneh (Jamnia), and Ashdod, and built Judaean cities in the Philistine area. On his eastern frontier he made sure of the fealty of the bedouin sons of Ammon. And he protected Judah against the Arab nomadic tribes of the desert which had constantly raided her borders.

He strengthened at strategic points the fortification of Jerusalem. He trained the fighting power of our nation in separate detachments and thoroughly equipped our troops for battle. He constructed skillfully contrived machines of war and installed them on the towers and at the corners of the city wall. King Uzziah also inaugurated an extensive agricultural program, building towers in the desert to control the bedouins and keep the caravan routes open. He dug cisterns for his large herds in the lowland and on the plains. Under his rule our hills and fruitful fields soon resounded with the happy-hearted songs of husbandmen and reapers (2 Chronicles 26. 6-15).

The last years of King Uzziah were clouded by his falling a victim to the plague of leprosy, which disease first manifested itself on the New Year's Day of his twenty-seventh year of reign, when having presumptuously exercised his royal prerogatives by usurping the functions of the priesthood, he clashed with the priests on the very day of the great earthquake.[1] This put an end to his active reign and to the exercise of any priestly functions, but he was permitted to dwell in his house at freedom (2 Kings 15. 5-7). So for eleven years the crown prince Jotham carried on the functions of king. Yet, during those shadowed years, we continued to cherish our stricken monarch, for he had loved Judah and had made her name great.

The public-minded Judaean youth of my own age were convinced, however, that we were at the end of an era. The days of prosperity and security which, thanks to the weakened condition of Assyria, Judah had enjoyed, were past. Pul, a vigorous Assyrian soldier under Ashur-nirari, usurped the kingship of Assyria toward the end of King Uzziah's days, taking the name Tiglath-pileser III, and had already begun to show his mighty hand in the Fertile Crescent. And, on the other hand, in Egypt, far up the Nile, Pharaoh Piankhi was soon to establish the Nubian kingdom with its capital at Napata. I shall always remember that fateful morning when I awoke to learn that King Uzziah was dead.

As a boy I had often seen him, ere his leprosy forced him into privacy, for from my childhood I have been familiar with the life of the royal court. Now the strong hand of the great king, which even in sickness had continued to shape the destiny of Judah, was cold in death.

The serious-minded of our people felt that we stood at a crisis hour in our nation's life.

Along with a throng of fellow Judaeans filled with reverent sadness, I was permitted to enter the palace to gaze upon the still form of our dead monarch as he lay in state. Then, in silence, I passed at once into the Temple, where, in a soul-shaking experience, the temporal scene merged into the eternal, and in a moving vision I saw the *living King*,[2] the Lord, not merely of Judah, but the Lord of the whole earth.

He was seated upon a lofty, towering throne and the skirts of his robe of splendor filled the Holy Place. Above him were standing the seraphs, fiery serpentine, superhuman beings, Yahweh's attendants and guardians of the threshold of his house. Each seraph had three pairs of wings. With one pair he kept screening his face from the unbearable radiance of Yahweh's glory. With another pair his nakedness was concealed from the eyes of the Lord. A third pair was for flight to perform Yahweh's errands. And these lofty beings kept singing antiphonally a majestic hymn such as I had often heard rendered in the Temple choirs:

> Holy, Holy, Holy, is Yahweh of Hosts:
> His glory fills the whole earth (6. 3).

At the thrilling melody of these singing voices celebrating in perfect harmony the glory of Yahweh—the luster of his unapproachable righteousness—the foundations of the threshold trembled and the Holy Place began to be filled with the smokelike cloud which, since the days of Moses at Sinai, had symbolized Yahweh's presence. I was deeply stirred, for I was conscious that I was in the presence of God. There I stood trembling in awe and fear, full of a crushing sense of contrast between the shining righteousness of Yahweh and the sinfulness of my own soul, darkened as it was by the sinfulness of my people in which I was implicated. How could one such as I see the Lord and live? In inexpressible lamentation of spirit I cried out:

> Alas for me, for I am ruined—for a man
> Unclean of lips am I,
> And among a people, unclean
> Of lips am I dwelling—
> For the King, Yahweh
> Of hosts, my eyes have seen (6. 5).

In immediate response to my heart cry of confession, one of the seraphs flew from the threshold of the Temple to the altar in front of the Temple porch, and with the altar tongs took up a glowing, red-hot stone used for the transfer of altar fires. Flying swiftly unto me he touched my mouth with it and said:

> See, this has touched your lips;
> So your guilt is removed,
> And your sin is forgiven (6. 7).

My sense of guilt seemed to drop from my soul as a filthy garment and there swept over me a profound realization that Yahweh had forgiven me. Thus freed from the burden of sin, my heart became sensitive to Yahweh's will. I could now hear him taking counsel with his heavenly court as to who should be sent as a messenger to Judah:

> Whom shall I send,
> And who will go for us? (6. 8a.)

80

The answer flew to my lips. In an overwhelming eagerness to render service to this majestic King, I cried:

Here am I, send me! (6. 8b.)

Swiftly came his summons:

Go and speak to this people— (6. 9).

In these first moments of realization that Yahweh wanted me to be his prophet I was conscious that he was forearming me against swift disillusionment. From the very beginning of my prophetic career I felt the stubborn difficulties I would encounter as I attempted to carry out my commission. My words would fall upon dull ears. I would preach to Yahweh's superstitious people message after message but they would not comprehend my meaning. They would be void of insight into the significance of events. Yet I was to keep on proclaiming Yahweh's word—how often in these latter days I have realized it—until Judah shall have been desolated, and Yahweh's people reduced to a mere remnant like the stump of a felled tree.

In a mood of awed exultation I left the Temple that day. Every detail of the ecstatic experience is as vivid in my memory today, after forty-five years, as though it had happened yesterday. And all that I have said or done as Yahweh's prophet throughout this stormy period of Judah's history has grown out of that creative hour.

The lofty sense of Yahweh's majesty which this vision had deposited in my soul colored my early ministry. And my teaching then stood also under the strong influence of the shepherd prophet of Tekoa, whom I had

heard speak Yahweh's word just five years before. He
had preached that the day of Yahweh was coming and
that it would bring darkness, not light, to Israel (Amos
5. 18). So in those same ominous tones I began speaking
words of rebuke and denunciation to Judah.

My country was then overflowing with material prosperity. Evidences of military preparedness were on every
hand. But the worship of Yahweh had given way to the
worship of idols—with what scorn I uttered the word!
My people had abandoned Yahweh, having substituted
for his worship the magical pagan rites that had swept
from east and west into Judah. So I proclaimed to the
Judaeans that Yahweh had abandoned his people and
was just at the point of bringing his day of darkness, when
in stern condemnation and awful destruction he would
manifest himself (2. 6-8).

> Go into the rocks,
> And hide yourselves in the dust,
> Away from the terror of Yahweh,
> And away from his splendid majesty,
> When he arises to terrify the earth (2. 10).

The proud cedars of Lebanon and every brilliant
product of Judah's haughty civilization that had vaunted
itself in antagonism to Yahweh's majesty are to be destroyed on Yahweh's day.

> And the haughtiness of men shall be prostrated,
> And the loftiness of men humiliated;
> And Yahweh alone shall be exalted
> On that day (2. 17).

Unless the spirit of Judah changed radically I could
see nothing but anarchy ahead, for the words and deeds
of my people were such as to provoke the pure eyes of

Yahweh's glory. Our leaders were corrupt. So I lamented:

> As for my people, their ruler is a child,
> And women have dominion over them.
> O my people, those leading you mislead,
> And confuse the paths you should take (3. 12).
> See, the Lord Yahweh of hosts
> Is about to remove from Jerusalem and Judah
> Staff and support (3. 1).

Consequently, instead of enjoying orderly, stable government, I told them, our nation would be at the mercy of inexperienced, capricious leaders, so that political tyranny and moral degeneracy would result. Citizens of rank from our old Judaean families who had previously furnished men of nation-wide influence would refuse to accept leadership in such depressing times (3. 6-8). I laid the responsibility for the imminent national collapse right at the door of the elders and princes of Judah, for they had prostituted their leadership, using their political power for graft, and growing rich by plundering the poor. I faced these leaders with Yahweh's stern accusation because of the way they had dealt with his beloved vineyard, the Jewish nation:

> Yahweh takes his stand to conduct a case,
> And stands up to condemn his people;
> Yahweh enters into litigation
> With the elders of his people and his princes.
> It is you who have devoured the vineyard;
> Plunder taken from the poor is in your houses.
> What do you mean by crushing my people,
> And by grinding the face of the poor? (3. 14-15a.)

Yet the male leaders of Judah were not alone in their guilt. Often in the streets of Jerusalem I had watched

young women of the capital as they tripped along, richly
gowned, and brilliantly girdled, luring attention by the
gentle tinkling of their prized anklets. They would
mince along, attracting admiring glances by their
fashionably set hair, and leaving in their train a seductive aroma of perfume (3. 16). Yet how shallow were
these haughty young women with their brazen flirtations!
How shamelessly indifferent to the tragic injustice ram-
pant in our nation which should have stabbed their
souls awake! How far from their present selfish thoughts
were the certain future disasters awaiting them—rape,
slavery, and exile—when they would be face to face with
Yahweh's judgment! So I cried out:

> The Lord will smite with a scab
> The crown of the head of the daughters of Zion,
> And Yahweh will expose their shame (3. 17).
> Instead of perfume there shall be rottenness,
> And instead of a girdle, a captive rope;
> And instead of an artistic set of hair, baldness;
> And instead of a rich robe, a girding of sackcloth;
> Branding instead of beauty (3. 24).

I pictured the desperate straits to which these haughty
young women will be reduced when the young men of
Jerusalem who might have been their husbands shall
have been killed in battle. Then as many as seven of
them will accost one man, begging to become his property so as to come under his protection and escape disgrace (4. 1).

Judah's fearless herdsman prophet had denounced the
degenerate worship of the Canaanite fertility god Dod,
as he had encountered it at the ancient Yahweh shrine
at Beersheba (Amos 8. 14). The ceremonies associated
with this worship were the fertility rites of the old

Canaanite religion, and those magical rituals were very popular in Judah. They had been absorbed by my people into Judaean worship with the result that the stern, righteous Yahweh, known to Israel since the days of Moses, had become in the popular thought identical with the licentious Dod. On every side I saw the resulting degeneracy of Judah's religion. The serious demand for obedience to the moral requirements of Yahweh had been replaced by a materialistic, sentimental, and even licentious attachment to him. One day at the Feast of Booths, when vintage songs were in the air, I sang to my fellow Judaeans a parable about Yahweh and his vineyard, the Judaean nation.[3] My song began in biting irony as I took upon my lips words that characterized Yahweh as a Dod deity and aptly gave expression to the magical and sentimental conception my people had of him. "My darling," I called him, and designated him by the name of that Canaanite fertility god which in the popular cult of the Judaean people he had practically become. How they did listen as they heard Yahweh's prophet begin to sing!

> Let me sing for my darling,
> A song of my Dod about his vineyard (5. 1a).

My song first represented Yahweh, "my darling," as though he were a fertility deity, preparing his vineyard for a bountiful yield:

> My darling had a vineyard
> On a fertile slope:
> And he dug it carefully about, and freed it of stones,
> And he planted it with choice vines;
> And built a watch tower in the midst of it,
> And a wine vat also he hewed out in it (5. 1b-2a).

Dod had a right to expect a good yield, for his devotees had sung the appropriate magical ritual words over the vineyard, but he was doomed to disappointment:

> And he looked eagerly for it to yield grapes,
> But it bore stinking things (5. 2b).

My device had succeeded. They now began to see meaning in my parable. No longer in irony but now in open sincerity I appealed in *Yahweh's* name to Judah's reason. What more could a husbandman do for a vineyard than he had done, I argued, and why was the yield so disappointing? Then I described the decision at which the master of the vineyard had arrived. He will cease these constructive measures and will submit it to a series of calamities that will lay it waste. He will remove its protecting hedge and break down its encircling wall, allowing it to be overrun and ravaged. No longer will men sing over it the vintage rituals. The weeds will take it and dearth will stultify it. The passion in my voice gave them the key to my meaning: the gardener was Yahweh, the vineyard was the nation of Judah, the plants of the husbandman's delight were the men of Judah. No Dod ritual, interested only in the fertility of the land, could bring the kind of fruitage Yahweh desires. For I saw that what he wanted was not primarily vines but men, not grapes but acts of justice and good will, for

> He (Yahweh) looked for rule, but, behold, misrule!
> For redress, but, behold, distress![4] (5. 7.)

Yahweh's vineyard was not Palestinian *land* but the Judaean *nation*. He was seeking to make out of Judah

86

a good society of Judaeans based on justice and righteous-ness. But the contemporary religion of my fellow countrymen in its crass materialism and shallow magic was leading straight to social anarchy and chaos. So Yahweh, who, like a gardener thrilling to his task, had nurtured and cared for his people, must now give them over to a series of calamities which their own acts had brought upon them, stern punitive and disciplinary measures.

My parable had caught their attention and I deter-mined to hold it, so I proceeded to point out the specific ways in which my fellow Judaeans had disappointed and violated Yahweh's reasonable expectation of Judah. In a mood of mingled lament and threat I uttered Yahweh's sevenfold woe upon the leaders of Judaean society (5. 8-23; 10. 1-3).

I condemned the greedy land grabbers who had ruth-lessly wrested property from small owners and concen-trated it in the hands of a few. I condemned them for their dissipation through strong drink and pointed out how their corrupt, gay living had blinded them to the spiritual insights of religion (5. 8, 11-12).

> Therefore, so Yahweh said, my people have gone into
>   captivity,
> Because of their lack of knowledge (5. 13).

I condemned them for their skeptical doubt as to the moral government of Yahweh and for their irreverent, presumptuous challenge to him to prove his power. I condemned them for their flagrant blurring of moral distinctions, calling what they knew was evil, good, and what they knew was good, evil. I condemned the self-

satisfied conceit of Judaean politicians. I condemned
the dilettantes of fast Judaean society—mighty (!) topers
of wine, I sarcastically called them—valiant (!) in mixing
drinks. Their self-indulgence had so blunted their official conscience that they were being repeatedly seduced
by bribes, and thus the innocent Judaean with a just
case was flagrantly robbed of his rights. And I condemned the corrupt judges who administered the laws or
arbitrated disputes with utter disregard of the rights of
the individuals concerned, distributing justice (!) in
proportion to the size of the bribe handed over to them.
Thus the righteous poor of Judah, the unprotected widows, and the orphaned children fell an easy prey to their
crookedness.

After concerning myself for several years with my own
people, my interest turned to Ephraim, Judah's brother
kingdom. Ephraim as well as Judah had experienced
the awful destruction of the days of Uzziah wrought by
the earthquake. How vividly I remember it! And
Ephraim had been greatly weakened by the exorbitant
tribute exacted by Tiglath-pileser from King Menahem
(2 Kings 15. 20). Yet from all that I could learn Ephraim
was dully complacent and superficially optimistic, quite
blind to any future peril which the suffering already experienced presaged. Just as Amos had journeyed to
Israel and delivered his message at Bethel where he could
best get the attention of Yahweh's people, so I went to
Samaria[5] to deliver Yahweh's rebuke. Upon every side
I heard expressions of their superficial optimism which,
in a quite unwarranted spirit of boasting, they uttered in
a popular proverb:

Bricks have fallen, but with hewn stone we shall
rebuild;
Sycamores have been hewn down, but with cedars
we shall replace them (9. 10).

I faced these superficial optimists of Ephraim with a
carefully planned address containing a reiterated refrain
which embodied the persistency of Yahweh's acts of judgment and their successive unfolding in the life of the
Northern Kingdom. I declared to the inhabitants of
Samaria that their land would be attacked from the east
by the Syrians, and from the west by the Philistines, yet

In spite of all this Yahweh's anger has not turned away,
But his hand is stretched out still (9. 12b).

I proclaimed a single day of awful disaster which awaited
Israel when leaders and common people alike would
perish. Even the brilliant flower of Ephraimite young
manhood and the helpless widows and orphans would not
escape, but

In spite of all this his anger has not turned away,
But his hand is stretched out still (9. 17b).

I described the horrors of a civil war which would sweep
through the Northern Kingdom like a fierce, devouring
fire, in which bloodthirsty Ephraimites and Manassites,
moved by old tribal jealousies, would destroy one another and both would at length turn against my people
Judah; still

In spite of all this his anger has not turned away,
But his hand is stretched out still (9. 21b).

Yet one more punishment Ephraim was destined to suffer. Yahweh will signal, he will "whistle" for Assyria
and the Assyrian will come! In vivid, imaginative words

I pictured the destructive advance of the intrepid Assyrian upon Ephraim:

> And see speedily, swiftly he will come.
> Not a faint one and not a stumbler in his ranks.
> He does not grow drowsy and he does not sleep;
> And the girdle of his loins is not loosened,
> And the thong of his sandals is not snapped.
> Whose arrows are sharpened,
> And all his bows bent;
> His horses' hoofs
> Are esteemed as flint,
> And his wheels are like the storm wind:
> And if one looks at the earth,
> Behold distressing darkness!
> Yes, the light about its beauty has grown dark
>   (5. 26b-28, 30).

My warning went unheeded in Ephraim. Indeed, this nation soon allied itself with a concerted political coalition of Westland peoples which was destined to result ultimately in its own destruction. I was back in Jerusalem when suddenly news came to me that the Syrian army had halted temporarily in the land of Ephraim (7. 2). King Ahaz, our young, timid monarch, who some seven years before had succeeded Jotham on the throne of Judah, was hurled by this news into a panic of fear which indeed the rank and file of my countrymen shared. What could this friendly halt of Syria in Ephraimite territory signify other than a hostile conspiracy of these two nations against him? But of still more immediate consternation to him was the rumor which would not down that this conspiracy aimed at dethroning him in order to exalt over Judah, as soon as it could be brought under Syrian control, an Aramaean puppet king, the son of Tabeel. Small wonder that this news occasioned such trepidation:

> And his heart and the heart of his people trembled,
> Like trees of a forest shake before the wind (7. 2b).

I kept hearing on every hand from the lips of the fear-stricken populace of Jerusalem about the "conspiracy" from the north. Amid these hectic days of national excitement I had a deeply moving experience of Yahweh. I became aware of his overpowering presence as he revealed his personal will for me, his prophet, in the crisis. He taught me that I must not allow myself to be swept up into this popular mania of fear because of any plot concocted by these nations of the north. Nor was I to approve the trend now rapidly gaining headway in Jerusalem, toward seeking Assyria's protection against the threatened invasion by the payment of tribute. Now it became clear to me that Syria and Ephraim were working to unite the small Mediterranean nations in order to shake off the dominion of Assyria in the Westland. But Yahweh showed me that I must withstand all such political action in Judah. In this moving experience of ecstatic seizure, Yahweh thus imparted to me his will:

> You shall not call "conspiracy,"
> All which this people calls "conspiracy;"
> And their fear you shall not share,
> Nor shall you dread (it).
> Yahweh of hosts,
> With him shall you conspire;
> And he shall be your object of fear,
> And he shall be your terror-inspirer.
> Then he will become a sanctuary (8. 12-14a).

This experience convinced me that my people should

neither surrender to the attempted compulsion of Judah
on the part of Syria and Ephraim to join them in an anti-
Assyrian alliance, nor seek its security at the price of
paying tribute to Assyria. Judah must rely solely upon
Yahweh and must develop such national policies as
would reveal that he, not Assyria, was Judah's real Lord
and the sole source of my nation's security and stability.
And if my people should ignore my prophetic counsel,
they would be ignoring Yahweh, who would then of
necessity become to them, even as to Israel as well,

> A stone to strike them,
> And a rock to stumble on,
> To the two houses of Israel;
> A trap and a snare,
> To those dwelling in Jerusalem (8. 14b).

While I was living under the first glow of this spiritual
illumination, I felt an impulse from Yahweh to take my
little son, to whom under Yahweh's revelation I had
given the prophetic name, A-Remnant-Shall-Return, and
directly confront King Ahaz with Yahweh's counsel.
Taking my little boy by the hand I took the Fuller's
Field road out of Jerusalem to the end of the channel of
the upper pool, where I suddenly encountered our agitated young ruler, under the threat of siege, anxiously
inspecting one of the aqueducts of the city. With my
own spirit calmed and steadied by Yahweh's revelation
to me, I keenly felt how groundless was the king's terror.
I knew that the two powers threatening invasion were
like the final flicker of two torches just going out. Oh,
if I could only help our king to see it, if I could but persuade him to resist the popular panic, and unite the
energies of our people behind him in confiding in Yah-

weh and in the development of a positive program of
national action which such confidence would generate!
With what deep earnestness I proclaimed to him Yahweh's word!

> See to it that you show quietness;
> Fear not; and as for your courage, let it not be soft,
> Because of these two stumps of smoking firebrands
>   (7. 4a).

Yahweh's revelation had convinced me that if my
people would but rest calmly in the all-sufficient strength
of its God, neither King Rezon of Damascus, nor King
Pekah, son of Remaliah, of Samaria, could ever domi-
nate Judah.   They, even at their greatest military
strength, were but human powers.   The real head of
Judah—if only I could get our king to see it!—was Yahweh, Jerusalem's unseen yet living Lord.   If Judah would
but trust in Yahweh and develop its national program
on the basis of the righteousness and truth that express
his nature and will, the threat of these northern nations
could be ignored.   Without such a line of action Judah
had no abiding power as a people.   Pouring my whole
soul into a trenchant appeal to our king and his people,
I cried in deep earnestness:

> If you will not confide,
> Surely you cannot abide[6] (7. 9b).

In tense eagerness I awaited his response.   But my
passionate words had made no impression upon him.
Shortly after this encounter I confronted Ahaz again.
Still hoping I could persuade him to accept my counsel,
and calmly certain of its truth, I challenged him to request from Yahweh any signal proof he might demand

that it was Yahweh's word. But King Ahaz cared not for Yahweh's word. He proudly responded:

> I will not ask and I will not put Yahweh to the test (7. 12).

But his pious-sounding refusal was but a bluff, for, as I was soon to learn, he had already begun negotiations with Tiglath-pileser III, king of Assyria, to secure Assyrian protection for his throne in return for Judah's payment of tribute (2 Kings 16. 7).

It was at that moment, when face to face with this timid, faithless monarch, that I felt, in a mighty mood of imminence, the pressure of the centuries-old hope of my people, that one day an ideal king would appear enthroned over Yahweh's people. *Now,* so it seemed to me, those ancient, treasured hopes were about to be realized! The king in hypocritical humility had refused to ask for Yahweh's sign, but Yahweh would give him a sign which would leave him in no doubt concerning his will. The young woman of wonder and hope, already revered in the pious longings of my people, would soon give birth to a child whose nature and bearing are summed up in the name to be given him—Immanuel, God-is-with-us. This child would both symbolize and guarantee the presence and power of Yahweh in Judah mediated through him. His food of curds and honey would be such as nourished infant deities. Before this child would be old enough to make ethical choices the land of Judah would be overrun and decimated by Assyria. This child will be Yahweh's Messiah, and his presence in Judah will, on the one hand, guarantee Yahweh's discipline and punishment of Judah by Assyria,

94

for eventually fruitful hills and fertile vineyards will be overrun and ravaged by that ruthless invader and the whole country will pass out of cultivation. But, on the other hand, the Messiah's presence will guarantee, in that day when Yahweh's discipline of Judah shall have accomplished its aim, that Yahweh will keep alive in the very face of general destruction, an inner nucleus, a disciplined and repentant remnant of Judaeans, who, reduced to utter simplicity, would yet live in comfort and plenty. I painted in glowing terms this life of respectable simplicity: then,

A man will nourish a heifer and two sheep;
And it shall come to pass that because of the abundance
Of yield of milk,
Everyone who is left in the land
Shall eat curds and honey (7. 21-22).

Such conceptions were beyond Ahaz. Yet, while the policy which the king would follow hung in the balance, I received an impulse from Yahweh to lodge in the mind of the close counselors of Ahaz a timely and pertinent warning against appeal to Assyria, toward which policy it was rumored the king was about to turn. In the presence of two well-known official witnesses who stood close to our king, upon a large tablet, conspicuous enough to attract general attention, I wrote in Hebrew characters a mystic sentence which in dream experience Yahweh had deposited in my mind:

"Concerning 'HASTENING-TO-THE-PLUNDER — SPEEDING-TO-THE-BOOTY.'"

Then I went home to my wife, whom I lovingly called the prophetess, for as truly as I, she was a dedicated soul,

sensitive to Yahweh's communications, my counselor and
my comrade. I left the mystic inscription unexplained,
for Yahweh had not yet revealed to me its enigmatic
meaning. But nine months later when our second son
was born, Yahweh revealed its significance to me.
It was to be the name of my second child. That
strange name, "HASTENING-TO-THE-PLUNDER—SPEEDING-
TO-THE-BOOTY," wherever the lad went, even in his infancy, was to preach to Judah the near-at-hand raiding
of Syria and Israel by Assyria. Even before our second
son shall have learned to call myself and the prophetess
"papa" and "mama" (8. 4), the Assyrian king shall have
invaded Palestine and plundered rich booty from Damascus and Samaria. Then Judah's similar fate would be
perilously near.

But all such warnings went unheeded. At a price that
impoverished the royal and temple treasuries King Ahaz
negotiated for the protection of Assyria (2 Kings 16. 7f.).
When this had become a matter of common knowledge,
Yahweh, in another luminous moment of insight, caused
me to see how Ahaz's policy, which encouraged Tiglath-
pileser to invade the Westland, would prove suicidal to
my nation. I had counseled Ahaz to turn away from
foreign alliance and in calm national confidence trust
in Yahweh's sufficiency for Judah. But instead Ahaz
had melted with fear before King Rezon of Damascus
and King Pekah of Israel, and had invited the ruthless
Assyrian monarch into Palestine. I told them that in
rejecting Yahweh's counsel it was as though they had
spurned the gently flowing, life-nourishing waters of
Shiloah which flowed from the only true spring in Jerusalem, in order to give preference to the destructive

Euphrates which I pictured as overflowing its channels in a devastating flood, sweeping down through Israel and on into Judah, where it would threaten the very existence of our nation. Swiftly changing the figure of speech, I described the Assyrian as a hostile vulture with his powerful wings outstretched, just ready to swoop down upon its prey, the Judaean nation (8. 8).

I now realized that this open rejection of Yahweh's word by King Ahaz ended a stage in my prophetic ministry. I knew that as long as a king of Ahaz's spirit was on the throne of my people it would be useless to try to get his ear. For a while my public ministry ceased, yet I was by no means idle. I seized upon this time of withdrawal from public teaching to give practical embodiment to my conviction that even after the Assyrian had exerted his desolating power upon Judah, a remnant would be saved. I began to develop in Jerusalem a religious society of my disciples, a spiritual nucleus of receptive and responsive minds in Zion, distinct from Judah's political parties, which might become the foundation and nucleus of a new society based on faith in Yahweh, and composed of those who believed in his presence and power in the nation's life. So I formulated my plan. There was nothing for me to do except

> Preserve the revelation,[7]
> Seal up the teaching among my disciples,
> And then I will wait for Yahweh,
> Who is hiding his face
> From the house of Jacob:
> And I will look eagerly for him (8. 16-17).

My disciples were to be the living documents upon whose hearts, in unforgettable meaning, I was to write my teaching. I was convinced that the presence of such a group of master and disciples in Jerusalem would keep alive the revelation of Yahweh, rooted deeply in this nucleus of faithful Judaeans, and would be in itself an effective witness to the validity of Yahweh's truth. When people saw me with my disciples and wondered who we were and what we were about, I explained to them:

Lo, I and the children whom Yahweh has given to me,
Are for signs and symbols in Israel,
From Yahweh of hosts,
Who dwells in Mount Zion (8. 18).

I saw just ahead an era of great uncertainty when necromancy and the magical arts would be given unwonted place in the popular religion. In such a time this inner nucleus would summon the people by precept and example to attend to Yahweh's words:

To the teaching and to the revelation! (8. 20.)

Such would be their challenge, and unless this challenge to study and absorb the truth which Yahweh had revealed to me were followed by this inner nucleus of Judaeans, I could see no dawn for my benighted people.

For the time being King Ahaz was able to defend his capital against the combined Syrian-Israelite siege (7. 1). It must have seemed to him that his Assyrian protector took his time in coming to his aid. But within a year Tiglath-pileser came. His expedition moved down the old military route taken by Assyrian kings along the Mediterranean coast. He took and looted the old Philistine town of Gaza, the gateway to Egypt.[8] I knew that this coastal campaign was but preliminary to his main objective, Syria.   So as a warning to my own people who might well fear for Jerusalem I cried:

> See, Damascus is about to be removed from being a city,
> And it will become a ruins,
> Its cities will be abandoned forever (17. 1).

And I knew that another incident in Tiglath-pileser's campaign against Syria would be his overrunning of the kingdom of Israel, so I spoke of the suffering awaiting Judah's brother kingdom:

> The glory of Jacob shall be laid low,
> And the fatness of his flesh shall grow lean;
> And it shall be as when a reaper gathers standing
>   (corn),
> And his arm gathers the ears,
> Like one gleaning ears
> In the valley of Rephaim.
> Or as at the striking of an olive tree,
> Gleanings shall be left on it;
> Two or three berries
> At the tip of the topmost branch,
> Four or five on the boughs of the tree.
> On that day your cities shall be abandoned
> Like the desolations of the Hivites and the Amorites
>   (17. 4-6, 9).

As was the case with my own people, the worship of Yahweh in the kingdom of Israel was full of pagan fertility rituals which the Israelites had absorbed from the Canaanites.   In periods of stress and strain, such as the present, they plied their magical Adonis rites such as the Adonis gardens with great intensity, thus seeking to arouse Yahweh's help.   Israel's alliance with Syria, a people among whom such rites were exceptionally popular, had strengthened the lure of this cult.   So I lamented:

> Since you have forgotten the God of your salvation,
> And do not remember the rock that protects you,
> Therefore you plant plants of Adonis[9]
> And seed it with vine slips of an alien (god);
> In the day you plant, you fence it about,
> And on the morrow you make your seed to sprout,
> But the harvest flees away in the day of sickness
> And of incurable pain (17. 10-11).

It happened as I said. Tiglath-pileser fell upon the kingdom of Israel, made an Assyrian province of the old tribal area of Naphtali, and carried off most of the Israelite population with their possessions to Assyria. Only Samaria, King Pekah's capital city, did he leave untouched, in consideration of his cringing payment of tribute (2 Kings 15. 29f.).

Then Tiglath-pileser turned to punish Syria.[10] He utterly routed the forces of King Rezon and locked him up in his capital. He ruthlessly decimated the territory around Damascus, which at length submitted to the siege, and the famous old Syrian capital fell. As soon as Tiglath-pileser had mastered Damascus, our King Ahaz paid his new protector and overlord a visit. As a consequence of this political and cultural contact he introduced into our Temple in Jerusalem, with the cooperation of Urijah, the priest, an altar of Assyrian pattern. He placed it in front of the eastern door of the sanctuary, and moved the old bronze altar to the north of it, where it continued to be used as an altar for the practice of divination (2 Kings 16. 10-16). Many Judaeans, priests and people alike, detested this intrusion of Assyrian innovations, but the king had complete control over the priesthood and the cult of the Temple.[11]

I knew that the days of Samaria were also numbered.

100

It was a proud city and had been chosen by King Omri as his capital because it was almost impregnable. But to me those lovely white-terraced streets were comparable to a chaplet of flowers wreathing the flushed temples of a reveler, for Samaria's leaders, even her priests and prophets, were dissipated and ribald. But Samaria's dissolute life was nearly at an end. Under the persistent peltings of Assyria it must eventually succumb. So I predicted its imminent fall to the ruthless Assyrians, hungry for conquest:

Woe to the majestic crown
Of the dwellers in Ephraim,
And the withering flower of its glorious beauty,
Which is upon the head of those who are smitten down
   of wine.
Lo, the Lord has a hand, one strong and mighty;
Like a hailstorm,
A destructive tempest,
Like a flood of waters,
Mighty, overflowing,
He thrusts it (Samaria) down to the earth!
The glorious crown of the drunkards of Ephraim
Will be trampled under foot.
And the withering flower of its glorious beauty,
Which is at the head of the fertile valley,
Shall be like a first ripe fig
Before summer,
Which, when one sees it,
While it is yet in one's hand, one swallows (28. 1-4).

Seven years later, the third after his accession to the Assyrian throne, Shalmaneser V came against King Hoshea of Israel, who had shaken off the Assyrian yoke and allied himself with King So (Sibu) of Egypt (2 Kings 17. 4). Shalmaneser captured and imprisoned King Hoshea, and after a three years' siege the Assyrian forces captured Samaria, his capital, and King Sargon, who had just succeeded Shalmaneser upon the Assyrian throne, entered Israel's capital in triumph. He took as captives practically its entire population, nearly twenty-eight thousand people with their fifty war chariots, and settled them in various parts of Mesopotamia.[12] Our king was rewarded by Assyria in being handed the southern Israelite hill country, which was now incorporated into Judah.[13]

Sargon rebuilt Samaria, and, making it an Assyrian province presided over by an Assyrian governor, he settled captive peoples there whom he had taken from other conquered regions. Thus the kingdom of Israel came to a sad and solemn end. Now the responsibility of being in all reality the people of Yahweh rested solely upon my nation Judah.

The following year when Hezekiah had been king of Judah three years, a vigorous new leader began to show his hand in the affairs of the Westland, Merodach-baladan. He was a powerful Chaldaean prince of Bit Yakin, a region situated at the northern end of the Persian Gulf. He was a man of real ability and genius. With the vigorous military backing of the Elamites and the support of the Aramaean and Chaldaean tribesmen, Merodach-baladan took advantage of the change in succession to the Assyrian throne to make himself master of Babylon and to have himself proclaimed king on New Year's Day. His shrewd political schemes gave incentive to a number of intrigues which then began in the Westland against Assyria. One uprising centered in Hamath on the upper Orontes River, but it was crushed and Hamath was made an Assyrian province. In this campaign Sargon met in battle the allies of Hamath, Hanno of Gaza, and So of Egypt, at Raphia, just north of Gaza on the borders of Egypt, and decisively defeated them, deporting nine thousand captives.[14] Pharaoh Bocchoris of Egypt, at that time, warded off an invasion of his land by the payment of tribute.[15]

Another revolt soon broke out which centered in the old Philistine town of Ashdod. Azuri, king of Ashdod, withheld his tribute from Assyria and disseminated the spirit of revolt among the nations of the Westland. His messengers were lent a ready ear by the leaders of my people. But I was opposed to it from the start. I knew that the leaders of Ashdod and of the other nations whom Azuri was inciting to revolt, would never have attempted to throw off the Assyrian dominion unless they could depend upon Egypt's help. But I was convinced that this confident hope for Egyptian aid would bring to my fellow Judaeans bitter disillusionment. My people were utterly blind to this and were ready to grasp at any straw that might promise release from the galling Assyrian yoke. Under the impetus of an intuition from Yahweh I determined to warn my fellow Judaeans in a startling manner. I began to go about Jerusalem as though I were a captive, naked and barefoot (20. 2). For me it meant deep self-renunciation and annoyance, as many Judaeans scoffed at me.

In the meantime Sargon of Assyria quelled the revolt in Ashdod. But the Ashdodites, strongly anti-Assyrian, rebelled again, and this time Sargon with his bodyguard marched against the city. I vigorously resisted the strong tides of opinion in Jerusalem, which, under pledges of Egyptian backing, favored alliance with Ashdod. A new and vigorous dynasty in Egypt, the Ethiopian, had just emerged under Pharaoh Shabaka, who was showing fresh initiative against Assyria. This fact made the drift of opinion toward Egypt all the stronger in Judah.

But before any concerted plot had taken concrete form and ere Egypt could assert its hand, Sargon marched against Ashdod and took it, conquering its seaport and Gath as well.[16] Yahweh now led me to teach my countrymen the full import of my symbolic action. It was intended to impress upon Judah, with unforgettable emphasis, the folly of depending for relief upon a nation which would itself succumb to Assyria. Those who had scoffed at my strange actions now listened while I explained to them:

> Just as I, Yahweh's servant, have walked naked and barefoot three years, as a sign and a symbol concerning Egypt and concerning Ethiopia, so shall the king of Assyria drive off the captives of Egypt and the exiles of Ethiopia, little boys and old men, naked and barefoot, with their buttocks exposed (20. 3-4).

In spite of all that I could do, the drift toward Egyptian dependence continued to grow among my people. One day I saw ambassadors from Ethiopia at the court in Jerusalem. They had come down the Nile in swift papyrus vessels with pledges of support to Judah if we would but join the nations of the Westland revolt. I could not help admiring the tall, sleek physiques of these official envoys from their famed nation. Most of my people were in favor of accepting Egypt's offer of assistance. But I sharply opposed it. Judah needed no such assistance. Yahweh had granted me an ecstatic moment of insight which led me to direct Judah's attention above

Ethiopia to him alone for help. So seeking to influence
my countrymen against such alliance I cried out:

> Go (home), you swift messengers,
> To a nation tall and shining,
> To a people dreaded afar,
> A nation mighty and all-subduing (18. 2b).

I had become aware of Yahweh's mighty purpose which
was quietly ripening in history, just as the glowing, shimmering heat of the full noon and the dew cloud of the
night in quiet, unhurrying process ripen the harvest.
And that calm purpose of Yahweh, thus moving unerr-
ingly to its fruitage, was the destruction of Assyria (18.
4-6). It would be Yahweh, not the help of Egypt, who
would bring that scourge of nations to its end.

One day during this anxious period when I was doing
my utmost to save the political leaders of Jerusalem from
the folly of dependence upon Egypt, I encountered
Shebna, the financial head of our government, and member of the Egyptian party in Jerusalem. I found him
hewing out on the heights a death chamber for himself,
as though aping the Egyptian Pharaohs, carving out his
own elaborate tomb from the rock! I was indignant at his
self-seeking and bold presumption, so I declared to him:

> Yahweh is about to hurl you out violently,
> O mighty man,
> Forcibly seizing you.
> He will roll you up tight,
> Like a ball, to a land
> Broad in extent.
> There shall you die,
> And there shall be your glorious tomb,
> You dishonor to the house of the Lord!
> I will depose you from your office,
> And from your station I will demote you (22. 17-19).

In those strategic hours King Hezekiah became deathly sick with a painful inflamed boil. I went to the palace and was granted admission to his bedside. I saw that he was in a desperate condition so I ventured to counsel him:

> Give directions to your household;
> For you are about to die,
> And shall not live (38. 1b).

But he was in no mood to give any final charges or to talk with anyone. With a gesture that made clear to me his desire for privacy, he turned his face to the wall, and I heard his lips, through a voice of weeping, framing a prayer unto Yahweh. I left him for the time. But Judah needed the strong hand of our king who had now begun to heed prophetic counsel (Jeremiah 26. 19), and Yahweh awakened in me confidence that he would recover. I went again to see him and suggested that they bind a poultice of figs upon the angry-looking sore. To the great joy of King Hezekiah himself and to the rejoicing of all Judah, he recovered (38. 1-5, 21).

King Sargon was succeeded on the throne of Assyria by Sennacherib. Merodach-baladan, the Chaldaean, who had been ousted from Babylon by Sargon, again took advantage of the change of succession on the Assyrian throne, and with the help of his own Chaldaean tribes, the Aramaean tribes, and a contingent of fearless Arab nomads, he regained the throne of Babylon.[17] Then he turned to Judah, hoping that he might induce the small nations in the Westland to revolt at the same time that he was leading the Chaldaean uprising in the east. Merodach-baladan sent a friendly delegation under the safe conduct of the Arabs whose help he had secured, along the caravan route from Babylon to Jerusalem, with letters and a present to Hezekiah. Ostensibly their errand was simply to congratulate our king upon his recovery from illness, but I knew its hidden purpose.

Our monarch was flattered by this visit of Chaldaean envoys. He treated them with the greatest of courtesy and openly disclosed to them our national resources. I accosted King Hezekiah after they had gone, and questioned him about the delegation—where they had come from, what he had shown them, and what they had said —and the king answered me quite frankly. But I knew the spirit of Merodach-baladan well enough to be sure that the presence of his envoys in Jerusalem meant nothing good for my people. I spoke to the king in deep earnestness and gave him Yahweh's warning:

> Lo, days are coming when all that is in your house, and whatever your fathers have stored up until today, shall be carried off to Babylon. Not a thing shall be left. And some of your sons whom you shall generate, whom you shall beget, shall be taken, and they shall be eunuchs in the palace of the king of Babylon (39. 5-7).

King Hezekiah responded quite humbly:

> Good is the word of Yahweh which you have spoken. But in my days, at any rate, there will be peace and stability (39. 8).

At first Merodach-baladan succeeded in his schemes. Exploiting the hatred which Babylon, ancient home of science, religion, and commerce, had always felt toward the Assyrian overlord, and playing on the resentment held against the Assyrian by all of the small peoples in the Westland, he was successful in stirring up the fires of general revolt. Our political leaders were strongly committed to participation in this rebellion, and in spite of all that I could say or do they began negotiations to secure the backing of Egypt. With pain of heart I saw a delegation of Judaean princes and envoys setting out toward the cities of Zoan and Hanes[18] in the Egyptian Delta, on their way to the Ethiopian court. I knew their diplomatic errand would eventuate only in national humiliation and chagrin. So in Yahweh's name I spoke out my condemnation of their mission:

> Woe to the rebelling sons,
> Who take counsel,
> But not from me;
> Who pour out a libation,[19]
> But not of my spirit;
> So as to add
> Sin unto sin.
> Who are on their way to go down to Egypt,
> But have not asked at my mouth;
> To seek refuge in the protection of Pharaoh,
> Yes, to seek shelter in the shadow of Egypt!
> But the protection of Pharaoh will be a source of shame
>   to you,
> And the shelter in the shade of Egypt a cause of disgrace
>   (30. 1-3).

I pictured the caravan of our envoys with their asses and camels loaded down with presents for the Ethiopian court, making their perilous way through the death-haunted desert—and all in vain,

> To a people who cannot be of benefit,
> Who help with mere vapor and emptiness.
> Therefore I call it (Egypt)
> "Rahab, the Destroyed"[20] (30. 6d-7).

I was deeply aroused by these events. Repeatedly I declared to the political leaders of my people the folly of their resort to Egypt. They counted themselves prac-

tical, realistic politicians (29. 14f.). But they were rebellious toward Yahweh and utterly lacking in the
venture of faith. Their attitude toward the seers and
prophets who shared my views was that of superiority
and condescension. They wanted to control those of us
who dared to proclaim what the Holy One had caused us
to see and to hear. They encouraged us to preach not
truth but flatteries. They sought illusions, not reality.
We were obstacles in the way of their politics, so they
said:

> Get out of (our) way!
> Turn aside from (our) path!
> Give us a rest from
> The Holy One of Israel! (30. 11.)

They felt secure in their crookedness and craftiness.
But I saw—ah, how vividly Yahweh had revealed it unto
me!—that their godless policies were leading my people
to certain national ruin which I described as being,

> Like a lowering breach,
> In a high wall,
> Which all of a sudden
> Comes to its crash;
> And its crash will be like the shivering into pieces of
>   a potter's jar,
> Crushed without sparing,
> So that there cannot be found
> Among its broken pieces a potsherd,
> For snatching up fire from the hearth,
> Or for dipping up water from a cistern (30. 13-14).

Although my teaching had failed of its immediate objective, an intuition from Yahweh now led me to write
down for posterity the truth which he had revealed to
me, that my people might at length heed it, and return

to their only basis of hope. An impulse from Yahweh
thus directed me:

> Now, go in, write it
> Upon a tablet in their presence;
> And upon a book inscribe it,
> And it shall be for a later day,
> A witness forever (30. 8).

So I went into my house and I wrote the sentence which
summed up Yahweh's revelation to me in those critical
hours. In it is concentrated the quintessence of my message to Judah:

> By turning back and by calmness shall you be saved,
> In showing quietness and in confidence
> Shall be your strength (30. 15).

When Judah turns back from Egypt unto Yahweh, when
my people cease their alliances with other nations, and
in calm trust depend solely upon him for their security,
then and then only can Judah be secure. By this act I
appealed to time. I am confident that history will still
prove the truth of this teaching.

How blind were our Egypt-bent leaders, who thought
themselves very wise, as they carefully computed the
strength of Egyptian horses and chariots, yet ignored the
strength of God! I cried to them:

> Woe to those who are going down to Egypt for help,
> Who put their trust in horses;
> And base their confidence upon chariots, because they
>   are many,
> And upon horsemen because they are numerous;
> But do not gaze upon the Holy One of Israel,
> Nor resort unto Yahweh! (31. 1.)

How my country did exaggerate the wisdom and strength
of Egypt! Yet even at its greatest, Egypt's wisdom was
but human wisdom, its military resources, merely material strength, so I continued:

> Now the Egyptians are men and not God;
> And their horses are flesh and not spirit (31. 3).

Soon Sennacherib got into action to quell the rebellions against Assyria. First he ousted Merodach-baladan
from Babylon and forced him to flee in terror. Then he
placed Bel-ibni, a young Babylonian prince who had
grown up in Sennacherib's palace,[21] upon the throne of
Babylon, and I knew that the Assyrian monarch would
speedily turn westward to punish Judah.

These were exciting days in Jerusalem as the plans in
the Westland matured for concerted resistance against
Assyria. Yet I was inwardly calm and serene, for Yahweh had taught me the meaning of events, and I could
now see his mighty purpose at work in history and how
even Assyria was related to it. I had by that time come
to understand how this ruthless military nation, which
had in its heart only to destroy and to cut off nations, and
which sought to establish its empire by flaying, impaling,
mutilating, and burning,[22] was in reality a "rod" held
securely in Yahweh's hand to give vent to his indignation
against Judah. Assyria was an "axe" but it was Yahweh
who was hewing with it! It was a "saw" but Yahweh was
wielding it! And when Assyria had meted out Yahweh's
judgment upon my people, Assyria would itself be destroyed (10. 5-27). Soon Assyria would march toward
Jerusalem. Imaginatively I pictured the hostile Assyrian
drawing near:[23]

> He has come to Ai,
> He has come to Michmash,
> The inhabitants of Gebim they have brought into safety,
> He has crossed the path,
> He has made Geba his place of camp,
> In Migron he has deposited his baggage train.
> Madmenah has taken flight,
> Ramah is terrified,
> Gibeah of Saul has escaped.
> Cry with your voice, daughter of Gallim!
> Give attention, Laishah!
> Answer her, Anathoth!
> Yet today at Nob will he stand,
> He will brandish his hand
> Against the hill of the daughter of Zion (10. 28-32).

Yet I was not afraid for Jerusalem, for just when the destruction of our capital would seem certain and imminent, in vivid imagination I saw the Assyrian swiftly laid low like a felled forest in the Lebanon:

> The Lord, Yahweh of hosts,
> Is lopping off the boughs with a crash!
> And the high in stature shall be hewn down,
> And the tall shall be laid low:
> And the thickets of the forest shall be struck away
>   with an iron tool,
> And Lebanon in its majesty will fall (10. 33-34).

In those days my mind was full of Assyria as it lay within the range of Yahweh's purpose. I recalled to my fellow countrymen the age-long menace of its powerful army, composed as it was of diverse peoples, as it had repeatedly surged in mighty waves of conquest against the little nations of the Westland. I cried:

> Ah! the commotion of many nations,
> That are turbulent like the roaring of the sea;
> And the uproar of the people, like the din
> Of mighty waters, are they in uproar (17. 12).

But Yahweh had led me to see that this turbulent, ruthless, motley army would at length find in him its master, for

> He will rebuke them,
> And they shall flee far off (17. 13a).

The fate which awaits this terror-striking scourge of the nations is sudden, swift destruction, and that at Yahweh's hands:

> At evening time, lo terror!
> But before morning he has vanished.
> This is the fate of him that is plundering us,
> And the lot of him that loots us (17. 14).

I now began to see that Yahweh's purpose with regard to Assyria concerned not only Judah but our neighboring nations of the Westland as well, and indeed all the nations of the earth.   And Yahweh had taught me that as that purpose was unalterable, so it could neither be frustrated nor annulled, and I declared in Yahweh's name:

> Just as I have intended,
> So shall it come to pass;
> And just as I have devised,
> It shall stand:
> That I will shatter Assyria in my land,
> And upon my mountains I will tread him down;
> Then his yoke will be removed from them,
> And his burden will depart from their shoulder.
> This is the purpose that is purposed
> Upon all the earth;
> And this is the hand that is stretched out
> Upon all the nations.
> For Yahweh of hosts
> Has purposed, and who will frustrate it?
> And his hand is stretched out,
> And who will repulse it? (14. 24-27.)

113

Yahweh had made it clear to me that this release from the galling Assyrian yoke would not come about by the triumph of Judaean arms or indeed of any armed force of the nations, but by Yahweh's own power and zeal, mediated through his Messiah. Once again the mighty hopes of the past spoke through me in imminent expectation. I felt, in anticipation, the light of Yahweh flooding my people and his joy filling their spirits, as his hand put an end to ages of oppression, just as in the long ago Gideon had broken the power of the Midianites. So I sang a hymn of praise to Yahweh celebrating his near-at-hand blessing:

> The people who are walking in darkness
> Have seen a great light;
> Those dwelling in the land of deep shadow—
> A light has shone upon them.
>
> For the yoke of his tyranny,
> And the bar on his shoulder,
> The rod driving him,
> You have shattered
> As (in) the day of Midian.

Then I described the character and reign of the expected and awaited new leader:

> For a child is born unto us;
> A son is given to us;
> And the rule shall be upon his shoulder;
> And his name shall be called
> A wonder of a Counselor,
> A God-like Man of Valor,
> Father Everlasting, Prince of Peace.
> To the increase of his rule and to peace
> There shall be no end,
> Upon the throne of David,
> And upon his kingdom,
> To establish it,

And to sustain it,
Henceforth and forever.
The zeal of Yahweh
Of hosts will do this (9. 2, 4, 6-7).

The next year, just as I had anticipated, King Sennacherib turned to punish us rebel nations of the Westland. He started in the north, where he met no opposition. He mastered Sidon, made it a tributary, and set
up Tubalu as king of the whole Phoenician region.[24]
Several kings of the Westland, the rulers of Arvad, Ashdod, Ammon, Moab, and Edom, almost tumbled over
one another in their haste to make submission to Sennacherib.[25]

In southern Palestine, however, Sennacherib met with
opposition. In Ashkelon, the Assyrian's puppet king,
Sharru-lu-dari, had been dethroned by a popular upris-
ing against Assyria and Sidqa had been put in his place.
Sennacherib deposed this popular favorite, took him
captive, and replaced his loyal prince upon the throne.
He also conquered Beth-Dagon, Joppa, Banaibarka, and
Asuru, cities belonging to Sidqa.

At Ekron, one of the most active of the rebel cities, an
anti-Assyrian uprising had deposed the Assyrian king
Padi, and, partly because our capital was the best fortress
in Palestine, and partly to make sure of Judaean co-operation, the elders of Ekron had handed Padi over to King
Hezekiah, who kept him in confinement as an enemy.
At the approach of Sennacherib the leaders of Ekron
appealed to the dynast kings of the Egyptian Delta for
the Ethiopian bowmen, chariots, and horses. These
came to their aid, and at Elteqeh, a town halfway between
Ekron and Jerusalem, the Ethiopians fought with the

Assyrians and were decisively defeated. Sennacherib then besieged and captured Elteqeh and Timnath. He turned back to Ekron, put the governors and the nobles of the anti-Assyrian party to death and hung their bodies upon stakes around the city as a lesson to the plotters. He pardoned those who had not been active in the revolt, brought King Padi out of our capital city, and re-enthroned him over Ekron. But Sennacherib's greatest enemy in southern Palestine was our King Hezekiah. He did not proceed at once, however, against our capital. He first laid siege to the city of Lachish,[26] between Ekron and Gaza, captured it and made it his Palestinian center for the receiving of tribute.[27] Then he sent his troops to master our Judaean fortified towns in the neighborhood, and they captured forty-six of them and took over two hundred thousand captives, along with untold spoil. He stationed a detachment of guards around Jerusalem to block the roads and capture any who might attempt flight. Hezekiah himself like a caged bird he shut up in our capital.

Even though I had anticipated and preached Yahweh's judgment upon Judah at Assyrian hands, my heart now bled for my people. The suffering of my fellow countrymen was indescribable. The stern judgment of Yahweh touched me to the quick. I poured out my soul in lamentation:

> Ah, sinful nation,
> A people weighted down with iniquity;
> Offspring of those who do evil,
> Sons of corruption;
> They have forsaken Yahweh,
> They have spurned the Holy One of Israel.
> How long will you continue to be smitten,

Will you increase in apostasy?
The whole head is sick,
The whole heart is faint;
From the sole of the foot even unto the head
There is no soundness in it—
Bruises, stripes,
And raw wounds—
They have not been pressed out, nor bound up,
Nor softened with oil.
Your land is a desolation,
Your cities burned with fire.
As for your ground, in your presence,
Foreigners are devouring it;
It is a desolation like the overthrow of Sodom
    (1. 4-7).

Our situation became still more desperate. King Hezekiah's mercenary Arab troops, whom he had hired to protect our capital, deserted him. Our king, then hopeless, sent messengers to Lachish to ask the terms demanded by Sennacherib. He had to pay the tribute money already levied, but in addition a heavy indemnity of thirty talents of gold and eight hundred talents of silver,[28] along with valuable treasures of his palace, his daughters, his harem, his male and female musicians. These were severe terms. To meet them our king had to empty the treasuries of Temple and palace, and strip the gold from the Temple doors and doorposts and send it to the Assyrian monarch. Moreover, Sennacherib gave the cities taken from Judah to King Mitinti of Ashdod, King Padi of Ekron, and King Silli-bel of Gaza.

Severe as these terms were, our king appreciated their relative leniency, because he still held our capital city intact. For, contrary to his usual manner of dealing with rebels, Sennacherib had not deposed Hezekiah. But soon

Sennacherib regretted his all too lenient terms. Not satisfied with having plundered the cities and sapped the national treasury of my people, he now sent from Lachish, under his commander in chief, a strong detachment of troops, which included the chief of the eunuchs, along with his Rabshakeh as spokesman, to King Hezekiah. They came up to Jerusalem and stationed themselves at the very place where thirty-four years before I had confronted the youthful King Ahaz with Yahweh's counsel. The events of this very moment were proving how short-sighted had then been Ahaz's policy of summoning Assyrian aid. King Hezekiah sent a strong delegation composed of Eliakim, who had now succeeded Shebna as treasurer, Shebna the secretary, and Joah the recorder, to consult the Assyrian leaders. Although Aramaic, in which the Jewish delegation was skilled, was the customary language of diplomacy, the Rabshakeh began to speak in Hebrew. He demanded surrender, else the city would be destroyed, and argued vigorously for it on three counts. First, he reasoned, Judah's confidence in Egypt was baseless, for Egypt was too weak to render effective assistance. Second, to follow the counsel which I had steadily advocated, of trust in Yahweh for protection and security, would be futile. Here he appealed to the wave of national resentment in Judah which had followed upon King Hezekiah's reform. He argued that Yahweh had not protected his places of worship in Judah from Hezekiah's drastic destruction. And third, if the king would but surrender his city to Assyrian dominion, the Assyrians would provide sufficient horses to mount Judaean troops so that this part of the Assyrian domain would not be at the mercy of Egyptian revenge (2 Kings 18. 23-24).

At this point in the conference, our delegation, desiring that the discussion be not overheard by the sentinels on the wall but be kept strictly private, urged the Rabshakeh to speak in Aramaic. But the Rabshakeh refused, saying he was appealing not primarily to the king and to the officials of Judah, but to the citizens, who, in case of siege, would experience desperate sufferings. Then in a loud voice he openly appealed to the common people who were listening from the walls of Jerusalem. First, he emphasized King Hezekiah's inability to throw off the Assyrian dominion. Then he ridiculed the counsel I had given, to trust in Yahweh for the protection of his city, pointing to other rebel cities whose gods had not saved them from capture, such as Hamath, which had fallen to King Sargon in 720; Arpad, which King Tiglath-pileser had taken some twenty years before that; Sibraim near Hermon, and Imm in northern Syria. And he urged that if they capitulated to Assyria, they would remain unmolested in their country, enjoying the yield of their fig trees and vines, and drinking from their own wells, until such a time as Sennacherib would transfer them to a land akin to their own but more fruitful, where they would enjoy grain and wine, olive oil and honey! (2 Kings 19. 10-13.) Our king had commanded our delegation to greet any Assyrian proposals with non-committal silence so they strictly observed his orders, making no response to the Assyrian appeal.

The Judaean delegation reported to the king the Assyrian demands, tearing their garments in lamentation as they went. When King Hezekiah had received the report, clothed in torn garments and in sackcloth he went into the Temple to lament before Yahweh. He sent Eliakim, Shebna, and the oldest of the priests to me with a message. Its content was as follows:

> A day of distress and rebuke, and of contempt, is this day, for the children have come to the mouth of the womb and there is no strength to bring them forth. Perhaps Yahweh your God will hear all the words of Rabshakeh, whom his master the king of Assyria has sent to taunt the living God, and will rebuke the words which the Lord your God has heard; so lift up a prayer on behalf of the remnant that is left (2 Kings 19. 3-4).

I sent this reply to King Hezekiah:

> Fear not because of the words you have heard with which the retainers of the king of Assyria have blasphemed me. Lo, I am about to put a spirit in him so that he shall hear a rumor and return to his own land, and I will cause him to fall by the sword in his own land (2 Kings 19. 6-7).

Hezekiah accordingly refused to surrender and the Assyrian detachment, without striking a blow, returned to report back to Sennacherib. But already the Assyrian monarch had begun to retreat from Palestine and had reached Libnah, north of Lachish. Rumors had disturbed Sennacherib of the advance against the Assyrian forces of Taharkah of Ethiopia,[29] son of Pharaoh Shabaka, who was then in charge of the Egyptian army. Sennacherib had already measured swords with Taharkah at Elteqeh, and although he had then defeated him, he could not stand a second encounter. This started the Assyrian withdrawal from Palestine. It was hastened, however, by the outbreak of a bubonic plague in the army of Sennacherib, which proved fatal to a great number of his troops.[30] Still more decisive in turning Sennacherib homeward, was the rumor of a new Chaldaean revolt led by Merodach-baladan, who at his old stamping ground at Bit-Yakin had gathered his resources for a fresh move against Assyria, and was thus seriously threatening that empire's dominance in the East.

Yet even after Sennacherib had begun his withdrawal, hoping as a final resort to bluff our king into the surrender of Jerusalem, he sent another delegation of messengers to King Hezekiah with a letter threatening dire destruction. King Hezekiah received the letter, read it, and then went up to the Temple and spread it before Yahweh in prayer, appealing for his deliverance. I was deeply stirred when I learned that King Hezekiah was at prayer, and I sent him a reassuring revelation from Yahweh:

> Thus Yahweh says concerning the king of Assyria: he shall not enter this city, nor shoot an arrow there, neither shall he confront it with shield nor throw up a mound against it. By the way that he came, shall he return, but he shall not come into this city. For I will defend this city to deliver it on my account, and on account of my servant David (2 Kings 19. 32-34).

Yahweh had led me to see that in Jerusalem was the foundation stone upon which the community of the remnant was to be built. There were, therefore, spiritual forces in Jerusalem that were indestructible. No Assyrian arms, however powerful, could capture or control them. King Hezekiah held steady and sent the messengers back to Sennacherib bearing his refusal to surrender his city. Jerusalem was saved, and although the land of Judah remained tributary to Assyria, our beloved capital was still in our hands. It alone had escaped destruction, and now upon that handful of survivors rested the future of my people!

> The daughter of Zion is left like a booth in a vineyard,
> Like a hut in a cucumber field, like a lookout.
> Unless Yahweh of hosts had left us a little remnant,
> We should have been like Sodom, we should have been
>   like Gomorrah (1. 8-9).

You can scarcely imagine the transports of jubilation into which the people of Jerusalem were lifted with the departure of Sennacherib and his troops. The mood of celebration swept the city. The pent-up fears of the people were transformed into hilarious joy. They crowded to the flat roofs of their houses, where they could better see the city in its mood of gaiety and relief. I cried out, speaking to my city,

> What has happened to you, pray, that you have gone
>   up,
> All of you to the roofs,
> O boisterous city, full of noises,
> O jubilant town? (22. 1-2a.)

The people of Jerusalem acted as though it were their power and not Yahweh's protection which had brought about the Assyrian withdrawal. People tried to laugh me out of my depression, to lure me from my lamentations, but I said to them:

> Turn away your gaze from me,
> I will weep bitterly;
> Hasten not to comfort me,
> Over the destruction of the daughter of my people
> (22. 4).

For I saw that Yahweh's day had yet to come. His people had not repented. To him they had not turned, and when that day would come, amid the crack and crash of walls, in anticipation I imagined the cries of the distressed people which would resound to the surrounding hills:

For it is a day of tumult, and ruin, and confusion,
Of the Lord Yahweh of hosts,
In the valley of vision;
Of tearing down of walls,
And crying to the mountains! (22. 5.)

I expostulated with my people, who had been so concerned about their military defenses, but had paid no
attention to Yahweh, who had both purposed and accomplished Judah's release.   I said to them:

You paid attention on that day
To the equipment of the House of the Forest,
And unto the breaches in the city of David
You attended, for they were many;
And you collected the waters of the lower pool.
And the houses of Jerusalem you counted,
And you pulled down the houses
To fortify the wall;
And you made a reservoir between the two walls,
For the waters of the old pool;
But you did not pay attention to him who accom-
    plished it—
Nor did you look unto him who devised it long ago
    (22. 8b-11).

Yahweh had revealed to me his sharp displeasure at this
dullness and stubborn pride of his people.   The great
release should have turned them in repentance and
thankfulness to their Lord.   So I declared to them:

Now the Lord Yahweh of hosts, called,
On that day,
For weeping and wailing,
Yes for baldness and girding on sackcloth;
But lo! exultation and mirth,
Killing oxen and slaying sheep,
Eating flesh and drinking wine—
Eating and drinking, "for tomorrow we may die."
    (22. 12-13.)

THE PROPHETS TELL THEIR OWN STORY

The Temple worship of the leaders of Judah—"rulers of Sodom" and "people of Gomorrah," I called them in disgust—did not make me more optimistic. The desperate outlook of the times had greatly increased the number and size of the sacrificial offerings. The Temple courts were thronged. Choosing a day when I could best get the ear of Judah, I entered the Temple. For a time I watched the worshipers as they performed the magical rites. Many of them, as I well knew, were men of ruthless oppression, who constantly profiteered on helpless widows and orphans. Their lives were utterly inconsistent with this display of piety. At length I could hold in no longer, and I poured out upon them, in Yahweh's name, his invective:

> What does the multitude of your sacrifices mean to me?
> I am sated with whole-burnt offerings of rams,
> And with the fat of well-fed beasts.
> And I take no delight
> In the blood of bulls, and sheep, and goats (1. 11).

On regular and special feast days thousands of worshipers trampled the Temple courts as they brought these offerings to Yahweh, and I said to them:

> New moon, and Sabbath and calling convocations—!
> I cannot endure fasts and assemblies!
> Your feasts and your appointed seasons
> My soul hates!
> They have been a burden upon me,
> I weary myself in bearing them!   (1. 14.)

On those hands piously spread out in prayer, in yet darker hue than the blood spots upon them, Yahweh let me see the sins of their evil deeds, so I cried:

124

Your hands are full of blood.
Wash yourselves and make yourselves clean;
Remove the evil of your practices
From before my eyes;
Cease to do evil,
Learn to do well;
Seek justice,
Set right those ruthlessly dealt with,
Vindicate the orphan,
Plead the case of the widow! (1. 15c-17.)

They were indifferent about their own conduct. Their scarlet sins they reckoned as snow-white. I knew that no sacrifices could atone for these deep, moral sins of my people.

Yet Yahweh's protection of his city, his confidence in his saving remnant, had made my heart leap with hope. And King Hezekiah's attitude in the recent crisis encouraged me to look forward to a new society in Judah and to dream of what it might be like.[31] I was convinced that its foundations would be in good government. King and princes alike would reign righteously and justly. And in that new society there would be citizens of noble manhood bringing protection, inspiration, and comfort to their fellows. In that day I told them:

A man shall be like the hiding place from the wind,
And a place of concealment from the downpour of rain,
Like streams of water in dry parched ground,
Like the shadow of a great crag in a land where one is
    faint (32. 2).

In that Judaean society of the future there will be general enlightenment and increasing capacity. Men will be sensitive to their times, able to speak with ease and freedom and will be valued for their true worth (32. 3-6);

and although ungodly men will still be bent on their evil designs, yet,

> The noble will plan out noble things;
> And in noble things will he take his stand (32. 8).

Moreover, Yahweh's remarkable defense of Zion has awakened in my heart high hopes for that final period of the future which I now feel is included in Yahweh's purpose.[32] Zion will then have its own significant part to play, when that time comes. So in these days as the end of my ministry draws near, I am spending my energies in Jerusalem interpreting these high hopes to my disciples and sealing them up in their hearts. For Zion is to become the center of a new world in which Yahweh's will alone will be regnant.

Mount Zion will tower spiritually above the surrounding hills. And to it will stream up[33] representatives of all nations who have hitherto been at war with each other, making pilgrimages to Yahweh's Temple on the summit of Mount Zion, there to learn the great principles of Yahweh, and the program of action he approves and prescribes for all:

> And they shall hammer their swords into ploughshares,
> And their spears into pruning knives;
> Nation shall not lift up sword against nation
> And they shall not learn war any more (2. 4).

CHAPTER IV

MICAH OF MORESHETH-GATH

I WAS born at Moresheth-Gath, an outlying rural community in the vicinity of the city of Gath.[1] Until mastered by our king, Uzziah of Judah (2 Chronicles 26. 6), Gath had been the focus of Philistine power along the western border of our nation. It alone of all the Philistine cities had been intermittently in the possession of the kings of our Judaean nation. Indeed, our relation to Gath began when it was fortified by Rehoboam, Solomon's son, who was our king when the Northern Kingdom broke away from Judah (2 Chronicles 11. 8). My home was situated on a hill about thirteen hundred feet above sea level, just north of Wady-ej-Judeideh.[2] The only large town in the near vicinity was Beit Jibrin,[3] which lay at the eastern border of a series of low-lying hills between the maritime plain and the central highlands of Judah, a region which my people called the Shephelah. Beit Jibrin was the half-way house between Jerusalem and Gaza, and between Lydda and Hebron. I often went there, and as a boy, I found endless delight in exploring the caves characteristic of the region which were hewn out of the soft limestone rock.

I love this community of my birth and have ever been happy as a peasant farmer. I am convinced that it is the common people of the countryside, the shepherds and farmers of Judah, who are the backbone of my nation's life. King Uzziah was still king of Judah in the days of my infancy and early childhood, although, because he

127

had fallen prey to leprosy, the reins of the government were left in the hands of his son, Jotham, who acted as regent. During my lifetime there have been five kings upon the throne of Judah—Uzziah, Jotham, Ahaz, Hezekiah, and Manasseh.

My forebears too were peasant farmers. I have known from first-hand experience what it means to be under the heel of the commercial and political leaders in Judah, for we peasants have had to submit to age-long exploitation at the hand of wealthy Judaean landowners. The farmers of our community told me in my boyhood about the courageous shepherd of Tekoa—a town only seventeen and a half miles distant from my home as the crow flies—who had preached to the Israelite leaders of Samaria and Bethel Yahweh's stern summons to righteous conduct in their social relationships. They told me all they knew of the very words he had spoken. I have treasured them in my heart, and even in boyhood days I tried to understand their meaning. I am now aware that they have played no little part in the fashioning of my spirit.[4]

During my young manhood the prophet Isaiah was preaching Yahweh's message in Jerusalem. More than once when I was in our capital city, I heard him speak forth fearlessly Yahweh's condemnation of the leaders of Zion.[5] One memorable day I heard him courageously utter passionate words spoken in deep emotion, wherein he pictured Yahweh as taking his stand to judge the elders and princes of Judah, condemning them because they had exploited Yahweh's beloved "vineyard," by which he meant the people of my nation. I heard the great prophet pronounce Yahweh's oracle:

It is you, who have consumed the vineyard,
Spoil plundered from the poor is in your houses.
What is it to you, that you crush my people,
And grind the face of the poor? (Isaiah 3. 14b.-15.)

How my young manhood thrilled to this brave and
needed indictment! I was conscious of responsive fire
kindling in my soul. As he spoke, I felt my inner being
aflame with prophetic zeal. That day I knew that I too
must be Yahweh's prophet.

The message of the prophet Isaiah which had so
gripped my soul had described Yahweh as standing up to
judge his people (Isaiah 3. 13, LXX). With similar conceptions I began my prophetic ministry, in the last year
of the reign of King Ahaz. But when I started to utter
Yahweh's message, the most strategic point that needed
his word was Samaria, the capital city of the nation of
Israel, the northern section of Yahweh's people. In
familiar style loved by the prophets of my nation, I summoned the peoples of the earth to listen to my prophetic
revelation of Yahweh's indictment of Samaria. All the
eyes were on Samaria in those days, for while that northern capital had thus far withstood the shock of the Assyrian invasion of Israel, no one knew how soon it must
succumb to Assyrian attack. So I cried:

Hear, you peoples, all of you!
Give attention, O earth, and all that fills you (1. 2a).

Just as in the ancient poems of my people, our fathers
were wont to describe Yahweh's manifestation, so I now
pictured him as about to reveal himself to the people of
Samaria in earthquake and volcanic eruption. I por-
trayed him as about to descend upon the High Places of
the land, upon those very nature shrines of Israel, situated

in the hills and valleys, that have corrupted the religion of my people.[6] At those very places, so I believed, Yahweh's judgment upon the Northern Kingdom would set in:

> For lo, Yahweh is about to go forth from his place;
> And he will descend and tread
> Upon the High Places of the land;
> Then the hills will dissolve under him,
> And the valleys will burst themselves open,
> Like wax melts before fire,
> Like waters running down a slope (1. 3-4).

One mighty purpose will then move the heart of Yahweh as in majestic tread, leaving upheaval and destruction in his train, he will descend upon "Jacob," his people, upon Israel, his nation in the north.

It was from the standpoint of a Judaean peasant that I viewed the social situation in Israel, for I felt that the cause of its impending ruin lay where its royalty and commercial leadership were concentrated. The deepest root of the corruption the nation had suffered was what went on in its capital. So I delivered against "Jacob" Yahweh's indictment, and declared to Israel the cause of its imminent destruction:

> Because of the rebellion of Jacob is all this,
> Because of the sin of the house of Israel.
> What is the transgression of Jacob?
> Is it not Samaria? (1. 5ab.)

But how will Yahweh punish rebellious Jacob? How will he discipline his people because of their sin? Yahweh had caused me to see that the political status of Samaria would soon be brought to an end. Its fortifications would be destroyed and it would be reduced to a mere agricultural settlement. And this would come

130

about by the sudden intervention of Yahweh in earthquake and volcanic eruption. So I proclaimed in Yahweh's name:

> I will turn Samaria into ruins,
> And its precincts into a planting place for vineyards.
> I will hurl down its stones to the valley,
> And I will lay bare its foundations (1. 6).

Then I dealt with the peculiar nature of Samaria's corruption. That capital city, and indeed the whole kingdom of Israel, had been more directly exposed to the
immoral fertility cults of the land of Canaan than my
own people of Judah had been. And its most powerful
dynasty of kings, the house of Omri, had officially introduced these corrupting influences into the kingdom of
Israel. King Ahab, the leading king of that dynasty, a
century and more before my time, had not merely been
tolerant of Phoenician-Canaanite influence in Israel, but,
at the instigation of his fanatical Phoenician wife, Jezebel, had himself introduced into Samaria and all Israel
the cult of the Baal of Tyre, with its stone image of
Baal and its wooden idol of Asherah. He had built a
temple for Baal Melqarth in his capital, equipping it
with altar and characteristic images and idols (1 Kings
16. 29-34). I knew that these costly cultic images in
Samaria had been provided by the extravagant offerings
of the devotees of the sanctuary, and especially from the
"harlot's hire," the lucrative gains which accrued to the
sanctuary from the horrible practice of cultic prostitution. For the devotees who made pilgrimage to Samaria
from afar—"foreigners" my people called them—were
thus exploited through these immoral practices in order
to make provision for the materials and upkeep of the

cult. It was from such sensual rites, and the income to
the sanctuary they provided, that these idols were acquired, and consequently, as Yahweh led me to see, they
could have no permanence whatever. So of these cultic
objects in that sanctuary which was even then awaiting
imminent destruction I cried:

> And all its graven images will be crushed;
> And I will make a desolation of all its idols.
> For from harlot's hire were they acquired,
> And unto harlot's hire shall they return (1.7).

Hand in hand with these practices of nature cults in
Palestine there always went a devotion to the materialistic values in life which inevitably linked religion with
oppression. Here again the dynasty of Omri had played
an influential part in Israel. For just as King Ahab,
under the incitement of Jezebel, had ruthlessly violated
the rites of the peasant Naboth of Jezreel, so the customs
of the house of Omri, with their cruel disregard of the
human right to justice, had permeated the commercial
life of Samaria. One day when there was an important
assembly in Samaria, I sent a message which declared
unto its inhabitants Yahweh's word.[7] It directed their
attention to the wealth of Samaria, the accumulation of
which had come from the dishonesty and deceit of its
leaders in commercial transactions:

> Yahweh calls to the city:
> Hear, O tribe,
> And assembly of the city:
> "Can I forget the stores of wickedness,
> And the accursed scanty ephah?
> Can I justify dishonest scales,
> Or a bag of deceitful weights?
> The rich are full of violence" (6. 9-12a).

MICAH OF MORESHETH-GATH

I pointed out that Yahweh was indignant with Samaria's commercial heads because they had followed the customs of their paganized national leaders. So I declared that Yahweh himself would punish them by perverting, frustrating, and disappointing all their normal expectations. Their efforts would come to futility. Thus in Yahweh's name I announced his judgment upon Samaria:

> But I, on my part, have begun to smite you,
> To devastate you because of your sins.
> You shall eat, but not be satisfied;
> There will be strength in your inward parts,
> But you shall not bring to birth.
> And him whom you might bear, I will give to the sword.
> You shall sow, but you shall not reap;
> You shall tread out olives, but not anoint yourself with
>   oil;
> And you shall tread out grapes, but not drink (the) wine.
> Yes, you have observed the customs of Omri,
> And all the deeds of the house of Ahab,
> Consequently I am about to give you over to destruction,
> And your inhabitants to derision (6. 13-16).

The collapse of Samaria which I had thus anticipated came in the fourth year of the reign of our King Hezekiah, not however as I had expected, through earthquake and volcanic eruption, but as the result of a vigorous Assyrian blockade. For three years King Shalmaneser V of Assyria besieged the city and at length it was entered in triumph by Sargon, who had just succeeded to the Assyrian throne.[8] Practically its entire population of close to thirty thousand people were taken captive, and in their places the Assyrian monarch settled captives from other regions he had taken, in numbers that exceeded its former Israelite population. Nonetheless I viewed the real *cause* of this political disaster as the moral and spiritual corruption, the "disease" of Samaria.

Samaria was then no longer a part of Yahweh's people. Yet, although it was gone as a political possession, we Judaeans could not escape the consequences of the cultural influences that had poured down upon us from it. I came to realize that the cancer of Samaria's immorality and the infection of her injustice had spread in virulent form to my own people Judah. The fall of Samaria had been an effective shock to my countrymen, and had ominously startled them. I deemed it a fitting time to appeal to my own fellow Judaeans, and indeed to the people of my own immediate neighborhood. The kingdom of Israel was now a lost cause. But it was my eager hope that Judah might still be saved from national collapse and destruction.

All around me, among my neighbors and countrymen, with pain of heart I saw the degenerating influence of the fertility rites that had played such havoc with the religious and social life of the kingdom of Israel. The lamentation, wailing rituals that were a chief element in the fertility cults, were peculiarly attractive to Judaeans. So I decided upon a striking way of prophetic appeal to my people. To suggest the dire disaster which I was sure awaited them, I went about in the presence of my fellow countrymen, naked and barefoot like a slave. And to portray the deep sorrow of my own heart over the near-at-hand punishment my nation was to suffer at Yahweh's hands, and to contrast my own sincere sadness over Judah's threatened moral and spiritual collapse, with the feigned lamentation of the magical fertility cults, I lamented and wailed. I thus explained the meaning of my conduct:

> Because of *this* let *me* lament and wail;
> Let me go barefoot and naked,
> Let me make a wailing like the jackals,
> And a mourning like an ostrich.
> Because of Samaria's fatal disease;
> Since it has come unto Judah,
> It has reached to the gate of my people (1. 8-9).

Well did I know the nature of these corrupt fertility cults, for the baneful consequences of such religion had been flaunted in my face in neighboring towns.[9] Flagrant centers of it familiar to me were the towns of Gath, Ekron, Shaphir, Zaanan, Lachish, and Maroth. It was the mother goddess—the "mistress," I called her—as worshiped at these places, and her immoral devotees that were the evil sources of this corruption. And in recent days, when, through Samaria's fall, my nation had just been given striking warning that the destructive Assyrian was steadily drawing nearer, these magical cults had taken on new popularity in our neighborhood, and were carried on with unusual intensity. I knew how utterly futile they would be for rescuing Judah from imminent destruction. So I taunted each of these cities and its revered mother goddess, calling attention to the impotence of such deities to help our nation in its critical hours. And, in the mood of irony, I lamented, touching on fertility and magical rituals characteristic of the cult as practiced at each place. I mentioned the whirling dance at Gath, and its aim, magically to coerce prosperity, as was evident in the cult at Maroth. There it will not bring prosperity but rather Yahweh's judgment! I described the ritual wailing of the devotees of the "mistress" of Ekron, and the lamentation ritual of the plucking out of the hair as seen at Mareshah. I pointed to the time in the near future when the mother goddess at Shaphir would no longer *have* any devotees to seek union with her by immoral rites. I mentioned the dignified sacred processionals at Zaanan, where the image of its "mistress" was carried forth, and I referred to the use in such processionals at Lachish of the horse and chariot to bear the idol of its mistress. Lachish, situated in the Shephelah, was one of the greatest cities in our region. King Rehoboam, over two centuries ago, had made it one of the chief Judaean frontier fortresses in the foothills between Judaean and Philistine territory (2 Chronicles 11. 5ff.). For centuries before our Hebrew Fathers had invaded Canaan and mastered Lachish, it had been a vigorous center of Canaanite worship, equipped with a temple and cultic implements.[10] So naturally it had played a major part in the introduction into the religion of my people of the immoral fertility rites. But now the image of its famed "mistress" was in Yahweh's power, and soon it would be bequeathed as a mere lifeless relic, Lachish's parting gift, to my own town of Moresheth-Gath. I solemnly summoned the "mistress" of Mareshah to *real* mourning, not to that *simulated* in the wailing rites that featured her worship, because the time was near at hand when her immoral devotees will all have been carried captive and she will be forced to acknowledge Yahweh as her subjugator. Thus in the mood of irony, I uttered my lament:

In Gath you shall not dance!
In Ekron you shall not wail!

MICAH OF MORESHETH-GATH

Caress yourself, O mistress of Shaphir!
The mistress of Zaanan goes not forth in processional!
Who has danced for prosperity,
O mistress of Maroth,
So that evil has come down from Yahweh?
Bind the chariot to the steeds,
O mistress of Lachish!
(A beginning of sins was it to the daughter of Zion)
For in you was found the source of the transgressions of
  Israel.
Therefore you shall be given as a parting gift
To Moresheth-Gath!
Moreover, your dispossessor shall be " my Father" to you,
O mistress of Mareshah!
Become bald, yes shear your hair,
On account of the sons of your delights!
Extend your baldness like the eagle,
For they shall go into captivity from you (1. 10-16).

It was but a few years later than this when the entire
region where I lived was thrown into great excitement by
an expedition into the Westland of the bodyguard of
Sargon, the Assyrian monarch, consisting of a few hundred soldiers. It was headed by Sargon's tartan, and the
purpose of the invasion was to punish a rebellion against
the Assyrian overlord which centered in Ashdod. There
a strong anti-Assyrian faction of the citizens had dis-
placed Sargon's official representative, Ahimiti, and had
enthroned a mercenary Greek soldier from Cyprus, by
name of Yamani. But my country also, along with Edom
and Moab, was implicated in the revolt, and negotiations
were already in progress for help from Ethiopia, when
the Assyrian force appeared. Ashdod and its seaport,
Ashdudimmu, were captured.[11] All this was of deepest
interest to us, for from the heights of Moresheth-Gath
we could see Ashdod. But then the Assyrian turned

toward Judah and captured Gath, just at the edge of Judaean territory. My town on the heights less than eight miles away watched these movements of the Assyrians with excited concern.

But the impending peril had no salutary influence upon the deeper life of my people. It did not arouse them either to heart-searching or to repentance. They kept on in their scheming injustice. So when the Assyrian force withdrew without invading the Shephelah, I was moved to condemn the avarice of the godless, land-hungry property owners of my people who, at night, when they should have been sleeping the healthy sleep of the innocent, concocted their ruthless schemes, and at the dawn of day started to put them into operation. I cried out:

> Woe to those who devise an evil scheme
> Upon their beds.
> In the light of the morning they carry it out,
> For their own fist is their god.
> Yes, they desire fields, so they seize them,
> And houses, so they take them.
> And they oppress a man and his house,
> Yes, a man and his inheritance (2. 1-2).

I know from bitter experience the conscienceless covetousness of these landlords and their high-minded dealings in wresting the fields from their peasant tenants, who were powerless to defend even a family inheritance. Just as my Judaean contemporary prophet Isaiah had dealt with this problem as a crying wrong in Jerusalem and vicinity, so I now took it up on behalf of the peasantry of Judah. My spirit was cut to the quick by such injustice. I told these scheming landlords that there

was another, who was devising a scheme—and that was
Yahweh—who was about to bring his judgment upon
his Judaean "clan" as a punishment for such oppression.
So I concluded:

> Therefore, thus says Yahweh:
> Lo, I am about to send evil against this clan,
> Which you shall not be able to remove from your necks;
> Then you shall not walk haughtily.
> For it will be an evil time (2. 3).

When this "scheme" which Yahweh has plotted, ma-
tures, Yahweh's people will know the galling experience
of a foreign yoke. When that day comes, so I told them,
Judah will listen in despair while one of her poets lifts a
mournful lament. Thus will he sing:

> The territory of my people is measured by line,
> And there is none to restore it.
> Among our captors our land has been divided,
> We are utterly ruined (2. 4bc).
> There is none who casts line or lot
> In the congregation of Yahweh (2. 5).

In the present these acquisitive landowners seize for
themselves as much as they have power to take, but this
clan of Judaean materialists will not be able by such
means to seize any share in Yahweh's congregation of the
future.

Such sharp words of condemnation and threat against
these ruthless leaders angered them. They were not accustomed to hear such criticisms of Yahweh's people, for
this they claimed to be in spite of their conduct, and,
furthermore, they counted on Yahweh's protection.
They took my words as insults and broke into my threat-

ening speech with indignant response. One of them said to me:

> You shall not prophesy at all!
> They do not prophesy like this! (2. 6ab.)

Then turning to his fellow oppressors he angrily asked:

> Shall he not remove the insults? (2. 6c.)

One of the others of this resentful group, piously declaring my condemnations to be blasphemy against Yahweh, Judah's God, and the house of Jacob, his people, told me the kind of words they expected from the lips of a prophet. Said he:

> Is the house of Jacob accursed?
> Has the spirit of Yahweh become powerless?
> Or are these things what he (Yahweh) does?
> Does he not make his words pleasing
> Toward his people Israel? (2. 7.)

But I was convinced that such unscrupulous men had no right to be called "Yahweh's people." Rather were Yahweh's people the oppressed poor, whose unfortunate lot I was championing. So in an oracle from Yahweh, I described the ruthless robbery of peaceful citizens of which these leaders were guilty. I pointed to their inhuman evictions of defenseless women from their homes and the consequent separation of mothers from their children. I said to them:

> But you are not my people!
> Against my people you stand up as an enemy;
> From peaceful men you strip off their cloak,
> From those passing quietly along.
> The wives of my people you drive out
> Of their comfortable houses:
> From beside their children you take
> Their mothers forever.

"Get up and go along with you," you say,
"This is no resting place!" (2. 8-10a.)

To such men money meant everything—humanity and honor meant nothing. I continued:

For anything
You will break a strict pledge (2. 10b).

Yet such conscienceless men as these wanted a prophet to prate to them about something pleasant! With my prophetic spirit rising to the height of righteous indignation I bitterly lamented—

If a man should go around
Dishing up wind and deceitful falsehood,
Prophesying to you of wine and strong drink,
He would be a prophet for this people! (2. 11.)

From these whose conduct had left them no claim to be called Yahweh's people I turned to the aristocracy of Judah, to the heads and rulers of the nation. The first demand of government is justice, and my people had a right to expect this from their rulers. But here too they were disappointed. I found in these national leaders no concern whatever for goodness but a greedy bent toward evil; indifference to the rights of men, and even brutal cruelty in their treatment of them. This inexcusable corruption of high office touched me to the quick, and with unaccustomed passion and sharpness I poured out upon them Yahweh's invective:

Hear, you heads of Jacob,
And rulers of the house of Israel,
Is it not your responsibility to know justice,
You haters of what is good, and lovers of what is evil?
(3. 1-2a.)

141

In graphic words I told how they had continually exploited Yahweh's poor. They were as rapacious as cannibals, and in passionate speech I so caricatured them:

> They eat the flesh of my people,
> And strip off the skin from upon them.
> They spread it out like meat in a pot,
> And like flesh within a caldron (3. 3).

But Yahweh's day of reckoning was coming wherein his retribution would overtake them. Then they will be dealt with just as they have dealt with others:

> Their skin will be stripped from upon them,
> And their flesh from upon their bones (3. 2b).

Then when it is too late they will turn to Yahweh:

> Then they will cry to Yahweh,
> But he will not answer them;
> Yes, he will hide his face from them,
> Because their deeds have brought evil (3. 4).

Then I turned to the false prophets. They carried on their prophetic mission as though it were a commercial business. They gauged the content of their prophetic oracle to the people who sought Yahweh's will at their mouth, by the sum paid them for it, by the size of the bite put in their teeth, rather than solely in accordance with Yahweh's inward revelation to their souls. For those who fed them well they were ready with an optimistic oracle of blessing. But they had no scruples about changing Yahweh's word from salvation to doom upon those who refused or neglected payment for the oracular revelation received at their hands! How I abhorred this travesty on true prophecy! In Yahweh's name I faced these deceivers whose practices brought into disrepute the calling of being Yahweh's prophet, and his true mes-

sengers into shame and disgrace, and delivered to them
Yahweh's stern oracle:

> Thus Yahweh says to the prophets
> Who mislead my people,
> Who bite with their teeth,
> Then cry, "All is well!"
> And as for him who does not put something in their
> mouth,
> They sanctify war against him! (3. 5.)

When his stern day comes bringing its solemn experiences of national judgment, humiliation, and collapse,
such faithless stewards of Yahweh's word will have to
confess in shame that they have no authentic word of
guidance to give his wistful, inquiring people. So I said
to these unworthy representatives of my calling:

> Therefore night shall come upon you with no vision;
> And distress shall fall upon you with no divination.
> And the sun shall go down upon the prophets,
> And the day shall grow dark over them.
> Then the seers shall be ashamed,
> And the diviners shall be abashed.
> Yes, they shall cover up their lips, all of them,
> For there will be no answer from God (3. 6-7).

Even while I gave expression to Yahweh's oracle, thus
sharply criticizing the shallow, degenerate prophetic
order in Judah—prophets who simulated an insight they
did not have, and boasted of a revelation from Yahweh
which they had never received—I felt burning in my own
soul Yahweh's living word. I was suddenly most vividly
aware of the awful contrast between an insight illumined
by Yahweh and words that lacked divine light. And to
this genuine prophetic consciousness I bore public witness, drawing aside the veil of my soul, and giving my

fellow Judaeans, to whom Yahweh's word was sent through me, a glimpse into my most secret self:

> But as for me, I am filled with the spirit of Yahweh,
> And of justice, and of courage,
> To declare to Jacob his transgression,
> And to Israel his sin! (3. 8.)

With this mighty consciousness of power and courage to bear Yahweh's message astir in my soul, I then journeyed to Jerusalem, where the political leadership of our nation was largely concentrated, to declare Yahweh's will. There was located the Temple, which, since the days of King Solomon, its builder, has been the most influential sanctuary of Judah. Moreover, as I looked out upon my nation from the quiet countryside of Moresheth-Gath, it had been borne home to my soul that even as had been the case with the kingdom of Israel, so was it now true with Judah, the capital city was the chief source of national licentiousness and corruption. So to those who asked me why I went to Jerusalem on such an errand I replied:

> What is the sin of the house of Judah?
> Is it not Jerusalem? (1. 5b.)[12]

I sought a time when the leaders of Jerusalem, the rulers, the priests, and the prophets, were in large numbers present in the Temple. Then I seized the opportunity to summarize Yahweh's condemnation of these national leaders.

I dealt first with the civil officials of Judah, who, by their violent, even criminal profiteering, at the expense of the rank and file of Judah, were squeezing the very life out of Yahweh's people. The stately palaces of Jeru-

salem had been built by blood money. Leaders whose
official position obligated them to be exponents and
distributors of justice, were in fact skilled evaders of
justice, themselves taken captive by the unhealthy lure
of money. The priests, whose sphere it was to teach my
people the knowledge of Yahweh and to give directions
and instruction with reference to his will, came next
under consideration. They were the recognized authoritative religious leaders who should have set the standard
of righteous conduct, but they too had surrendered to the
subtle sway of the mercenary motive, and gave the priestly
guidance and directions only to those who paid them
well for it. They manipulated the priestly oracle so that
they themselves would be enriched. Then I turned to
the prophets. Yahweh's special word of revelation was
their province. But they too had become infected with
this same acquisitive virus. They had prostituted their
lofty calling and had sold themselves to the highest
bidders. They proportioned the content of Yahweh's
"revelation" to the amount of money paid them for their
prophetic divination. So upon these money-mad national leaders I poured forth Yahweh's indictment:

> Hear now, you heads of Jacob,
> And rulers of the house of Israel,
> You who abhor justice,
> And who make the straight crooked!
> Who are building Zion out of blood,
> And Jerusalem with injustice.
> Its heads judge for a bribe;
> And its priests teach for a price;
> And its prophets divine for silver (3. 9-11a).

Thus the three most influential classes of my people had
sold out to the lure of money. Yet these first citizens of

Jerusalem were presumptuously confident of the protection of Yahweh in whose Temple they felt secure! Of all three classes I lamented:

> Then upon Yahweh they lean, saying,
> "Is not Yahweh in our midst?
> Evil can not come upon us" (3. 11b).

Ah! but evil was coming and Yahweh was about to bring it! And I must utter his oracle! I can still remember the solemn awe of my spirit when I sensed the word I was about to utter as the stern, authentic oracle of Yahweh. And I vividly remember the startled expressions on the faces of the leaders as they heard for the first time from prophetic lips of the certain annihilation of our beloved capital and its Temple hill. Only by the courage with which Yahweh had endowed me could I utter such critical words of judgment and doom. For I then pronounced to these leaders Yahweh's oracle, speaking slowly, with great solemnity, and weighing every word:

> Therefore on account of you, Zion
> As a field shall be plowed,
> And Jerusalem shall become a heap of ruins,
> And the mountain of the Temple as a wooded height
> (3. 12).

These words were wondrously used of Yahweh to reach the heart of King Hezekiah. They aroused the conscience of Judah as no other words of mine had yet done. Along with the great influence of the preaching of the prophet Isaiah, who had the ear of the king, I am convinced that they played some part in inspiring our monarch to undertake a significant religious reform in Judah such as no king before him had dared to attempt (Jere-

146

miah 26. 16-19). In the face of great popular misunderstanding and disapproval, but sensitively aware of the degenerate influences in our nation of the old Canaanite elements still stubbornly persisting in the public worship of Judah as carried on at the high places and even in the Temple at Jerusalem, King Hezekiah launched upon a revolutionary program to reform the national religion (2 Kings 18. 5-6). He removed the High Places where the old fertility cults still carried on. He broke down the pillars which in the old Canaanite religion had been symbols of the Baals, and he chopped down the Asherim, wooden poles or trunks of trees which were symbols of Asherah or Astarte, the feminine counterpart of the Baal. And he broke into pieces the bronze serpent image in the Temple, popularly called "Nehushtan," originally the symbol of the Canaanite deity of healing. Although at that time these idols had all become associated with Yahweh, our king well knew the heathen elements their presence had brought into the religion of my people as popularly practiced.

Disillusionment, however, was near at hand. The reform thus inaugurated by King Hezekiah did not have the heart of Judah behind it. And at best it touched only the conduct of the public worship. The repentance of the people of Judah was superficial and short-lived. The inhuman leadership of my people continued unchecked. And the hard lot of the peasants of Judah remained unchanged.

At length the expected Assyrian invasion of the Westland took place. King Sennacherib, who four years before had succeeded Sargon on the Assyrian throne, first settled the rebellions in Phoenicia and western Palestine, defeated at Elteqeh, a city only eighteen and a half miles from Jerusalem, the army of Ethiopia for which the Ekronites had sent to re-enforce them, then turned eastward toward Judah. Sennacherib had made Lachish his Palestinian army base of operations.[13] This city, second only to Jerusalem in its fortifications, was only about four and one half miles from my home town, so along with others of my people who could make their escape, I fled to our capital.[14] Sennacherib now demanded the release from confinement in the fortress of Jerusalem of Padi, his chosen head over Ekron, and reinstated him. The Assyrian forces then mastered forty-six Judaean fortresses and small towns in their neighborhood, employing all their famed Assyrian military tactics, leveling the walls with battering rams and siege engines, using mines and tunnels, and attacking and storming on foot. Sennacherib counted as spoil 200,150 people, as well as their horses, mules, asses, camels, cattle, and sheep. He shut up King Hezekiah in our capital and threw up earthworks against him. Anyone who ventured out of the city was punished for his misdeed.

The crowded populace of our capital, augmented by its host of Judaean refugees, was in a panic of fear. All the swagger had now gone out of the leaders of our nation. King Hezekiah, depending as he was not upon Yahweh's protection but upon Ethiopian help, was playing what seemed to me a contemptuous rôle. I believed that the judgment I had preached was now about to come upon Jerusalem. I thought then that the fall of our beloved city was at hand. Pouring my words forth in a lamentation which was tinged with sarcasm and irony, I questioned the tense, anxious throngs of Jerusalem:

Why do you cry out a lament?
Is there not a king in you?
Has your leader perished,
That there has taken hold of you
Anguish like one bearing a child? (4. 9.)

I knew there was good reason for their lamentation. No wonder the whole community was in mental anguish, comparable in severity to the travail of a mother in child-birth. For soon those lamenting Judaeans would be forced to flee from the fortified city into the open fields, shelterless and defenseless! So I cried:

Writhe and cry and groan,
O daughter of Zion, as one bearing a child,
For now you must go forth from the city
And you shall dwell in the field! (4. 10ab.)

I brought my lament to an end, picturing the Assyrian siege-wall thrown up against the invested city, our king treated with insolent contempt, his people passionately lacerating themselves and wailing in tragic hopelessness. To the tense city I called:

Lacerate yourself frantically!
A siege wall they have laid upon us! (5. 1a.)

And I pictured the indignities likely to be suffered by King Hezekiah from the leaders of the Assyrian expedition:

With the rod they strike upon the cheek
The ruler of Israel! (5. 1b.)

The destruction of Jerusalem which I had so confidently expected did not yet come. The catastrophe which I had preached was delayed. Suddenly and unexpectedly the Assyrian forces lifted the blockade of

Jerusalem and departed. The anxious distress of the inhabitants of our capital was swiftly replaced by a sense of self-sufficiency and a superficial feeling of security. And with this release of tension came a corresponding loosening of moral conduct. During the late years of King Hezekiah's reign the social corruption and the moral depravity of my countrymen increased apace. Up to this time I had largely concentrated my prophetic teaching upon the officials and leaders of my people, for the corruption of Judah had centered in them. But after the Assyrians withdrew from Palestine, the evil became more widespread and, indeed, almost universal. And although I still felt that the major responsibility for the moral and spiritual condition of my people lay with its leadership, civil and religious, it had now been borne in upon me that the whole nation was corrupt and depraved. The destruction which I had thought would come mainly upon Jerusalem I now saw must come upon the whole land of Judah. As I observed the spirit of my people it seemed to me that good men were few and far between. A righteous man in Judah was as rare as were the gleanings after the corn harvest had been thoroughly gathered. Good men were as hard to find as grapes after the vines had been stripped of their vintage and as figs after the trees had been picked of their fruit. So in the mood of sad lament, disillusionment, and pessimism, I poured out my heart:

> Alas for me, for I am as one who gathers after the harvest,
> Like gleanings after vintage,
> Not a cluster or a fig to eat,
> Which my appetite craves.
> Good men have perished from the land,
> And as for the upright among men, there is none (7. 1-2a).

MICAH OF MORESHETH-GATH

Everywhere I looked among my people I saw moral anarchy and social chaos. I continued:

> All of them lie in wait to murder;
> A man hunts down his own brother (7. 2b).

It seemed reasonable to expect that among the judges and high officials of Judah, after all the suffering and discipline my people had experienced, some honorable, faithful leaders could be found. But wheresoever I looked for kind, constructive leadership I was confronted only by graft and greed, such as reminded me of prickly thorns:

> They make their hands well disposed toward crooked dealing,
> The magistrate demands what is dedicated (to God),
> And the judge demands a reward,
> And the great speaks but to ruin.
> Justice they abhor.
> The best of them is like a briar;
> The most upright of them is like a (thorny) hedge (7. 3-4ab).

With such conditions so widespread in Judah, I saw clearly that Yahweh, moral Being that he is, could do but one thing to his people. So with the shadow cast by that prophetic certainty darkening my soul, I gave expression to the most sweeping conviction of national destruction which I had as yet uttered to my people:

> The day of their punishment has come!
> Now shall their confusion set in!
> And the land shall become a desolation,
> Because of those dwelling in it, on account of their evil deeds (7. 4cd, 13).

It was the opening years of the reign of King Manasseh that summoned me anew to engage in my prophetic task.

He was the son of King Hezekiah and a man of great power, but a monarch of an entirely different stamp. Contrary to the policy of his father he acquiesced in the protectorate of Assyria over our nation and continued the tribute paid King Sennacherib by like acknowledgments to King Esarhaddon, who had succeeded to the Assyrian throne.[15] King Manasseh gave national leadership among my people to a great wave of popular reaction against the reforming spirit that had characterized King Hezekiah. He rebuilt the High Places his father had destroyed, restoring the altars for Baal and the images of the deities. He introduced the worship of the heavenly bodies and erected altars for these deities in the inner and outer courts of the Temple. Under such temper of leadership the old Canaanite rite of child-sacrifice surged back into Judah, and King Manasseh gave it the incentive of his own example by offering up his own sons (2 Kings 21. 6, LXX). He resorted to the use of magic spells and omens, and attached to his court diviners, necromancers, and wizards, all skilled in professional magic.

As was to be expected, along with this mighty resurgence of these pagan practices, came an ignoring of the rightful claims upon the monarch of Yahweh's people of righteousness and justice toward his subjects. His acts of oppression led him to resort ruthlessly to the murder of innocent Judaeans who stood in his way (2 Kings 21. 16). With such leadership upon the throne of my people, the religion of Yahweh suffered a great setback and a corrupting reaction to the higher trend of public worship as it had been fostered by King Hezekiah now set in. The true Yahweh worship was no longer in evidence. Yahweh's real nature and his requirements of his people became vague and indistinct. The sacrificial cults were plied with frantic devotion. There was crying need in Judah for a prophetic interpretation of the religion of Yahweh. As I brooded over the depressing religious situation I was led of Yahweh to make a last attempt to reach in unique measure the intelligence and conscience of my countrymen. I was in Jerusalem when I made this final appeal.

I presented Yahweh's appeal to Judah in a form of expression familiar to the leaders of Jerusalem, that of a lawsuit, but between Yahweh and his people. I opened it at a time when the Judaean leaders thronged the Temple courts at a national feast, where sacrificial offerings were being presented in great numbers at the altar of Yahweh's house, with a plea for their attention. I challenged them:

Hear, pray, the word which Yahweh is speaking (6. 1a).

Yahweh's reason for thus appealing to Judah was the spoken, and even when not uttered, the nonetheless strongly felt, criticism by my countrymen of the way Yahweh had dealt with his people. They were Yahweh's people, yet Judah's lot had made them question the reality of Yahweh's leadership and care. So Yahweh spoke through me, summoning his people to present their accusation of him and their claim to different treatment at his hands. He appoints the everlasting mountains, the ancient hills to be witnesses in this case of Israel against him:

Arise, contend before the mountains,
And let the hills hear your voice.

> Hear, O hills, my dispute,
> And listen, O foundations of the earth.
> For a case has Yahweh with his people,
> And with Israel he would argue (6. 1b-2).

Then, directly to Judah, Yahweh spoke through me:

> My people what have I done to you?
> And how have I exhausted your patience? (6. 3.)

But Yahweh's people had no answer to give him, no defense to make. So Yahweh, on his part, stated his case against Judah. In a sweeping interpretation of the history of his people and his leadership of them in their formative past, Yahweh both defended himself against Judah's implied accusation, and laid the basis of his claim to the trust and obedience of all Judaeans. Thus he reasoned:

> For I brought you up from the land of Egypt,
> And from the house of slaves I ransomed you.
> And I sent before you Moses,
> Aaron and Miriam with him (6. 4).

In Yahweh's name I challenged his people to remember those heroic days when, under his guiding hand, the tribes of Israel were making their way up triumphantly through Transjordan. I recalled to the memory of Judah the thrilling story of Balaam, the noble Aramaean seer, who thrice defied the command of the Moabite King Balak to curse the invading Israelite tribes, saying:

> How can I curse whom God has not cursed?
> And how can I denounce whom God has not denounced?
> (Numbers 23. 8.)

Thus had this high-minded seer defended himself before Balak the king, for Yahweh had revealed to his soul in ecstatic visionary experience that his people were under his protection, and no seer's curse was powerful enough to veto the blessing of Yahweh (Numbers 23-24).

Then I brought Yahweh's people to remembrance of a creative moment of Israelite history, held as precious in our sacred traditions. It was when the invading tribes under Joshua left Shittim, the last camping station east of the Jordan River, crossed the river into the land Yahweh had promised them and set up at Gilgal their first camp in the land of Canaan (Joshua 3. 1; 4. 20). Behind all of this early history of my people, and that which alone made it possible, was the mighty arm of Yahweh executing his righteous acts on his people's behalf. In Yahweh's name I next summoned them to recall the thrilling story of their own past, to the end that they might ponder their relation to him in the present hour:

> Pray, remember what Balak counseled,
> And what Balaam answered him.
> Mark your crossing from Shittim to Gilgal,
> That my righteous acts may be revealed (6. 5).

It was customary among my people for Yahweh worshipers to consult the priests and the prophets at the sanctuary as to how rightly to come into Yahweh's presence so as to win his approval.[16] I could see that my interpretation of Yahweh's case against his people had touched the conscience of some Judaeans whose religion was undergirded by a consciousness of our nation's history. My words expressing Yahweh's appeal had now rendered them teachable, but what is yet more significant, had awakened in some of them their consciousness of sin. Just as worshipers often came to the sanctuary or Temple seeking light from Yahweh's ministers as to how rightly to approach him so as to meet fully his requirements, so now a group of the serious-minded of my people came to me, seeking my counsel as to just what Yahweh requires of his people. Their questions were such as I expected, for they implied the orthodox views of the generally accepted religious practice of the time. One of them first spoke for the group:

> With what should I come to meet Yahweh,
> And bow myself toward the high God?
> Should I come to meet him with burnt offerings,
> With calves a year old? (6. 6.)

For centuries the whole burnt offering of a year-old calf had been presented to appease the wrath of Yahweh (Leviticus 9. 3). Moreover, the only way they knew to approach him was by means of sacrifice. But another of the group broke in, feeling that perhaps what pleased Yahweh yet more was the significant ceremonial occasions in the nation where would be held a great sacrificial feast unto Yahweh. Then vast throngs of worshipers would participate; the rams for the feast would have to be exceedingly numerous; and the libations of olive oil might flow in myriad-streamed abundance. Such was that memorable day centuries ago at the dedication of the Jerusalem Temple when the vast number of peace offerings had cheered the participating multitudes (1 Kings 8. 63-66). So this member of the group asked,

> Would he be pleased with thousands of rams,
> With myriads of rivers of oil? (6. 7a.)

But a third—I could feel the mood of the devotee in this questioner—driven by the hunger for release from the burden of his sin, was ready to meet Yahweh's utmost requirement if it be necessary. What this might entail, the still persisting Canaanite practice made all too clear. And the recent public example of King Manasseh's acts made his question critical and pertinent (2 Kings 21. 6). Is it the sacrifice of my infant male child that Yahweh wants?

> Should I give my first born for my transgression,
> The fruit of my body for the sin of my soul? (6. 7b.)

So they questioned me. And Yahweh had already revealed to me the answer. He had led me to see that in spite of the centuries-old persistence of sacrifices and offerings as the appropriate and expected way to seek Yahweh, and in spite of the almost universal acquiescence of my people in the practice of such rites, it was not the true way to him. He had led me to see that these ways of approaching him to propitiate his wrath, induce his forgiveness, and win his favor, were in reality an inheritance absorbed by my people from the magical fertility cults of the Canaanites. With sharp clarity he had revealed to me that they represented no part of Yahweh's unique revelation to his people. Those who practiced them were not seeking to know his will and submit to it, but to control his power in their own interests.

Moreover, Yahweh had revealed to me that what he does desire of his people he has made clear to them. My own experience of Yahweh had taught me this. Not alone in the precious intuitions of my own soul did this knowledge come to me. For the prophets whom Yahweh had already sent to his people had shown us the way to the good life. The words reported to me as uttered by the shepherd prophet Amos of Tekoa had taught me Yahweh's insistence upon justice in human relationships. Yet more profoundly into truth had I been led by the teaching of the deep-souled poet-prophet Hosea, Ephraim's great gift to Yahweh's people, who was still preaching in the north in the days of my early ministry, before Samaria had fallen prey to the Assyrians. For he had unveiled the merciful kindness of Yahweh, and in his own personal life had revealed its unspeakable depth when it comes alive as a motive in a human soul. And the majestic teaching of my illustrious contemporary prophet Isaiah, whose words for nearly a half-century have brought light and challenge to Judah and Jerusalem, had helped me to see how confidence in Yahweh's presence with his people, and dependent, trustful humility toward him is what Yahweh most desires of Judah and Judaeans.

So I answered the questions my most responsive Judaean seekers brought to me in words which, brief and simple as they are, represent to me the very essence of religion. They sum up the best that my people have been taught and they represent the ripe fruit of my years of revelation as Yahweh's prophet. They set in clear, sharp relief the requirements of Yahweh, stripped of all unessential accompaniments. And I leave them as the most significant contribution of my prophetic experience to Judah and to humanity:

> He has declared to you, O man, what is good:
> And what is Yahweh seeking from you,
> But to do justice, and to love kindness,
> And to show a humble walk with your God? (6. 8.)

158

CHAPTER V

ZEPHANIAH OF JERUSALEM

I WAS born in Jerusalem, about the middle of the reign of King Manasseh.[1] From my earliest childhood it was often recalled to me by Cushi, my father, that royalty was in my veins, for my great-great-grandfather was Hezekiah, king of Judah.[2] I grew up among the princes of the court and was naturally deeply interested in the politics of my people. In the late years of his reign King Hezekiah had shaken off the Assyrian domination of Judah. But my people have told me how King Manasseh restored Assyria as protector over them. Indeed, in the nineteenth year of his reign, King Manasseh had contributed dues to King Esarhaddon for the building of an Assyrian arsenal at Nineveh. Along with other kings of the Westland, including the kings of Edom, Moab, and the Ammonites, the kings of the Philistine cities of Gaza, Ashkelon, Ekron, and Ashdod, the kings of the Phoenician cities of Byblos, Arvad, and Samsimuruna, and twelve other subject rulers, he had taken his tribute in person to King Esarhaddon at Tyre.[3]

During my boyhood our section of the world was in swift movement. Assyrian power was rapidly expanding. I often listened as the leaders in the court would speak of it. Sometimes they would tell in awed tones of how, nearly a century before, the great prophet Isaiah had warned our nation that the Ethiopian kings of Egypt would at length succumb to the expanding Assyrian power (Isaiah 20. 3-6). For exactly that had taken place

159

only a few years before I was born. The elders told me, in response to my questions, how in the last year of the kingship of the Ethiopian monarch Taharkah, King Ashurbanipal, the Assyrian, had driven him out of Memphis and had sacked Thebes.[4] Yet more vivid was the story the elders told me of Ashurbanipal's second invasion, while Tanutamon was Pharaoh of Egypt. For then Thebes was recaptured by him, its wealth looted, and the great city laid waste. In our section of the world the Assyrians had thus become without question, the dominant political and cultural force.

Even as a child I began to see for myself how perilous this situation was to the deeper life of my people. For our subjection to this dominant power resulted in the worship of Assyrian deities and the practice of Assyrian rites. I have since come to understand better how this came about, for to the rank and file of Judaeans the best gods were naturally considered to be those who could lead their people to conquer. And during most of the reign of King Manasseh, Assyria was absolute lord in the West-land. The elders of Jerusalem were far too conservative to approve the reforming trends which my great-great-grandfather had introduced. They had been able to control the young King Manasseh when, at the tender age of twelve, the kingship of my nation fell to him, so at once a great wave of reaction to the reforms of King Hezekiah had set in.

At first this reactionary party was content simply to rid themselves of King Hezekiah's innovations and to restore the worship of the Jerusalem Temple and of Judah to what it had been before the Judaean prophets had exerted their purging influence upon it. The High

Places were rebuilt. Altars for the worship of Baal were again erected. Just as, two centuries before, King Ahab had done in Samaria, King Manasseh now set up in the Temple of Yahweh in Jerusalem an Asherah, the symbol of the feminine counterpart of Baal in the old Canaanite religion. Royal protection was given to the worship of the dead, an ancient pagan rite which even the genius of my hero prophet Isaiah had been unable to stamp out in Judah, and necromancers and wizards were officially appointed. The old Canaanite rite of child sacrifice was revived and King Manasseh gave royal prestige to it by the sacrifice of his own sons (2 Kings 21. 3-7; 23. 13).

Soon, however, the trend toward things Assyrian became more conscious and purposive. The magical arts of the diviners and enchanters, famous in Assyrian religion, were given official protection in Judah. Astral religion, which played so great a rôle in the Assyrian worship, now became popular in Judah. On the roof of the upper chamber of Ahaz, King Manasseh erected altars for the sun, the moon, the signs of the Zodiac, and all the host of heaven; and a chamberlain, Nathanmelech, was put in charge of processional chariots, dedicated to the worship of the sun (2 Kings 23. 11f.). The worship of the mother-goddess, which already had its roots deep in the popular religion of my people, now received new impetus as she was revered particularly in her Assyrian-Babylonian expression as Ishtar, Queen of Heaven. Her cult was inordinately attractive to my people, and in Judaean households entire families—father, mother, and children—all had distinctive parts in the ritual of her worship (Jeremiah 7. 17ff.). Thus did my people, in the wake of this reaction, come to admire and imitate things Assyrian.

Particularly was this the case with the court princes, who could not help being awed by the scope and character of the Assyrian world dominion. Not content with this aping of Assyrian culture, King Manasseh set out to rid himself of the factors in the nation which opposed his policies. Some of the elders in Judah have told me the tragic story of his tracking down the members of the prophetic party who were then living, and naturally who were sharply opposed to the king, and great numbers were put to death.[5]

It was the invasion of the Scythians into Palestine, however, that aroused me to awareness that Yahweh was calling me to be his prophet. They were barbarians, the fiercest of them all. King Josiah had been on his throne but eleven years when these barbarian hordes poured down into Asia-Minor and Palestine, where for twenty-eight years they raided the whole region, even up to the borders of Egypt, spreading terror wherever they went. Psammetichus I of Egypt bribed them to retreat from his borders. On their way back toward the north they plundered the Temple of Aphrodite, located in the old Philistine town of Ashkelon, and also made themselves master of Beth Shean, warden city of the road which led from the Jordan across the plain of Esdraelon.

With horror and dismay I witnessed these raiding, sacking, barbarian hordes. Their overrunning of Palestine then seemed to me to mark the beginning of the end for all civilization. I could view it only as the judgment of Yahweh. These raiding hordes I believed to be the harbingers of a cataclysm which Yahweh was about to bring. It was to be of gigantic proportions and was to embrace in its scope the whole world, and every living thing in it. My mind was full of the horror of this imminent world destruction, as I began to proclaim to Judah, Yahweh's oracle:

> I will gather up completely and remove all things
> From upon the face of the earth.
> It is the oracle of Yahweh.
> I will gather up and take away man and beast;
> Birds of the heavens
> And fish of the sea.
> Yes, I will cause the wicked to stumble,
> And I will cut off man from the face of the earth (1. 2-3).

By this awful catastrophe my people of Judah, so I was convinced, would likewise be overtaken. The basic reason for Yahweh's destructive judgment upon his people was the corruption of the religious life of the nation. This was in part due to the stubborn vigor of the old pagan Baal worship which King Manasseh had encouraged to flourish anew in Judah. And partly it was because of the evil influence of the degenerate order of idolatrous priests, such as had ministered to the Bull cult of Bethel a century before my time, and who now, with royal approval, burned incense at the High Places in Judah and in the environs of Jerusalem (2 Kings 23. 5).

But a new factor which was heightening Judah's apostasy from Yahweh was the now popular fad of the Assyrian astral cults. For Assyrian religion was interwoven with the worship of the planets, especially the sun, the moon, and the planet Venus, with which the deities Shamash, Sin, and Ishtar, respectively, were associated.

King Manasseh's sanction of this worship had given prestige to these astral rituals, that were performed from the Judaean housetops, and they led my people far astray from Yahweh. Indeed, my countrymen had become hospitable toward all cults and had ignored Yahweh's requirement of exclusive allegiance to him. Although formally worshiping Yahweh, they doubted the adequacy of his power, so swore by Moloch the old Canaanite king deity to whom, as in old Palestinian paganism, now anew children of Judah were being sacrificed. Some had entirely given up even the appearance of Yahweh worship, and hosts of my countrymen did not worship him at all. It was because of this religious situation in Judah that I now pronounced Yahweh's judgment upon all the people of our nation and its capital:

> And I will stretch out my hand against Judah,
> And against all the inhabitants of Jerusalem.
> And I will cut off Baalism to its last vestige;
> And the name of the idolatrous priests;
> And those who worship upon the housetops
> The host of heaven;
> And those who worship Yahweh
> And swear by their (god) Moloch;[6]
> And those who have turned themselves away from following Yahweh,
> And those who have not sought Yahweh (1. 4-6).

From my life in the court I was familiar with the princes of the royal house. They had been the leaders in introducing into Jerusalem and Judah things Assyrian. They had started the vogue of wearing Assyrian modes of dress. This in itself did not disturb me, but I saw that this new fashion symbolized an attitude toward Assyria which had turned the back on Yahweh and left him utterly out of account in Judah. Moreover, these princes, through contact with Assyria, had become impregnated with Chaldaean magical rites such as the Assyrians themselves had docilely absorbed. One of these was the ritual of leaping over the threshold. The Assyrians believed that the thresholds of the houses were inhabited both above and underneath by evil demons. It was thought that these demonic spirits crouched down on the threshold. So by leaping over it they prevented and avoided the peril which contact with these spirits might bring. I was against this rite, for its performance was a tacit recognition of spiritual powers alien to Yahweh.[7] Moreover, hand in hand with such magical superstitious rituals practiced by the princes went immoral avarice. These princes occupied various offices in the palace, and used their exceptional positions to perpetrate such shameful acts of violence and trickery in commercial transactions as could only proceed from unhealthy souls. In the presence of these young leaders of royal blood I pronounced the certain punishment Yahweh was about to bring upon them:

> And I will punish all the princes,
> And the house of the king;
> And all who clothe themselves in foreign garments,
> And I will punish all who leap over the threshold,
> Who keep filling the house of their master with violence
> and fraud (1. 8-9).

Yahweh then led me to deal with the merchants, the leaders in business and commerce in our capital. They plied their wares at various areas in the city—at the Fish Gate in the northern wall; in the recently added Second Quarter, "the New Town," which was the northern suburb of Jerusalem, just outside the wall of Manasseh; in the hills, a residential quarter toward the north; and in the "Maktesh," the Mortar, the trough of the cheese makers in the Tyropoean valley southward of the city, which was the Merchants' (people of Canaan) chief resort, and the center of Jerusalem's industry and trade.[8]

The focus of dishonesty and trickery in commercial transactions was in these business quarters of the capital. The moral sense of these scheming leaders of Jerusalem's business had become so blunted and dulled that they were utterly indifferent to ethical ideals. A stolid conservatism characterized them. They were opposed to every reform movement and were a drag on the deeper life of my people. I compared them to wine grown thick upon the lees. For just as wine, when left upon its lees without being strained from vessel to vessel, becomes thickened and coagulated, so the moral sense of these merchants had become muddy, sluggish, and clogged. Their colossal inertia and their moral indifference had issued in a practical atheism. They doubted that Yahweh had any interest in their affairs and were skeptical as to his power in their lives. Their own lethargy and inaction they excused on the ground of what they interpreted as the inactivity of God.

But Yahweh had granted me insight into their lives and into his imminent judgment that awaited them. In anticipation my sensitive ears could already hear the bitter laments originating in these teeming business sections, when the Scythian hordes would invade and plunder the commercial quarters of Jerusalem. I could not wipe out of my imagination the hopeless deep-throated cries that were soon to be heard from these complacent

Jerusalem business men. In the ears of my soul I kept hearing those despairing cries, and I uttered Yahweh's oracle against these men, to whom silver was life's greatest treasure:

> And there shall be in that day,
> Oracle of Yahweh,
> A voice crying from the Fish Gate,
> And a wail from the New Town;
> And a great crash from the hills.
> So howl, you who dwell in the Mortar!
> For all the merchants shall be ruined;
> All who are loaded down with silver
> Shall be cut off (1. 10-11).

The life of both the princes and the merchants of Jerusalem had the marks of a godless civilization, and I knew these leaders could not escape Yahweh's judgment. So to these profane politicians and merchants, who ignored his claim upon their lives, I pictured Yahweh with lamp in hand tracking them down, turning their brilliant homes into desolate ruins, and confiscating their material wealth, thus dishonorably won. Said he:

> I will search Jerusalem with a lamp,
> And I will punish those who feel secure,
> Thickened upon their lees,
> Who keep saying in their hearts,
> "Yahweh does not do good,
> And Yahweh does not do evil."
> Yes, their property shall become plunder,
> And their homes a desolation (1. 12-13a).

I felt that the end of Judah was near at hand and set myself to interpret it so that it would grip my people. I had often been impressed with the rapidity and completeness with which my hungry countrymen could consume a sacrificial meal. Just like that will the hungry Scythians put an end to my people. I compared my people to sacrificial victims that were being prepared by Yahweh to be slaughtered. And the rapacious Scythians I interpreted as the guests invited by Yahweh to consume the sacrifice thus prepared. Even now just as priests sanctify and prepare the summoned worshipers for partaking of the sacrifice, so I told them, Yahweh is getting the Scythians ready to consume completely the Judaeans.

The picture struck terror to my own soul. The Lord Yahweh was host, presiding at the sacrifice where the Scythians, invited of him for the very purpose, would utterly consume his people! And this would take place on Yahweh's awful day! For strange as it seemed to me, Yahweh had shown me that the Scythian hordes were his chosen instruments to execute judgment upon his people. Before such a God, controller of nations and of men, Judah can but hold her peace, and submit to her sovereign Lord! In awed solemnity I admonished my people:

> Silence! before the Lord Yahweh,
> For near is the day of Yahweh!
> For Yahweh has prepared a sacrifice,
> He has sanctified those he has invited! (1. 7.)

But the day of Yahweh meant nothing to my people. The great shepherd prophet of Judah, more than a century before, had told Yahweh's people that the day of Yahweh for which they were longing would mean for them darkness, not light, thick darkness without an extenuating ray. But my people now neither longed for it nor feared its coming. They were utterly indifferent

168

to the day of Yahweh. It was meaningless to them. As
for me, in those days I could think of nothing else. Yahweh had lodged the terror of it in my very soul. It
shadowed my spirit night and day. I brooded over it
and strove to penetrate to its incomprehensible meaning.
Then at length I could keep silent no longer. I began
to describe it to my people in tense, picturesque words.
And the solemnity of my own soul caught and held their
attention as I strove to teach Judah the tragedy it would
bring. First I described the speed with which Yahweh's
great and bitter day was steadily nearing Judah, like the
swiftness of invading warriors:

> Near is the great day of Yahweh;
> Near, speeding along rapidly!
> Swifter comes Yahweh's day than a runner,
> Yes, speedier than a warrior! (1. 14.)

Then I interpreted it as the day of the outpouring of
Yahweh's moral wrath against his people, bringing them
pain and destruction. And not only human beings
would experience its awful destruction, for portentous
disturbances would be wrought by it in the world of
nature as well:

> A day of wrath is that day;
> A day of trouble and distress,
> A day of crashing ruin and devastation,
> A day of darkness and calamity,
> A day of clouds and gloom! (1. 15.)

Our people of Judah stood in mortal terror of the Scythians. We had heard their sharp bugle blasts and their
savage battle shouts as they had surged across Palestine
toward Egypt. My people feared for their fortresses
before the onslaught of such vigorous warriors. And

now I showed my fellow countrymen how these fierce
barbarians were the forerunners of Yahweh's day:

> A day of trumpet and battle cry,
> Against the fortified cities,
> Against the lofty battlements (1. 16).

Yet the Scythians were but *part* of Yahweh's day. More
awful than the desolation they would leave in their
train would be the blinding, destroying, supernatural
forces which Yahweh was about to release, not merely
upon Judah but upon mankind in general:

> And I will bring trouble upon men,
> So that they shall walk like blind men;
> And their blood shall be poured out like the dust,
> And their fat like excrement (1. 17).

Psammetichus I of Egypt, as I have said, by heavy payment of money, bribed the Scythians from overrunning
his land, and thus saved his people from destruction. My
people, while not despairing of the protection of our
fortress, yet were confident that we too, in case it came
to that, could in like manner secure the withdrawal of
these decimating hordes. But I had become convinced
that Yahweh's day embraced more than Judah in its
destructive scope, and the Scythians were but part of his
agents. Nothing less than a world destruction awaited
mankind, and no human power could frustrate it. So I
concluded in Yahweh's name:

> Yes, neither their silver nor their gold
> Shall be able to deliver them.
> For an end, yes, sudden and terrifying, I will make,
> Of all the inhabitants of the earth (I. 18).

Thus far I had spoken to my countrymen in vague and

general terms of Yahweh's day, when his righteous fury would overflow the world. The solemn words in which I had painted the various features of that day had arrested the attention of my people. So I began to describe in more detail and definiteness how Yahweh's impending judgment would affect various nations with which we Judaeans were intimately concerned. I began with the Philistines, the "Cherethites," we Judaeans call them (Ezekiel 25. 16), the people nearest at hand, whose territory is bordered by the great sea. Judah had been allied with their famous cities a century ago when the nations of the Westland were together trying to shake off the domination of Assyria. I described in prophetic anticipation the imminent devastation of the famous Philistine cities, Gaza, Ashkelon, Ashdod, and Ekron, when these now populous towns and villages would be reduced to pastoral solitudes. In the mood of lamentation and in vivid words, I painted the sad picture:

> For Gaza shall be deserted,
> And Ashkelon a devastation.
> As for Ashdod,—at noon they shall expel her,
>   And Ekron shall be uprooted.
> Woe to those dwelling by the sea-coast,
> O nation of the Cherethites!
> I will humble you, O land of the Philistines!
> And I will destroy you until there is no inhabitant.
> And you shall become pastures for shepherds,
> And folds for flocks;
> By the sea they shall feed,
> In the houses of Ashkelon.
> In Ekron shall they lie down (2. 4-7b).

Then I turned to the imminent fate of Egypt. Psammetichus I, in the beginning of his public career, was a prince of Sais in the Delta under the overlordship of

Assyria. But some fifteen years before I began my prophetic ministry he had thrown off his Assyrian allegiance, asserting his independence. Assyrian domination of Egypt had thus far merely rid Egypt of its Ethiopian monarchs. And now the Egyptians had begun to show new designs upon Asia. Even then they were besieging Ashdod, the first movement in a new attempt at conquest of Palestine and Syria. But strong as they were, the Egyptians—Ethiopians I scornfully still called them, because of the long subjection to Ethiopian rule Egypt had experienced—would likewise fall in the imminent destruction that is drawing near upon the world. I put this certainty in a brief, decisive word:

> Also you Ethiopians
> Shall be slain by the sword! (2. 12.)

But still more terrible and more momentous than the destruction of all our neighbors, was that which Assyria, age-long enemy of Yahweh's people, was to suffer. Often had my nation trembled in terror when the news was heralded in Judah that the Assyrian forces had crossed the Euphrates at Carchemish and were descending upon Yahweh's people. But soon the tables were to be turned. I had become aware that the hand of Yahweh was already stretched out to destroy this enemy, most hated by all the Westland peoples. Already the barbarous Medes, precursors of the still more barbarous Scythians, had repeatedly attacked Nineveh on the east, and now the Scythians, yet more ferociously, were swooping down upon the Assyrian empire, threatening its very existence. This onslaught of Assyria by these decimating barbarian

forces I interpreted as the scourging hand of Yahweh. So
I declared what Yahweh was about to do:

> He will stretch forth his hand against the north,
> And cause Assyria to perish.
> And he will make of Nineveh a desolation,
> A land of drought like the desert.
> And herds shall lie down in its midst,
> All the beasts of the field (2. 13-14a).

I pictured the capitals, windows, and thresholds, of the
once proud Assyrian palaces, now merely the haunt of
screech owls, porcupines, and ravens!

> Both screech owl and porcupine shall lodge in her capitals.
> The owl shall hoot in the window,
> The raven on the threshold! (2. 14bc.)

My soul was moved with awe as I contemplated the
approaching fall of mighty Nineveh. Yahweh's judgment upon it, thus mediated by these destructive bar-
baric hordes, I saw would be final and irrevocable, and
would reduce the proud city to an unpopulated region,
the haunt of wild beasts. The passer-by will not then
try to conceal his scornful hate of the fallen tyrant. So in
anticipation of her ignoble collapse I taunted her with
a mock lament:

> This is the exultant city,
> That dwelt in security!
> That kept saying in her heart, "I am,
> And there is none to compare with me."
> How has she become an appalling waste,
> A lair for wild beasts!
> Everyone who passes by her
> Will hiss, he will shake his fist! (2. 15.)

As I thus contemplated the destruction of the neighbors of my people far and near, an insistent question kept

forcing itself upon me. Would like destruction engulf Judah? Or would Yahweh's people escape, when he executed his judgment upon the world? Gradually my mind achieved certainty at this point. Yahweh led me to see that his people were under the same condemnation as were the other nations. Yet I came to realize that there was one way of escape for Judah. The day of Yahweh's anger had not yet come. If my people, now so shameless in their iniquity, and so careless regarding his requirements, would but honestly seek Yahweh! If they would but reveal a humble spirit of dependence upon him rather than such stolid, proud indifference! If they would but aim to be righteous in social dealings and turn from their ruthless oppression so characteristic of them at the present! Then when the day of Yahweh should come, his wrath would pass Judah by. With eagerness of heart and with voice thrillingly tender in appeal, I accordingly summoned my people to repentance:

> Sanctify yourselves and become clean,
> O nation unadmonished;
> Before you are ground to dust,
> Like the chaff which blows away.
> Before there comes upon you
> The heat of Yahweh's wrath!
> Before there comes upon you
> The day of Yahweh's anger!
> Seek Yahweh,
> All you meek of the land,
> Who do his justice.
> Seek righteousness, seek humility;
> Perhaps you may be hidden,
> In the day of Yahweh's wrath (2. 1-3).

Then with great enthusiasm and with passionate hope I set myself, as Yahweh's prophet, to awaken the leaders of Jerusalem, the princes and judges, the prophets and priests, to the critical nature of the times and to arouse them to repentance. The time was short, for Yahweh's day was near at hand. If I could but arouse our capital city and make her responsive to Yahweh's will, our city and nation might be saved from overwhelming disaster.

Reformation was desperately needed. Her princes who ruled the city were comparable to ravenous lions, leaping with a terrifying roar upon their victims. For these rapacious political leaders treated my poor countrymen as their prey. Her judges were corrupt, insatiable in their lust for gain. Like prowling evening wolves they were accustomed to plan out and execute their schemes under cover of darkness. But her religious leaders were no better. Her prophets were presumptuous and faithless, declaring not the mind of Yahweh but the false product of their own imaginings. The priests, whose supreme task was instruction in the knowledge of Yahweh and directions for his rightful worship, had been false to their high office. By their own corrupt lives and in their poor instruction of my people they had blurred the distinction between what is holy and common, and had twisted Yahweh's directions to suit the wishes of those who consulted them. So in solemn, specific indictment, I pronounced Yahweh's woe upon Jerusalem, and his impending judgment:

> Woe to the rebelling and defiled one,
> The oppressing city!
> She has not listened to a voice;
> She has not accepted correction!
> In Yahweh she has not trusted;
> To her God she has not drawn near!

> Her princes in her midst
> Are ravenous lions.
> Her judges are wolves of the night,
> They do not long for the morning.
> Her prophets are reckless, treacherous men;
> Her priests profane what is holy;
> They deal violently with instruction (3. 1-4).

How dull has been our beloved capital in giving heed to the warnings of Yahweh's prophets! How slow to submit to Yahweh's discipline! Yet Jerusalem is still *Yahweh's* city. *He* dwells within her, in his holy Temple, righteous in his innermost nature, dealing justly with his people every morning, as persistent and constant as the sun! But in awful contrast to this lofty Being of unchanging justice and of unfailing dependableness, I pictured these corrupt, shameless leaders of my people:

> Yahweh in her midst is righteous;
> He does not do wrong.
> In the morning he gives his judgment:
> Like the light he does not fail.
> But the wicked do not know shame (3. 5).

The prophets of my nation who preceded me had taught Yahweh's people how his judgment had been manifested in history. The destruction of mankind at the flood, the fall of the cities of Sodom and Gomorrah, Admah and Zeboim, the fall of Damascus, the fall of Samaria—all such events should have warned Yahweh's people, for he spoke to them in those catastrophes. It was his intention that these calamities experienced by other nations and cities, should have warned his own people of Judah. They should have made Jerusalem sensitive to his presence and open to his correction. Thus Yahweh spoke through me:

> I have cut off the nations;
> Their battlements have been destroyed.
> I have made their streets desolate,
> With no one passing by.
> Their cities have been made destitute of men,
> So there is not an inhabitant.
> I said, "Surely she will fear me,
> She will accept correction,
> And what I have laid upon her
> Will not vanish from her eyes" (3. 6-7c).

Then I gave expression to Yahweh's disappointment with his people because of their dullness to perceive and their unresponsiveness to obey his will:

> But in fact they have actively and strenuously
> Made all their deeds corrupt (3. 7de).

So my mind returned to my earlier thoughts of universal catastrophe which, on Yahweh's day, was soon to engulf the world. Then he would appear as a lone witness against all nations gathered by him, to pour out upon them the fire of his indignant wrath. I uttered, as Yahweh's oracle, his decision to consume the earth.

> Therefore wait for me, is the oracle of Yahweh,
> For the day when I will rise up as a witness,
> For it is my decision to gather nations,
> To assemble kingdoms,
> In order to pour out upon them my wrath,
> All the heat of my anger.
> For in the fire of my zeal shall be consumed
> All the earth (3. 8).

But Yahweh had led me to see this awful impending catastrophe in a new light. Destruction, certain as it was, and widespread as it was to be, was not the last word in Yahweh's purpose. Well do I remember the thrill of spirit that came to me when I first grasped this thought. I had been meditating upon the universal destruction that awaited the world—Judah as well as the nations. But not all my people were evil. Some of them whom I knew, the lowly and poor among us, had sympathized with my message and had shared my hopes for a nobler nation. They were the quiet in the land. Socially they were of little importance, yet I was convinced that in the hands of this inconspicuous minority among my people rested the future of the religion of Yahweh.[9] Now I saw that Yahweh's destruction would not embrace *them*. It will destroy the proud and profane in the nation. It will purge Yahweh's people of all liars and deceivers. When Yahweh's day has come, the community of the faithful will no more experience humiliation because of the sinful and proud in its midst, for these on that great day will be removed. But in Yahweh's holy mountain, our beloved Temple hill, there will be left a righteous remnant of Judaeans whom Yahweh will not destroy. This community of the faithful in Judah shall live on, freed from all disturbance from without, with hearts fearless and at peace. This was my gospel to Judah. This I shall now continue to proclaim. It is with a heart thrilled to the core, and in words vibrant with tender emotion, that I utter it as Yahweh's final word, the zenith of his revelation to Judah through me, his prophet:

> For then I shall remove from your midst
> The proudly insolent ones of you;
> And you shall no more be haughty
> In my holy mountain;
> For I shall leave in your midst a people,
> Humble and poor.

ZEPHANIAH OF JERUSALEM

And they shall take refuge in the name of Yahweh—
The remnant of Israel!
They shall do no iniquity,
And they shall not tell lies.
And there shall not be found in their mouths
A tongue that is deceitful.
For they shall all feed and lie down,
With none to disturb them[10] (3. 11b, 13).

CHAPTER VI

NAHUM OF ELKOSH

MY birthplace was at Elkosh, a town in southwestern Judah, in the region where the tribe of Simeon had settled, close to the Philistine and Egyptian borders, between Beit Jibrin and Gaza.[1] For some time now, however, I have been one of the prophets connected with the Temple at Jerusalem, and reside there. It was the fall of Nineveh that moved me to this act of prophecy, for the reverberations of that event were felt by all the nations of my day. The collapse of mighty Assyria marked the end of an epoch in the history of all the peoples in Western Asia. With amazing vigor and ruthless energy the Assyrians had created the first imperial State known to history. For seven centuries all of us peoples in the Mediterranean area had felt her harsh hand. For nearly three centuries her armies had constituted the most feared fighting machine in the world, and the most barbarous and cruel as well. For more than a century now she had been the terror of my people. King after king had cowered before her, and the vast tribute my nation had paid into her coffers had impoverished our economic life, as well as compelled the surrender of our political freedom. Indeed, Assyria's exhaustive drafts on the treasuries of Judah and of our neighbor nations were too high a price to pay for her seductive "protection." I could only think of it as "harlot's hire" paid to this greedy and immoral mistress of the peoples by these nations, her "paramours." The "harlot of the nations"

I called her, for what we Judaeans had experienced from our relationship with her was the common lot of all our neighbors.

In order that you may understand the exultation that thrilled my people when famous Nineveh, Assyria's capital city, finally fell, I must lead you upon a brief excursion into the past and tell you what I have learned at the lips of the fathers of Judah. I must swiftly trace for you the story of the expansion of the Assyrian dominion in the Westland until the Assyrian Empire stretched from Babylonia, on the one hand, to Thebes in upper Egypt, on the other. Then I must tell you what took place in the generation immediately preceding my time, just as the elders of my people have told it to me, for it was in that generation that the forces were taking shape which led to Yahweh's judgment upon Assyria, and at length to her collapse.

The elders of Judah have transmitted to me what their fathers had in turn told them—how our great Judaean prophet, Isaiah, in the days of Hezekiah, a century before my time, had warned his people of the futility of rebellion against Assyria. They have told me how the leaders of our nation at that time, ignoring the prophet's counsel, had turned to the Ethiopian kings for help in their concerted attempt, along with other nations of the Westland, to throw off the oppressive Assyrian yoke. Isaiah, in those days, had prophesied that the Ethiopians themselves would be carried captive by Assyria, in abject humiliation. He had accordingly summoned my people to seek stability and permanence solely by trust in Yahweh.

But King Manasseh had sought this security through alliance with Assyria and by his admiration and imitation of things Assyrian, and accordingly was consistently loyal to his overlord well into the reign of Esarhaddon, the successor of Sennacherib. At length the realization was forced upon our monarch of what Yahweh had revealed so clearly to the prophet Isaiah, that Assyria would not rest until Egypt was in her control. Moreover, he saw clearly that if Egypt too should be mastered by Assyria, the days of any kind of independence for our nation and for the other small Westland peoples, even under an Assyrian protectorate, would be at an end. Accordingly, King Manasseh forsook his Assyrian loyalties, and, along with the heads of the Phoenician cities of Arvad and Tyre and the Philistine city of Ashkelon, chose to take his chance with Egypt and allied himself wholeheartedly with Taharkah, who was now Pharaoh of Egypt. In this period of his Egyptian loyalty, King Manasseh even named his son and successor, "Amon," after the chief god of Egypt. He constructed an outer wall to the city of David on the west side of the spring of Gihon in the valley at the entrance to the Fish Gate and thus fortified our capital for his revolt against Assyria. He surrounded Ophel with a strong wall and raised it to a great height. This region of Jerusalem was a tongue of rock two thousand by four hundred feet in area, which combined seclusion for the city of David with safety and a good water supply, for the spring of Gihon was on its eastern front. He stationed valiant captains in the various Judaean fortresses. This change in my nation's political allegiance was accompanied by significant changes in the national religion, as fostered by our king. He removed from the Temple the Assyrian gods and the idols, which included the images of Ashur and of the king of

Assyria. All the altars he had erected to the foreign
deities were taken away and the regular offerings and
sacrifices to Yahweh were restored (2 Chronicles 33. 14-
16.)

The Assyrian domination of Egypt, thus long ago anticipated by the prophet Isaiah, at length began. The
elders of Judah who remembered it, have told me of the
great excitement and fear it aroused among my people.
Under terrific difficulties, Esarhaddon, the Assyrian king,
invaded Egypt in the last years of his reign, captured
Memphis and tore Ethiopia away from the Egyptian
Empire. On his triumphal march homeward he put our
King Manasseh in chains as a punishment for his perfidy.
After a period of imprisonment, however, he restored
our king to his throne.[2]

But the height of Assyrian expansion came in the reign
of Esarhaddon's successor, Ashurbanipal. King Taharkah the Ethiopian, who had been wounded five times in
his battles with Esarhaddon, now tried to wrest Egypt
back from the hands of the new Assyrian monarch.
Ashurbanipal accordingly, in his fifth year, made his first
campaign into Egypt. He defeated Taharkah's army,
and seized and occupied Memphis. He pursued the fleeing Pharaoh to Thebes, whereupon he seized that famous
city, occupied it, and, plundering it of its rich treasures,
returned to Nineveh.

The local rulers in Egypt, whom Ashurbanipal had
installed, and of whom the leader was Necho of Memphis
and Sais, realized their need of the powerful Taharkah
as a bulwark for their own hold upon Egypt. So they
plotted with him to parcel out Egypt between them and
himself, hoping thus to expel Assyrian dominion en-

tirely. The officials of the resident Assyrian army, however, got word of this plot, and putting these rebelling rulers in fetters, they horribly massacred the inhabitants of the plotting cities, and took their disloyal chieftains to Nineveh. Necho, however, was forgiven and was restored to his post in Sais.

Tanutamon, a son of Pharaoh Shabaka, reigned as co-regent with Taharkah during the latter's final year, then he seized the throne of Egypt and fortified his kingdom at Thebes and Heliopolis. He defeated the Delta rulers, who, as subject chieftains of the dominant Assyrian power, opposed him, and captured Memphis, where he settled, as Pharaoh of all Egypt. The news of this usurpation was relayed to Ashurbanipal by his Assyrian officers in the Delta. It stirred him into action, and he made straight for Egypt and Ethiopia. He drove Tanutamon from Memphis and pursued him to Thebes. When Tanutamon saw the approach of the Assyrians he forsook Thebes and fled. This famous city was called by my people "No Amon," which means, the city of the god Amon, for it was there that Amon the chief god of Egypt had his seat. Ashurbanipal, then in the seventh year of his reign, recaptured that great city in its entirety, helped, as he himself piously maintained, by the Assyrian deities Ashur and Ishtar.

No Amon was the greatest of the then existing cities in the east. Its final and complete fall and the sacking of its treasures, including those of the famous Temple of Amon at Karnak, stirred the world of my day. In mighty triumph, and with his hands full of precious booty, Ashurbanipal returned in acclaim to Nineveh. Thebes was the greatest depository of Egyptian treasures. From there he brought with him silver, gold, precious stones, brilliantly colored linen garments, two tall obelisks made of electrum which stood by the gate of the Temple, great horses, and many male and female captives. This remarkable fulfillment of the prediction which Isaiah had announced to my people just fifty years before made an unerasable impression upon my countrymen. Still today the very name, "No Amon," awakes informed Judaeans to attention.

Now I must tell you how this victorious, masterful Assyria gradually loosened her grip upon the east and west alike, and began to crumble. Upon the death of the Ethiopian chieftain Necho, whom Ashurbanipal had reinstalled at Sais, Psammetichus, his son, fled to Syria, where he was under Assyrian protection. Ashurbanipal then placed Psammetichus upon the throne of his father, as chieftain of Sais and Memphis. He was a man of brilliant power and great political sagacity. He soon saw that the times were ripe in Egypt for throwing off, with decisive finality, the Assyrian yoke, for Ashurbanipal had just then become involved in a life-and-death struggle with his crown prince of Babylon. For Shamash-shum-ukin rebelled against Ashurbanipal in the latter's sixteenth year, thus beginning the war that four years later ended in his suicide and the prostration of Babylon. Psammetichus took advantage of this preoccupation of Assyria with the Babylonian rebellion and recovered for Egypt her lost liberty.

In the meantime Bel-ibni, the Chaldaean, a descendant of Merodach-baladan of Bit Yakin, had been appointed ruler of the Sea-lands of the Persian Gulf, and, in southern and eastern Babylonia, was laying the foundations of the new Chaldaean Empire. The power of Ashurbanipal was now steadily weakening, and he died in his forty-second year. The following year, building on the foundations laid by the Chaldaean Bel-ibni, Nabopolassar of Babylon threw off the Assyrian dominion and founded the Chaldaean Empire. This new empire was the greatest threat to Assyria that had yet appeared upon the stage of history.

Another threat to the last shreds of Assyrian dominion in our area of the world was the emergence of the Medes. Cyaxares, king of the Medes, as early as the year which saw the founding of the Chaldaean Empire, had laid siege to Nineveh. While this siege was in progress, however, a great horde of Scythians, marching eastward along the northern slope of the Caucasus Mountains, then turning south between the end of that range and the Caspian Sea, poured down upon Media and defeated the Medes, forcing the withdrawal of Cyaxares from the siege of Nineveh. They marched through Palestine to Egypt, but were bribed by Psammetichus to turn back from his domain. On their way back through Palestine they pillaged the Temple of Aphrodite at Ashkelon. For twenty-eight years they lorded it over Asia, exacting heavy tribute and plundering wherever they went. Cyaxares, however, swiftly won back his Median Empire.

And now it was our turn to throw off the Assyrian yoke from the shoulders of Judah. King Josiah, in Ashurbanipal's thirtieth year, had succeeded to the throne of my people. Assyrian authority over Judah was then at a very low ebb. Our break with Assyria came contemporaneously with the Scythian invasion which had contributed greatly to the relaxation of Assyrian control. In the eighteenth year of King Josiah my people virtually proclaimed our independence of Assyria. Our king, on the basis of a new lawbook found in the Temple by Hilkiah the priest while the repair of the Temple was in progress, set in motion a religious reform. It aimed at purifying the public worship of Judah of all foreign intrusions (2 Kings 22-23). But this program of reform had its political angle as well. The movement thus inaugurated by King Josiah was in part an attempt to do for my people what king Psammetichus of Egypt and the Chaldaean king, Nabopolassar of Babylon, had just done for theirs—throw off the Assyrian yoke and revive the national spirit.[3] This reform did away with the High Places, where primitive elements of Canaanite heathenism still continued to exert a corrupting influence upon the Judaean religion. And it did away with the remnant of the Assyrian astral cults which King Manasseh had introduced. Moreover, it involved the extension of King Josiah's political authority into Bethel, thus reclaiming for Yahweh's people territory which, since Samaria's fall, had actually become an Assyrian province (2 Kings 23. 15).

The young son of Ashurbanipal, Ashur-etil-ilani, secured his father's throne in the same year that Nabopolassar threw off the Assyrian dominion in Babylon. He reigned four years, during which time he interested himself chiefly in restoring shrines of the Assyrian deities. He was succeeded by Sin-shar-ishkun, another son of Ashurbanipal, who was likewise devoted to the restoration of the Assyrian cult. But all this devoted attention to shrines and Temples could not recover Assyria's strength nor stave off its crumbling collapse. Sin-shar-ishkun, however, proved to be a vigorous soldier as well as an enthusiast for famous Assyrian shrines, and for several years he held his enemies at bay, and with considerable political skill, turned his erstwhile vigorous opponents into loyal Assyrian allies.

At length Nabopolassar, the Chaldaean, after making forays into Assyria and Akkad, and after getting all Babylonia well under his control, mobilized his army against Assyria. In the spring of his tenth year, marching up along the Euphrates, he defeated the Assyrian army at Qablinu.[4]

Egypt then took a new hand in eastern affairs. No longer now did she fear Assyria. Rather had she transferred her fear to the emerging Chaldaeans, who were rapidly becoming a mighty obstacle to Psammetichus' ambitions for conquest in the East. Consequently, Psammetichus allied himself with decadent Assyria, and came to her help against Nabopolassar. The allies found that the Chaldaean king had retreated from Qablinu but they could not overtake him. Nabopolassar then turned and fought the Assyrian army near Arrapha and inflicted upon the Assyrians a decisive defeat.

In his eleventh year Nabopolassar the Chaldaean crossed the Tigris and attacked the city of Ashur, one of the four principal towns of Assyria. He was repulsed and pursued by Sin-shar-ishkun to Takritain, but Nabopolassar then turned and decisively defeated the Assyrians.

Then the Medes got into action against Assyria. In the autumn of that same year they descended upon the Assyrian province of Araphu, and the following year, under Cyaxares, they went down the Tigris and, attacking Ashur, captured and destroyed it, and carried its people captive. Nabopolassar, marching to Cyaxares' aid, arrived too late for the assault, but established an alliance with the Medes, sealing it by the marriage of Nebuchadrezzar, his son, with Amyitis, granddaughter of Cyaxares.

At length the final assault upon Nineveh took place. Nabopolassar, the Chaldaean, and Cyaxares, the Mede, besieged the city from June until August of Nabopolassar's fourteenth year, and at last the proud Assyrian capital fell. Its common people and nobility were slaughtered and its king, Sin-shar-ishkun, fled. The Assyrian army deserted and Nineveh was destroyed and turned into a heap of ruins.

Never will I forget the day the news reached Jerusalem — that mighty Nineveh had fallen! It stirred my people to transports of joy. Already King Josiah's throwing off the Assyrian yoke, and his vigorous religious reform in Judah, had awakened new national and religious hopes among my people. And now the thrilling tidings that the capital of Judah's most feared and most hated enemy had finally fallen added fuel to the already leaping flames of patriotism and religion. Near at hand was the festival of the New Year which we are accustomed to celebrate in connection with the great autumnal Feast of Booths, the popular feast of rejoicing, and the most important festival of our whole Temple year. Since the inauguration of the reformation of King Josiah, just nine years ago last spring, our Temple had attained new prestige and now had achieved a far-reaching national influence. For not only had the corrupt worship of the High Places of the Judaean towns and cities been destroyed and abolished, but the reform had the more positive aim of making the Temple of Jerusalem the one authoritative religious center of our nation. And now it was the accepted law of my people that in spring, summer, and autumn pilgrims would come from all over Judah to celebrate respectively, the Passover, the Feast of Weeks, and the New Year's and Booths' festival. Greatest and most popular of all for my people was the New Year's festival, which was celebrated as the climactic day of the Feast of Booths. On this day it was the custom in Jerusalem to celebrate the enthronement of Yahweh over Judah. Moreover, this festival looked to the future and its celebration anticipated the time when Yahweh would be king over all the nations also.

It was clear to me that this year, because of the fall of Nineveh which had just occurred, the festival of the New Year would be celebrated with unprecedented enthusiasm and with mounting passion of Judaean nationalism. Yahweh led me to seize upon this as an opportunity to impress upon his people that the destruction of Nineveh, now an accomplished fact, was but the outworking in contemporary history of Yahweh's judgment. The fall of Nineveh, as I was now led to see, was the expression of the divine Nemesis. Most of my fellow Judaeans thought it had fallen merely before the superior power of the armies of the Chaldaean Nabopolassar and Cyaxares' rough hordes of Median troops. But there was now revealed to me behind these fierce pagan powers the mighty irrevocable hand of Yahweh, Lord of all the earth, using these forces to accomplish his awful judgment upon Assyria, that harlot of the nations.

Connected with the Temple, and under the oversight of its head priest, there were now a number of Temple prophets, of whom I was one, who had their residence there, and in connection with the Temple worship, uttered Yahweh's oracles. Our New Year's festival included in its celebration a liturgical recitation of the story of the creation of the world by Yahweh, and the recall of those qualities in his nature and of the acts of his hand that merited his universal sovereignty over the world.[5] So I put my message into the form of a prophetic liturgy for use at the Jerusalem Temple at the approaching New Year festival. I created it with the consciousness of being Yahweh's prophet, and with the intention of uttering, at appropriate points in its rendition, the oracles of Yahweh to his people. I hoped thus to make sure that the memory of Yahweh's decisive judgment upon Nineveh might never perish from the soul of Judah. I shall now tell you of its content.

I began it with the majestic hymn of praise to Yahweh, as the jealous and avenging God, whose might had destroyed Nineveh. To fasten this hymn imperishably in the memory of my people I composed it as an alphabetic poem, carrying the acrostic through the first half of our Hebrew alphabet.[6] This hymn was to be sung by the throng of worshipers at the feast. It opened with the celebration of Yahweh as the God of vengeance who manifests himself in hurricane and in swirling dust storm, as he comes forth to judge his enemies:

> (Aleph) A God jealous and avenging is Yahweh;
> An avenger is Yahweh and a wrathful Lord;
> Yahweh is slow to get angry and great in strength,
> And he will not at all acquit (his enemies).

(Beth)   In storm wind and tempest is his way,
            And a cloud is the dust of his feet (1. 2a-3).

My hymn then takes up the theme of the terrified response of physical nature to Yahweh's revelation of himself in power. The waters of the sea and rivers evaporate before the heat of his wrath. Pastureland as fertile as the luxurious plains of Bashan, forests as dense as cover the slopes of Mount Carmel, tree sprouts such as would grow into the majestic cedars of the Lebanon mountains, all wither at his approach; mountains tremble from earthquake, streams of molten lava from erupting volcanic mountains pour down the slopes, and the earth crumbles in destruction. Thus I pictured nature reacting in terrified awe to the presence of her creator:

(Gimel)   He rebukes the sea and dries it up;
           And all the rivers he makes dry.

(Daleth)   Bashan and Carmel have languished;
           And the sprout of the Lebanon grows weak.

(He)   The mountains quake before him;
           And all the hills melt.

(Waw)   The earth crashes to ruins from before him;
           The world and all who dwell in it (1. 4-5).

My hymn then celebrates the righteous wrath of Yahweh, for mighty Nineveh had gone down to destruction before its unearthly fury:

(Zayin)   As for his wrath, who can stand before it?
           Who can stand the heat of his anger?

(Heth)   His wrath is poured out like fire;
           And the rocks are broken down before it (1. 6).

Then the hymn proceeds to the praise of Yahweh as the mighty protector of his people. In these days of in-

ternational turmoil and threatened national collapse
there were some among my people who had never lost
their faith in Yahweh's protection. The decisive downfall of Nineveh had given signal evidence of his overthrow of the powers of evil, of which Nineveh was the
very incarnation. Yahweh's worshipers thus utter their
praise of his protection and their gratitude for his destruction of his enemies:

> (Teth) Good is Yahweh to those who wait for him,
> A protection in the day of trouble.

> (Yodh) Yahweh knows those who seek refuge in him,
> And makes them pass through an overflowing
> flood.

> (Kaph) A complete destruction he makes of his oppo-
> nents;
> And his enemies he drives into darkness (1. 7-8).

My liturgy moves on into an antiphonal rendition.
The congregation's hymn of praise is for a moment si-
lenced by the priests, who address a question to the worshipers:

> Why do you praise Yahweh? (1. 9a.)

In antiphonal response the worshipers answer. They
give, as a reason for their hymn of praise, the final and
irrevocable destruction of Nineveh, just accomplished
at Yahweh's hand. It is comparable to a fire that sweeps
everything before it:

> A complete destruction is it that he makes;
> The oppression will not arise a second time.
> For the adversaries, (like) thorns and briars,
> Have been consumed, like stubble in the fire (1. 9b-10).

At this point of the liturgy Yahweh's oracle, which he

had revealed unto me in a moment of deep receptivity,
is delivered unto the congregation by me, the prophet.
It pledges Yahweh's rescue of his people from the hand
of the once powerful Assyrian which now has lost its grip:

> Thus Yahweh says:
> Neither intact nor many are they;
> And so they shall vanish and disappear.
> And I will no more bow you down with affliction;
> I will break his rod from upon you;
> And I will snap your bonds (1. 12-13).

Such is Yahweh's oracle to Judah, a promise of blessing. But Yahweh had caused me to hear likewise his
oracle of judgment upon the king of Nineveh. So the
oracle of blessing for Judah is followed immediately by
this oracle of doom upon Nineveh's ruler. It is a doom
which has now been accomplished and thus it has immediate interest for my fellow worshipers. In Yahweh's
name I pronounced his judgment upon Assyria, the destruction and devastation of Nineveh by his hand. The
hour has struck![7] No longer will the name and repute
of Nineveh sow terror in Judaean hearts! Even the
brilliant idols adorning the great sanctuary of Nineveh
are destroyed. And Yahweh's curse will pursue the Assyrian monarch even to his grave:

> Yahweh has laid charge upon you;
> The fullness of your days has gone forth,
> O deviser of evil against Yahweh!
> Counselor of ruin!
> Of your repute no more shall be sown;
> From the house of your god I will cut off
> Graven and molten images;
> I will devastate your sepulcher;
> For you are accursed (1. 14a, 11, 14bc).

NAHUM OF ELKOSH

I then lift an exultant song of triumph. I picture a messenger, striding down the mountains, bringing to Judah the first glad tidings of the great deliverance which Yahweh has accomplished. I summon my fellow Judaeans to keep the feast, to perform their vows, to pour into the familiar rituals of the festival their gratitude and devotion. I summon Judah to new vigilance. Let the watchmen of Judah mount their battlements, for Yahweh, who has destroyed Nineveh, will now restore Israel's lost glory! The pillaging Chaldaeans and Medes have torn up Assyria's power by the roots. Thus with stirred spirit and thankful heart I sing triumphantly:

> Behold, upon the mountains, the feet of the bringer of
>   good tidings,
> Publishing deliverance!
> Keep, O Judah, your feasts!
> Pay your vows!
> For they shall not pass through any more.
> The Demon is entirely cut off!
> The watchman has gone up upon your battlements!
> Guard the rampart!
> Watch the way!
> Strengthen your loins!
> Make your power very strong!
> For Yahweh is in process of restoring
> The majesty of Jacob,
> Like the majesty of Israel.
> For pillagers have pillaged them;[8]
> And their roots they have destroyed[9] (2. 1-3).

My song of triumph ends. And at this precise moment there unfolds in the liturgy a dramatic actualization of the attack and collapse of Nineveh.[10] When the news of Nineveh's fall had reached Jerusalem, the account of the attack upon it by the Chaldaean and Median troops had been vividly told us.[11] So, imitating the mysterious, veiled style of speech which the prophets of my people were wont to use in their narrative of vision experiences,[12] and combining actual description of the event with its significance as Yahweh unfolded it to my inner vision, the attack upon Nineveh and its issue is actualized. Throwing a veil of mystery over the scene, yet with vivid glimpses of the actual conflict shimmering through, I first describe the assailants as they begin to concentrate their forces. I distinguish the infantry with its two divisions of warriors and men of valor. Then I picture the chariots of war driven by their charioteers, and finally the cavalry as the vanguard. As though in vision, I picture the nobles gathering around their standards, then advancing in assaulting columns against the walls, meting out destruction. I describe the moving up of the machines of war[13] against the walls. Thus in mysterious tones the dramatic re-enactment takes place:

> The shield of their warriors is reddened;
> The men of valor are clad in scarlet.
> The charioteers make ready (the chariots) with flaming steel;
> The horsemen form their squadrons.
> The chariots whirl like mad through the streets;
> They rush to and fro in the open places.
> Their appearance is like flaming torches,
> And they dart, swift as the lightning.
> Their nobles are summoned and join themselves round their banners.
> With columns of assault they precipitate themselves against her walls;
> And the machines of war are prepared (2. 4-6).

The dramatic re-enactment continues. I picture the breaking open of the gates of the canals of the Tigris, its waters tearing down two and one-half miles of the walls and coming up into a part of the city,[14] thus making Nineveh a pool of water, and hurling the palace and court into despair. And I describe the queen being brought forth in ignominy from the flooded palace to be carried into exile, followed by her wailing, lamenting maids-in-waiting:

> The gates of the canals are opened,
> And the palace melts away.
> Her queen is brought forth, she has gone into exile.
> And her maids are lamenting,
> Like the voice of doves,
> Beating upon their breasts.
> And Nineveh is like a pool of water,
> Its waters in tumult (2. 7-9b).

The scene changes. I portray the Assyrians in precipitate flight, leaving behind them the inexhaustible treasures of their capital city, taking no heed of the mocking cries which suggest that they stop and take their treasures with them. Their life is dearer to them than their property! The conquerors of Nineveh then leap upon the fabulous riches of the captured city and reduce it to a mere heap of ruins, carrying off great quantities of spoil beyond computing. I picture the once proud Ninevites, now wounded, defeated, and in abject humiliation.

> They flee and no one turns back.
> "Halt! Halt! there is no end to the treasure!
> Pillage silver! plunder gold!
> And the jewels, numberless"!
> Waste and void!
> And courage fails!
> The knees totter;
> Torture is in all loins;
> And the faces of all of them glow with shame (2. 9c-11).

The dramatic representation and realization of Nineveh's fall is ended. Then comes an ironic lament, sung by the festal congregation. Where now is Nineveh, they ask, which once was like a lion's den, to which nations were dragged as its prey?

> Where is the den of lions,
> And the cave of the young lions,
> Whither the lion went to enter,
> A lion's whelp with no one terrorizing him,
> A lion tearing in pieces for the need of his whelps,
> Strangling for his lioness?
> Yes, he filled with prey his dens,
> And his lair with torn flesh (2. 12-13).

I then answer with an oracle of Yahweh which pronounces his judgment upon Nineveh. I utter it in Yahweh's name and in the mood of passionate invective. It is the judgment that has just been accomplished. No longer will the barbarities of Nineveh terrify and shock the nations:

> Behold, Nineveh, I am against you;
> Oracle of Yahweh of hosts,
> And I will burn up in smoke your chariots,
> Your warriors the sword shall devour,
> And I will cut off your prey from the earth,
> And no more shall be heard the noise of your deeds
> (2. 14).

Immediately after Yahweh's oracle has thus been pronounced, the choir responds with a wild mock lament, describing vividly, as though in extension of my vision, the miserable fate of Nineveh. By her magic spells, for which Assyrian religion was famous, this harlot of the nations had laid many peoples prostrate, but now the Ninevites themselves are but a mass of dead bodies. Yahweh's judgment has thus brought back upon her her own evil deeds. In the style of lamentation, but with fierce joy of soul, the congregation cries out its wail:

> Woe to the bloody city, in its entirety;
> It is full of lying and robbery!
> Prey departs not from it.
> The crack of the whip, and the noise of the rattle of
> chariot wheels!
> And of dashing horses,
> And of jolting chariots!
> Charging horsemen,
> And the flash of the swords, and the glitter of the
> spears!
> And the multitude of slain, and a mass of corpses!
> Yes, no end is there to the dead bodies!
> They stumble over the corpses!
> Because of the many fornications of the harlot,
> Beautiful in form, the mistress of sorceries,
> Who lays nations prostrate by her harlotries,
> And clans by her magic spells (3. 1-4).

This lamentation thus uttered in irony, leads to my pronouncement of Yahweh's oracle upon Nineveh, now accomplished, the judgment and shameful humiliation of that harlot of the nations, who in her ignominy will have none to comfort her or lament her destruction. Again in Yahweh's name, I speak:

> Lo, I am against you; oracle of Yahweh,
> And I will uncover your skirts to your face,
> And I will let nations see your nakedness,
> And kingdoms your dishonor.
> And I will throw filth upon you,
> And I will treat you with disgrace, and make a spec-
> tacle of you;
> And it shall come to pass that every one who sees you,
> Shall flee from you and shall say:
> "Nineveh is ruined!
> Who will show grief for her?
> Whence shall I seek comforters for her?" (3. 5-7.)

199

At this point the congregation bursts forth with a
taunt song of satire upon Nineveh, comparing her fall
with the sack of No Amon, mighty Thebes, chief city of
Egypt and the world, which memorable catastrophe took
place a half century ago and was still fresh in Judah's
memory. At low water the Nile is divided into four
channels, the "arms of the Nile," by mud banks that are
opposite the city. During the Ethiopian domination
of Egypt the resources of Ethiopia and those of Egypt
proper—upper and lower Egypt—were joined together.
Moreover, the mercenaries of Put, a country situated on
the African coast of the Red Sea and extending from the
desert east of Upper Egypt to Somali,[15] and the mercenaries of the Libyans who were located in northern
Africa, west of the Nile Delta, were then allies of Thebes.
The fate which, within the memory of many of my fellow
countrymen had come to No Amon, Nineveh too, in spite
of her proud feeling of superiority, could not escape. So
the worshipers lift the taunt:

> Are you better than No Amon,
> Who dwelt in the arms of the Nile?
> Waters were round about her,
> Whose rampart was the sea;
> Waters were her wall.
> Ethiopia was her might,
> And Egypt, and no end!
> Put and Lybians were among her helpers.
> Yes, even *she* was for exile,
> *She* went into captivity.
> Her children also were dashed in pieces,
> In the chief of all the streets.
> And upon all her distinguished men they cast lots;
> And all her great ones were bound with fetters.
> You also shall be broken,
> You shall swoon away,

Even you shall seek
Refuge from the enemy (3. 8-11).

The taunt song continues. Nineveh's fortress has
fallen prey to the rapacious Chaldaeans and Medes, just
as first ripe figs are devoured by hungry men, for her pro-
tectors were effeminate and traitorous:

> All your fortifications shall be as fig trees,
> Your people like first ripe figs;
> If they be shaken, they shall fall
> Into the mouth of the eater.
> Behold, women are in your midst;
> Fire has devoured your bars;
> To your enemies they have surely opened
> The gates of your land (3. 12-13).

My liturgy then moves into a theme of prophetic irony.
As though speaking directly to Nineveh before her already accomplished fall, I summon her to preparedness
for the siege. I urge her to shape great numbers of bricks
by which to replace the walls, damaged by attack and by
flood-waters from the Tigris. For Nineveh's great walls,
one hundred feet high and fifty feet wide,[16] must be kept
intact. I cry in biting irony:

> Draw waters for the siege.
> Strengthen your fortifications.
> Tread down clay, and
> Trample it with mortar.
> Take hold of the brick mold (3. 14).

Yet toil as furiously and feverishly as she may, Nineveh's
strengthening of her defenses will be in vain. For the
king has already perished in the palace in the suicidal
fire he himself had kindled.[17] So I continued:

> There fire shall devour you;
> The sword shall cut you off;
> It shall devour you like the young locust (3. 15a).

Moreover, numbers of warriors will be of no avail for Nineveh, and increase in commerce and trade cannot halt her collapse. Though her military officers should become as numerous as the countless locusts in a swarm, Nineveh will look like a region that has been stripped and desolated by such destructive pests. So I taunted:

> Make yourself dense like the locusts!
> Multiply yourself like a locust swarm!
> Multiply your traffickers,
> More than the stars of the heavens!
> Locusts have stripped you and vanished! (3. 15b.-
>   16.)

> Your princes are like a locust swarm.
> Multiply your marshalls like a swarm of locusts!
> Those camping on the hedges,
> In a cold day,
> When the sun has risen,
> Flee away,
> And their place is not known (3. 17).

For the Ninevites, numerous as they were or might again become, will disappear as swiftly and as completely as locusts vanish after an invasion.

— My liturgy comes to its close with a final woe upon Nineveh which I put into the lips of the congregation—a death song of lamentation. Yet even while they are uttering this solemn dirge, my people will be glorying in Yahweh's triumph, for they well know Nineveh's destruction to be final and irrevocable. All the other nations felt as did we Judaeans, for they too had been ground under the harsh heel of this oppressor, and all alike

exulted in her fall. Thus the congregation will sing
their triumphant lament:

> Woe to you, your shepherds were drowsy!
> Your nobles, O king of Assyria, have been asleep!
> Your people are scattered upon the mountains,
> And no one gathers them together!
> There is no healing for your break-up;
> Severe is your blow.
> Everyone who hears tidings of you
> Claps his hands over you,
> For against whom has not your wickedness contin-
> ually gone forth? (3. 18-19.)

In the fall of Nineveh, Yahweh had led me to see con-
clusive evidence of his lordship in history. He had thus
shown me the sure working out of his moral judgment
in the life of our world. And in this liturgy, prepared
for the use of the congregation of my people, I have
sought to give imperishable expression to this faith.

CHAPTER VII

HABAKKUK OF JERUSALEM

I GREW to manhood during a time when my country enjoyed peace with other nations and had entered into commercial and cultural relations with them. Our great King Josiah had introduced an era of righteousness and justice in Judah. Under the impulses from the reform that he inaugurated, our Temple at Jerusalem was given an unprecedented dignity and strength. From my boyhood I have loved the Temple, and have always felt greatly attracted to the teachers of the law who taught in its courts, having enjoyed intimate converse with them.[1] Yet it was not the priests of the Temple and their functions to whom I felt most drawn, but, rather, to the prophets connected with the Temple, for early in my life I became aware that the spirit of prophecy was alive in me. I had vision experiences and became conscious that Yahweh's voice was sounding in my inner soul.[2] These ecstatic experiences often shook me to the depths of my being. It was my habit to prepare myself for such moments of revelation from Yahweh by climbing to my watchtower, where, removed from all the commotion of the world, I would set myself to search for Yahweh's will—to see with inner vision, and to listen for his voice. When his revelation came to me, I would declare to the congregation at worship what Yahweh had caused me to see and hear.[3] As one of the Temple prophets, I belonged to the Temple singers,[4] and, on occasion, stirred by a revelation from Yahweh, I would compose a psalm for public rendition in the Temple.

It was but a few years after our King Josiah had thrown off from the shoulders of Judah the yoke of the decaying Assyrian power that the rising Chaldaean Empire, founded by King Nabopolassar of Babylon, began to usurp the center of the stage in our section of the world. This new, vigorous, pagan people, with the help of the armies of Cyaxares, king of the Medes, dealt Nineveh its fatal blow in the twenty-third year of King Josiah's reign, and the proud Assyrian capital fell.

However, although the capital of the Assyrian Empire had thus succumbed to attack, the remnant of that once great empire itself manifested a stubborn and tenacious hold upon life. An Assyrian noble, Ashur-uballit by name, at once set up his throne at Harran, as king of Assyria. This famous city of Harran was situated on the main route from Nineveh to the Mediterranean Sea and was the residence of the commander in chief of the Assyrian army, an officer second only to the king. It was chosen as the capital of this remnant of the Assyrian nation so as to be near Egypt, which country was now Assyria's new ally. We Judaeans followed these events, as news of them reached Jerusalem, with the keenest interest, and we recalled to one another how a century before the prophet Isaiah had predicted Yahweh's destruction of Assyria (Isaiah 10. 5-34).

As master of Nineveh, Nabopolassar, the Chaldaean, now in his fifteenth year, went into action to destroy this torso of the Assyrian Empire and captured Rugguliti. Then the following year, supported by the Medes under Cyaxares, he marched against Harran. Ashur-uballit forsook his capital and fled. Harran was taken by the Chaldaeans and rich plunder beyond computation was carried away,[5] but even this victory did not spell the complete end of Assyria.

In the spring of the following year, Necho II, having just ascended the throne of Egypt, with a great army advanced to the help of his Assyrian ally. On his way to the Euphrates he met with opposition from our King Josiah, who, resisting the Egyptian Pharaoh's advance toward Carchemish, met him in battle at Megiddo, but was there mortally wounded and was brought back home to Jerusalem to die.[6] This tragic loss of our beloved monarch at the zenith of his power touched deeply the heart of my people.

Leaving matters in our stricken country for the time being without further interference, Pharaoh Necho crossed the Euphrates, marched against Harran, and strenuously assaulted it. He was unable, however, to wrest it from the hands of the Chaldaean garrison. Nabopolassar then marched to the aid of his army in vigorous military strength, and made himself master of the regions as far north as the province of Armenia.[7]

Pharaoh Necho returned from his unsuccessful attempt to aid his Assyrian ally, making his way through the territory of Judah. A popular uprising among my people following directly upon King Josiah's death, had placed upon the throne of Judah, Jehoahaz, our deceased king's younger son, who was preferred because of his strong and independent national policy. But Pharaoh Necho, upon reaching Judah, abruptly terminated King Jehoahaz's three months' rule. He banished him to Riblah, on the Orontes River, about fifty miles south of Hamath, and from there removed him to Egypt, where he was soon to end his days. Necho established in his place over my people, Eliakim, Jehoahaz's two-years-older brother, whose sympathies were with Egypt, and gave him the throne name of Jehoiakim (2 Kings 23. 31-34).

At once the fortunes of my nation began to fall. Our Egyptian overlord demanded from us a heavy tribute of one talent of gold and a hundred talents of silver, which was paid, but grudgingly (2 Kings 23. 35). We Judaeans, who for just a few years under King Josiah had tasted sweet freedom, were now again sadly conscious of being a subject people. Yet we knew that Necho, our overlord, had yet to face the greatest crisis of his reign, for soon, as we Judaeans knew to be inevitable, his army would have to meet that of Nabopolassar, the Chaldaean, in the contest for supremacy in the Westland. The news came to Jerusalem that Nabopolassar, upon hearing of the defection from him of the satrap he had put in charge of Egypt, Coele-Syria, and Phoenicia, had sent his eldest son, Nebuchadrezzar, with part of his army against Necho. The Egyptian monarch collected his forces and met the Chaldaeans at Carchemish, one of the old Hittite capitals, but now an Egyptian dependency, Necho's northern frontier, situated on the northern bank of the Euphrates. At the battle of Carchemish the Egyptians were decisively defeated, and Pharaoh Necho lost the territory extending from Wadi el-Arish, the extreme northeastern border of Egypt, to the Euphrates (2 Kings 24. 7). This decisive defeat of Egypt at Carchemish was a culminating stroke by the Chaldaeans, for it determined once for all which power, Egypt or Chaldaea, was to be dominant in Palestine. For that rebellious Hittite capital, ever since Egypt had regained her independence from Assyria, had turned eyes of hope to the Nile, trusting that with Egypt's help Carchemish could throw off, formerly the Assyrian, and now the Chaldaean yoke.[8]

Many of my countrymen exulted in the defeat of our Egyptian overlord at Carchemish, whose dominant hand we had felt in Judah since the battle of Megiddo, among them being our great poet-prophet Jeremiah. They gloated in the thought that Egypt's days were now numbered (Jeremiah 46. 10-12, 19). And Nebuchadrezzar probably would then have invaded Egypt had it not been for the sudden death of Nabopolassar, the Chaldaean. This led Nebuchadrezzar to force a swift understanding with Pharaoh Necho which involved the latter's relinquishment of any Egyptian designs upon Asia. Then as master of Syria and Palestine he returned to Babylon to secure the throne that had just been vacated by his father.[9]

Jehoiakim, our king, was left in a difficult position. He was pro-Egyptian in his sympathies, and, indeed, most of our people—the soldiers, the court, and the populace generally—believed that Pharaoh Necho, the implacable foe of the Chaldaeans, was now our only hope. So naturally, even though the Chaldaeans by their triumph at Carchemish had obtained mastery over Egypt, Coele-Syria, and Phoenicia, and had decisively defeated Necho, my people did not yet surrender their Egyptian loyalties and leanings. I myself had not been sympathetic with the prophet Jeremiah's outspoken convictions that we should reject help from Egypt and humbly submit to Chaldaean sovereignty.

Nebuchadrezzar's hasty return from the Westland to Babylon had given fresh opportunity for Egyptian intrigues against the Chaldaean to get under way. Necho's confidence was restored and he now built a new fleet to protect his coastal cities from falling prey to the Chaldaeans.[10] But Nebuchadrezzar in a two years' campaign, his first undertaking against Judah, was able to frustrate the plots of Egypt.[11] For three years our King Jehoiakim, while not surrendering his real Egyptian leanings, made formal submission to Nebuchadrezzar, but then rebelled. At first Nebuchadrezzar punished him merely by sending against our country raiding bands of Aramaeans, Moabites, and Ammonites, who, assured of Chaldaean protection, gladly marauded us (2 Kings 24. 2). But the opposition of our people generally to Chaldaean overlordship was too strong to be put down in that manner. The death of Jehoiakim set his eighteen-year-old son, Jehoiachin, upon the throne, and he had been king but three months when Nebuchadrezzar besieged and took Jerusalem. Our young king, accompanied by Nehushta, daughter of Elnathan, the queen mother, and our royal officials, went out to him, appealing for clemency. But Nebuchadrezzar carried our hapless monarch, the queen mother, the officials and courtiers, the army and the craftsmen, indeed, the very flower of our national leadership, to Babylon.[12] Jehoiachin's uncle, Mattaniah, was then placed on the throne by Nebuchadrezzar and given the throne name of Zedekiah. Nebuchadrezzar forced our new king to swear a solemn oath of allegiance to Babylon (Ezekiel 17. 13).

Such events naturally hurled our people once more into political and social chaos. Amid these momentous political changes the great truths of the religion of Yahweh seemed utterly impotent. National collapse stared us Judaeans in the face. I myself was deeply agitated for my intimate contact with the Temple had daily forced upon my view the disastrous consequences to the religion of Judah from these tragic events. I found relief for my own spirit by preparing a liturgy for a great service of national intercession in the Temple.[13] I hoped through its rendition to put heart and courage into my people in the face of the awful destruction and distress wrought by the Chaldaeans. I thus sought in those days of testing in the furnace of national suffering to lift the soul of my people from disillusionment, bitterness, and despair to faith in the presence and power of Yahweh.

My liturgy began with a lamentation of our nation over the situation that had been created in the whole world of nations by the violence and pagan ruthlessness of the Chaldaeans. The cries of Yahweh's faithful worshipers had apparently gone unheeded, and before the cold brutality of Chaldaean dealings, the forces of law and order had congealed and had impotently allowed the harsh hand of our overlord to prevail over Yahweh's righteous people. We could see no evidence that Yahweh's judgment was operative in the political events of the time. So I thus pronounced the lamentation of my people over the oppressive violence of this mighty empire:

> How long, Yahweh, have I cried for help?
> I keep crying to thee: "Violence!"
> But thou dost not save.
> Why dost thou let me see wickedness,
> And look upon oppression?
> Yes, havoc and violence are before me,

HABAKKUK OF JERUSALEM

Contention and strife I must bear.
Therefore law is frozen,
And justice never goes forth.
For the wicked ensnare the righteous;
Therefore justice goes forth warped (1. 2-4).

Then I gave Yahweh's first answer, and indeed a strange one it was, to this complaint. I already knew that the cause of the awful disturbance which had struck not only Judah but, indeed, all the nations was the Chaldaeans. I had seen, as had all who lived in Jerusalem, those brutal soldiers that day, never-to-be-erased from our memory, when they poured into our beloved capital in triumph. But Yahweh had now caused me to see that these same Chaldaeans, fierce, savage, and pagan as they were, and violaters of all international proprieties, were nonetheless being used by him as his instruments. Moreover, Yahweh had further revealed to me that the Chaldaeans were yet something more than this. For he had shown me that they were the embodiment of the age-old conviction, which we prophets had kept alive in our people, that there would take place an ultimate catastrophe when the forces of wickedness in a final challenge to the powers of right, would overwhelm the world.[14] We believed that whenever that final struggle should take place, Yahweh would victoriously lift himself against this climactic assault of evil as supreme Lord and Master. So partly in conceptions belonging to this long-cherished prophetic faith, and partly in terms descriptive of the Chaldaeans as my own eyes had seen them, I interpreted Yahweh's response to the lament voiced on behalf of my people. His answer was designed to lift the vision of my nation from immersion merely in its own bitter experience to embrace the suffering of the whole contemporary world. For all the nations had felt the pressure of those ruthless Chaldaean captors, who knew no source of national dignity other than human, and worshiped no god but might. Thus came his answer:

> See among the nations and look,
> And astonish yourselves, be astounded!
> For a deed am I about to do in your days,
> You would not have believed it had it been told.
> For I am raising up the Chaldaeans,
> The nation fierce and impetuous,
> Which strides through the length of the earth,
> To take possession of dwellings not his.
> Terrible and dreadful is he;
> His claims proceed from himself.
> And his horses are swifter than lions,
> Yes, keener than evening wolves.
> And his horsemen, his horsemen gallop;
> They come flying from afar;
> Like an eagle hastening to eat,
> Every one of them comes for violence;
> The terror of their countenance goes before them;
> And they gather captives like the sand.
> And he mocks at kings;
> And rulers are the butt of derision to him!
> He laughs at every fortification;
> He throws up a mound and captures it.
> Then he sweeps along like the wind,
> And makes his strength his god (1. 5-11).

But such insights, in spite of my conviction that they correctly revealed Yahweh's hand at work in our troubled world, were in themselves unsettling to me. This seemed a strange work if truly it were being done by Yahweh, astounding indeed to the nations as well as to my own people. How could the righteous and holy Yahweh thus use this treacherous and pagan power, even though it be to judge, rebuke, and discipline his own people? How could Yahweh allow this brutal world force—whose only god is its own craftiness and whose power expands solely through the forced subjection of smaller nations—to catch these peoples in his dragnet, Yahweh's own nation among them? So in the name of the congregation of Judah I voiced, in a second prayer of lamentation, my challenging complaint unto Yahweh:

> Art thou not of old, Yahweh?
> My holy God, thou diest not.
> O Yahweh, thou hast ordained him for judgment!
> Yes, O Rock, thou hast established him for rebuke!
> Too pure of eyes art thou to see evil,
> And thou canst not look upon mischief.
> Why dost thou look upon the treacherous,
> Why dost thou keep silent when the wicked swallow up
>   the righteous?
> Yes, thou hast made men like fish of the sea,
> Like gliding things, having over it no dominion.
> All of them he has drawn up with hooks,
> And drags them off in his casting net,
> And collects them in his dragnet.
> Because of this he rejoices and exults;
> Because of this he sacrifices to his casting net,
> And burns incense to his dragnet.
> For with them his share has become rich,
> And fat has come to be his food.
> Shall he then continue to cast his net,
> To ruin nations without sparing?   (1. 12-17.)

Long and earnestly did I brood over this problem that so concerned my people. It was to me the cause of great mental and spiritual anguish. At times I felt as though my faith in Yahweh were uncertain and insecure. One day in profound inner distress of spirit I climbed to my high retreat, where, removed from all the activities of the world, I waited in eager receptivity before Yahweh.[15]

And as I waited he revealed to me in a vision the message I knew I must deliver to my people. So in my liturgy I uttered to Yahweh's congregation his second oracle. Yahweh had shown me that I must engrave the teaching content of the vision upon stone tablets in letters so large and plain that a runner would not need to slacken his pace to read the words. He had made it clear to me that I must not expect the content of the vision to be realized immediately but must wait in certain confidence that in time it would become a reality. So I uttered Yahweh's answer to the complaint of my people but first described how the vision and its meaning had been revealed to me:

> Let me take my stand upon my watch,
> And let me station myself on the lookout;
> And I shall look forth to see what he will say to me,
> And what he will answer to my complaint.
> So Yahweh answered and said:
> "Write the vision
> And engrave it upon the tablets,
> So that one may read it as he runs.
> For the vision awaits its appointed time,
> And it will open in the end and not fail.
> If it should tarry, wait for it;
> For come, it surely will, and delay not!" (2. 1-3.)

Then I gave the oracle itself. It had truly come to me as a revelation from Yahweh. It was at once a comfort and a warning. It brought comfort and hope, for it taught that the domineering ruthlessness of the Chaldaean Empire, which we Judaeans now knew from tragic experience, was but a temporary thing, for that empire had no hold upon permanence. Even now the fever of decay was at work in it. But the oracle also brought warning and challenge to my people. For it revealed at the same time that Judah could endure as a nation only if it were righteous. Through faithfulness to Yahweh, and loyal dependence upon him—in that direction lay the sole way to hope for the future of Judah. With a clearness such as I had never before attained, I now saw that the basis of all security, national or personal, was confidence in Yahweh and faithfulness in the performance of his holy will. The seeming strength of the proud, oppressing Chaldaean had in it nothing that could last, even though to all appearances his power was limited only by his insatiable desire for conquest. So thus reporting Yahweh's oracle in my liturgy, I strove to make its teaching my people's faith:

> Behold, as for him who is not upright,
> His life in him will swoon away:
> But the righteous shall live by his faithfulness.
> Though indeed the oppressor deal treacherously,
> A man who is proud cannot be established,
> Who increases his appetite like Sheol,
> And like death cannot be sated;
> Yes, he gathers all the nations to himself,
> And collects to himself all the peoples (2. 4-5).

Yet in spite of the calm assurance which this revelation from Yahweh gave me, I could not keep my soul from crying out in burning indignation at the ruthless acts of the Chaldaean. I could not at all share our prophet Jeremiah's wholehearted acceptance of his domination of Judah and his counsel of friendly submission to the harsh mastery of Nebuchadrezzar. For in spite of its brief history, without question the Chaldaean Empire had already revealed that, just as had been the case with Assyria, it too was built upon bloodshed, plunder, and the enslavement of whole nations. And even though Yahweh had revealed to me that this Chaldaean policy was hastening that ungodly nation to its doom, I still felt moved to pronounce Yahweh's sharp rebuke upon the Chaldaean king, as the representative and incarnation of the spirit of his nation. His recent outrage, which had so decimated my people, his inhuman uprooting from Judah of the leaders of Yahweh's stricken nation, made my words all the more poignant. So in the next movement of the liturgy I pronounced Yahweh's five-fold woe.

I likened this series of woes to a mocking parable on the lips of the nations, taken up by them against the Chaldaean king. Yet the nervousness and delicacy of the times demanded that my references to the Chaldaean be veiled, for already his harsh hand had come down heavily upon my people. But no Judaean could possibly have doubted my meaning. I began:

> Do not all of them (the nations) lift up a proverb,
> And an enigmatic satire against him? (2. 6a.)

In my first woe I dealt with Nebuchadrezzar's ambitious lust for conquest, emphasizing the severe tolls demanded by him as tribute from the nations. I compared these severe exactions to heavy pledges of payment demanded by a merciless creditor:

> Woe to him who keeps increasing what is not his,
> And weights himself down with pledges!
> Will not your debtors suddenly arise
> And cut you off, violently shaking you?
> And you will become booty for them.
> All the rest of the peoples will plunder you,
> For you have plundered many nations;
> Because of human bloodshed and violence done to the
>   land,
> To a city and all who dwell in it (2. 6b-8).

I was convinced that what the Chaldaean had done to others would be done to him, when the peoples whom he is now dominating shall have become strong enough to lead an insurrection against him.

In my second woe I dealt with the object which the Chaldaean had in view in all his pillaging and plundering. It was to erect a Chaldaean dynasty so strong that no other national power could challenge it. So I cried:

Woe to him who by violence gets evil gain for his dynasty,
To place his nest in the height,
To deliver himself from the grip of calamity (2. 9).

I was convinced that all the schemes of this ruthless plunderer would come back like a destructive boomerang upon the Chaldaean. Nebuchadrezzar was a mighty builder. Already he had begun to dazzle the world with the riches and treasures of Babylon.[16] His first building enterprises were directed toward the strengthening of the defenses of Babylon. He finished the great wall, then he built the eastern wall some distance from the city, a huge wall like a mountain made of brick and mortar. He laid this great upper wall upon the moat wall which had been built by his father, Nabopolassar. Nebuchadrezzar now fitted strong city gates into it which were made of great cedar beams covered with copper. He restored the Temple of Shamash, the sun god, at Sippar. And from tribute money assessed upon all the lands he had mastered, he built the zikkurat of Babylon. All these magnificent structures built by Nebuchadrezzar had been made possible solely by the blood money of the peoples he had conquered. It seemed to me that my ears, made sensitive by Yahweh to human wrong, could hear the very stones of the walls crying out against him, the great cedar beams of the gates joining them in bitter indictment. So Yahweh's rebuke continued:

> You have advised what is shameful for your dynasty,
> You have crushed many peoples,
> And your soul has sinned.
> For a stone cries out from the wall,
> And a rafter from the timber-work answers it (2. 10-11).

My third woe concerned itself with the cruel oppression that had made possible the magnificence of these architectural structures of the Chaldaeans. For by using his captives Nebuchadrezzar had unbounded command of naked human strength, and the cities which he built or rebuilt, those of upper Babylonia, Babylon itself, Sippara, Borsippa, Cuth, and others, thus had arisen on the foundations of human blood. So in my third woe I cried:

> Woe to him who builds a town with blood,
> And founds a city upon injustice,
> So that nations have toiled but for fire,
> And peoples weary themselves for nothing (2. 12-13).

I was convinced that all the wealth which had been slowly built up by the weary toil of nations, then ruthlessly wrung from them by the rapacious Chaldaean, would at length come to nought. For such wealth wrested by his greedy hands from the nations has no permanence. It is Yahweh's judgment upon the Chaldaean that property thus acquired will go up in smoke.

Our neighbor kingdoms had all shared a like fate with Judah. This pagan power had made their national experience bitter like ours. With my heart sore because of the cup of wrath which my people had been forced to drink from Chaldaean hands, I composed the fourth woe. I could not but see in the unprecedented stupor of my shocked and diminished countrymen the effect upon them of the fury of Yahweh, for I well knew that my nation was not innocent. But Yahweh caused me to realize that from the same cup of his wrath which Judah had been forced to drink, the Chaldaean would himself eventually have to drink. The Chaldaean nation, now in the heyday of its glory, I was convinced would itself someday experience our bitterness of being shamed and disgraced in the eyes of the nations. So in my fourth woe I taught that the ruthless dealings of the Chaldaeans would rebound upon their own heads. And I cried:

Woe to him who makes his neighbor drink his wrath,
And from the goblet of his fury makes him drunk,
In order to look upon their shame!
You are sated with ignominy rather than glory.
Drink, even *you,* and reel!
The cup of the right hand of Yahweh shall come round
  to *you!* (2. 15-16c.)

In imagination I saw the primeval dragons of chaos and disorder, Leviathan and Behemoth,[17] when the hour of judgment had struck, covering the proud Chaldaeans with confusion, and dealing out shattering destruction. And repeating as a refrain the closing lines of the first woe, I ended my fourth woe as follows:

And disgrace will come upon your glory.
For the wrath of Leviathan shall cover you,
And the havoc of Behemoth shall shatter you,
Because of human blood and the violence done the land,
The city and all who dwell in it (2. 16d-17).

In my own youth I had witnessed the great reform which King Josiah had set going in Judah, in which every

graven image and every molten image among my people
had been destroyed. Young as I was when this reform
got under way, I recalled how my heart rejoiced to see
these lifeless idols destroyed and banished from Yahweh's
people. Even then I realized to some extent the havoc
they had made in Judaean religion. And now the dominant overlord of Judah, Yahweh's people, was an idolater,
and at many a brilliant temple built by his zeal for his
Babylonian deities, he had installed his idols. Especially
loved by the Chaldaeans were the images to the gods Bel,
Shamash, and Marduk.[18] The oracles of the Chaldaean
priests, their incantations, and magical formulas, I
viewed as a gross hoax by which they had ignobly deceived the people. All this was of more concern to us
now because all this empty elegance of the Babylonian
worship, performed with pomp and brilliancy at Chaldaean temples, would be the daily environment of the
thousands of my fellow countrymen now exiled in Babylon. So my final woe was hurled against the Chaldaean
as a worshiper of idols. Thus I proclaimed:

> Woe to him who says to the wood "Awake!"
> "Rouse thyself!" to a dumb stone.
> Behold, it is sheathed with gold;
> But no breath whatever is in it (2. 19).

In vivid contrast to these lifeless, material nonentities,
my mind was sharply aware of the towering, unseen,
spiritual presence of Yahweh, enthroned in the Temple
that I loved. And I ended this part of my liturgy with an
awe-struck summons to all the earth:

> But Yahweh is in his holy temple;
> Be silent before him, all the earth! (2. 20.)

When, on that strategic day of which I have spoken, in deep distress of spirit, I had climbed to my watchtower in order to discern Yahweh's will, he had caused me to hear his word which I have enshrined in my liturgy. And in that same creative hour, when I looked forth to see what Yahweh would say to me, he had also illumined the eyes of my soul by a deeply moving vision experience, which I now strove to communicate to my people through my liturgy. Yahweh had profoundly aroused my soul by this vision and through it had awakened me to renewed faith and confidence in him. It was a vision of the climactic struggle of Yahweh with his enemies, and their ultimate and final defeat at his hand.[19]

I introduced the content of this vision, which made up the next part of the liturgy, by reporting the experience itself and uttering unto Yahweh a prayer for the *speedy* realization of that which the vision assured;

> O Yahweh, I have heard tidings from thee;
> I have seen thy work, O Yahweh.
> In the near at hand years, realize it!
> In the next years make thyself known!
> In wrath remember mercy! (3. 2.)

Then I described the awesome vision I had experienced. I had always been fascinated by the descriptions of Yahweh's manifestation of himself to his people both in the strategic moments of their history and at the creation of the world. As our ancient poets had described these self-disclosures of Yahweh, he had come from his ancient home on Mount Sinai, beaming upon his people from Mount Seir, shining forth from Paran, and drawing near from the steppes of Kadesh (Deuteronomy 33. 2). Often had I brooded upon them and now I reported what I had seen in my vision. I saw the holy God coming from his mountain home in Sinai to Teman in Edom. I saw him march across Paran, the elevated region that lies between Sinai and Kadesh-barnea. His splendor flooded heaven and earth with light. He strode along in majesty, coming to the help of his people:

> God came from Teman,
> Yes, the Holy One from Mount Paran.
> His splendor covered the heavens,
> His radiance filled the earth.
> Brightness like light was under him;
> Rays he had at his side;
> Smoke was the veil of his might (3. 3-4).

In my vision I had seen his destructive power. The pestilence-bringing demon preceded him and the plague-dealing demon followed him. Where he stood the earth under him quaked. Great clefts broke up the mountain mass, and the age-old hills changed their shape. His glance fell upon the nations and they were startled into movement. The Midianite nomads in the neighborhood of Sinai, and their neighbors, the Cushites, were thrown into excited amazement.

> Before him went the Pestilence,
> And the Plague followed his steps.
> He stood and made the earth shake;
> He looked and made nations start up:
> The everlasting mountains split themselves asunder,
> The eternal hills bowed low.
> The tents of the Cushites were afraid;
> The tent-curtains of the Midianites were excited
>   (3. 5-7).

I was familiar with another manifestation of Yahweh, the description of which was likewise classic in the ancient traditions of my people. It told how Yahweh had appeared in majesty to battle against the primeval chaotic force of the raging, destructive flood, so that when he had mastered it, he might create his orderly world. Yahweh had then conquered the dragon of the deep.[20] So now as I saw Yahweh hurtling through the heavens, I asked him if this manifestation of himself were such a one as occurred when he created the world.

> Art thou angry with the floods,
> Or is thy wrath directed against the sea,
> That thou mountest upon thy horses,
> Thy chariot of victory?
> Thou barest completely thy bow;
> Thou fillest thy quiver with arrows.
> The earth bursts open into streams;
> The mountains saw thee and writhed;
> The cloud masses poured forth water.
> The deep gave forth its voice.
> The light forgot its appointed season,
> The moon stood still in its abode.
> For light thy arrows go forth,
> For brightness the flash of thy spear
>   (3. 8-11).

The answer to my question was clear. What I had beheld in vision was not such a manifestation of Yahweh as had occurred at creation, but such a one as took place at the exodus, when Yahweh discomfited the Egyptians and saved his people. It is not with the chaotic floods that he is now angry but with the destructive Chaldaeans. And as the Egyptians met their doom when their horses and chariots were overwhelmed in the Red Sea, so will the arch demon, the Chaldaean, be shattered when Yahweh goes forth to save his people and their king. So I continued:

In wrath thou dost tread the earth;
In anger thou tramplest down the nations.
Thou goest forth for the salvation of thy people,
For the salvation of thine anointed one.
Thou hast crushed the head of the house of wickedness,
Thou hast laid bare the foundation to the rock.
Thou hast pierced his head with thine arrow;
His riders are stormdriven like chaff.
It is their exultation to scatter the poor,
To devour the poor in their hiding place.
Thou treadest his horses into the sea,
Into the mire of great waters (3. 12-15).

So ended my liturgical description of Yahweh, victorious in his mighty duel with the Chaldaean world ruler. The vision shook me to the depths of my spirit by its emotional power and left its permanent deposit in my soul. It taught me to trust in the invisible might of Yahweh, and to rest in the secure confidence that in his own time he would intervene on behalf of his people. In the mood of awe which the vision had aroused in my soul, I composed as a climactic act of the liturgy a prayer for utterance by the congregation. It was the "Amen" of the nation to the vision of Yahweh's final triumph over the Chaldaean. It was a prayer of Yahweh's congregation which, in spite of the distress it had already suffered and was yet to suffer, had begun again to have hope. It expresses the certainty of Yahweh's day of calamity which at length would surely come upon the oppressor of Judah, bringing about his final and ultimate overthrow. But yet more notably than this, the prayer gave expression, on behalf of Judah, to a mighty confession of faith. With a soaring spiritual confidence which, from the depths of despair, had burst into a song, it voiced Judah's triumphant faith. The Chaldaeans had harassed and decimated our land and had made awful inroads upon it. Their overrunning of Judah and their siege had cruelly interrupted the normal processes of agriculture, the cultivation of the olive and the grape, the raising of cattle and sheep. Times were hard and material calamity stared us in the face. Yet my people would trust in Yahweh, who, as my vision had assured me, would eventually bring them to triumph. And even as the swiftness and sure footedness of the hind illustrates, so Yahweh will give his people freshness of life and power and confidence in action.[21] Psalms of praise will be uttered to Yahweh by my people, even though through starving lips.

This closing section of my liturgy began in the mood of trembling awe which the majestic vision had aroused in my spirit, and which I was confident its report would evoke in the congregation of Judah, for it had shaken me to the depths and had left me trembling, almost consumed with emotion:

> I have heard and my inmost soul is perturbed;
> At the sound my lips quiver!
> Decay comes in my bones;
> And my steps are atremble under me!   (3. 16ab.)

Through awe the prayer moved to confidence in Yahweh's ultimate intervention when his day of judgment upon the Chaldaean would come. My liturgy summoned my countrymen to patience as we wait expectantly for that day:

> I will wait for the day of trouble
> To go up upon the people that attacks us   (3. 16c).

Then came the closing words—a heart-cry of trust which

the congregation is to utter in words taught me only of
Yahweh, expressing the victory of faith over all material
misfortune or loss:

> For though the fig tree should not bear fruit,
> And there be no yield on the vines;
> Though the olive should disappoint in its product,
> And the field should not grow food;
> Though the flock should be cut off from the fold,
> And there should be no herd in the stalls—
> Yet, as for me, I will exult in Yahweh!
> I will rejoice in the God of my salvation!
> Yahweh, the Lord, is my strength;
> And he has made my feet like the hind's feet,
> And he makes me tread on my high places (3. 17-19).

In this liturgy I have set my soul Godward on behalf
of Judah. I feel impelled to share with my countrymen
what Yahweh has caused me to see and hear.

CHAPTER VIII

JEREMIAH OF ANATHOTH

I WAS born at Anathoth, one of the thirteen Levitical cities (1 Chronicles 6. 60), in the fifty-first year of the reign of King Manasseh.[1] This region where my boyhood and young manhood was spent has had a peculiar fascination for me. Anathoth lay at the very edge of the wilderness of Judah, about four miles northeast of Jerusalem, across Mount Scopus, and over a deep valley. It was the last Judaean village toward the east. Between it and the northern end of the Dead Sea lay nothing but broken, barren hills. That desert maze is indelibly imprinted in my memory. The wild outlook and the scorching desert air which sweeps across this barren waste to Anathoth, as I now realize, have left an abiding deposit in my soul.

My father, Hilkiah, was a priest whose line of spiritual descent reached back through Abiathar of King Solomon's time, lone survivor of Eli's line, to Shiloh, where my forebears had once guarded the most sacred symbol of our ancestral religion (1. 1). From his lips and under his instruction I imbibed the history and the ideals of my people. I cannot remember a time when religion was not a reality in my experience. Especially did I feed upon the thoughts of Hosea, the deepest prophetic soul my people Israel had given to our nation.[2]

Not until I was a young man did I discover that even before I had seen the light of day—while my mother was carrying me close to her heart—she had dedicated me to be a prophet of Yahweh. I was yet under twenty when I began to be conscious of inner leadings toward this holy calling, but it frightened me to think of it. Finally one day it seemed to me that I was in the very presence of Yahweh, and he was saying to me:

Before I formed you in the womb I knew you,
And before you came forth out of the womb I set you apart;
I have appointed you a prophet unto the nations (1. 5).

But I shrank from Yahweh's summons, pleading my youth and inexperience:

Alas! Lord Yahweh!
Behold, I know not how to speak,
For I am but a boy! (1. 6.)

With Yahweh's answer to me which sounded in the deep recesses of my being, there came strange assurance:

Do not say, "I am but a boy;"
For to whomsoever I shall send you, you must go,
And whatsoever I command you, you must speak.
Be not afraid in their presence;
For I will be with you to rescue you (1. 7-8).

I had never before been so conscious of a Presence as I was at that hour. It was so intimate and awesome that I can scarcely describe my sensations except by saying that I seemed to feel upon my lips the touch of the divine finger, as though Yahweh would so thrill with his own inspiring power my faulty human speech. That hour my task lay clearly before me. It concerned my people, but other nations and kingdoms too. I must announce sharp condemnation and destructive judgment. Yet the positive, constructive note was not to be lacking in my preaching. Thus Yahweh revealed more fully his will for me:

> Lo, I have put my words in your mouth;
> See, I have appointed you today
> Over nations and over kingdoms,
> To uproot and to pull down,
> To destroy and to tear down,
> To build and to plant (1. 9c-10).

During those days while I was accustoming my timid spirit to this high summons, I had two experiences that I have always counted part of my prophetic call. Just outside the door[3] of my home was my favorite tree, the almond tree. It was already bursting into blossoms, beautiful, delicate, and fragrant. My people call it the "wakeful tree," because it is the first Palestinian tree to flower in the spring. Whenever its blossoms appear we know that the spring has really come. But that day, as I drank in the vivid beauty of a twig of our wakeful tree, gloriously alive in its first spring radiancy, I became uniquely aware of the power of Yahweh alert in his world, his purposes flowering and issuing in fruitage, and I seemed to hear him say:

> I am awake[4] over my word to accomplish it (1. 12).

As a boy I was always interested in watching my mother hang the large pot over the fire. Soon it would begin to boil and overflow. Now as I saw this familiar sight it had peculiar meaning. For the mouth of the seething pot was turned away from the north. It appeared to be blown upon, fiercely heated by a blast of wind which swept in upon it from that direction. And I realized that through this sight Yahweh was speaking to me of a fierce and deadly evil which he was about to send down from the north upon Judah and the civilized world. And Yahweh's voice explained to me:

> From the north the evil shall be blown
> Upon all the inhabitants of the earth.
> For lo, I am summoning
> All the kingdoms of the north;
> And they shall come and set up, every one, his throne
> At the entrances of the gates of Jerusalem,
> And against all its surrounding walls,
> And against all the fortified cities of Judah (1. 14b-15).

Then I knew what the vision meant. The Scythians were coming! Already I had been aware of the threatening movements of these hordes of barbarous nomads from the north, but now for the first time I realized they were being stirred up against my people by Yahweh.

These deeply moving experiences soon took me to Jerusalem, where I might better begin my prophetic ministry. My first words to my countrymen in the capital were designed to interpret to them what Yahweh had revealed to me concerning the Scythians. I strove to awaken them to the dire disaster that threatened them:

> Blow the trumpet in the land:
> Call with a full blast.
> Hasten! Gather yourselves and go in
> To the fortified cities.
> Lift the banner Zionward;
> Take yourself to safety, don't stand still!
> For I am about to bring trouble from the north,
> And a great shattering.
> A lion has gone up from his thicket,
> And a destroyer of nations has set out;
> He has gone forth from his haunt,
> To make your land a desolation.
> Your cities shall be felled into ruin heaps
> With no inhabitant.

Because of this gird on sackcloth;
Lament and wail;
For the heat of Yahweh's anger
Has not turned away from us (4. 5b-8).

I appealed to the people of Jerusalem to save themselves from the stormlike menace of the Scythian by sincere repentance:

Lo, like storm clouds he comes up,
Yes, like the storm wind are his chariots;
His horses are swifter than vultures.
Woe to us for we are made havoc!
O Jerusalem, wash the evil out of your heart,
In order that you may be saved.
How long shall your iniquitous thoughts
Find lodgment in your heart? (4. 13-14.)

As I contemplated the awful destruction they would mete out to my people, I suffered mental anguish. In my mind's eye I kept seeing the signal that would indicate that they were upon us! My vivid imagination kept me hearing with the ear of my soul the trumpet-blast of alarm.

In anguish over the imminent suffering of my people I cried out:

My anguish, my anguish! let me writhe,
O walls of my heart!
My soul is in commotion within me;
I cannot keep silent;
For I hear the blast of the trumpet,
The alarm of war.
Crash upon crash is reported;
For all the land is devastated (4. 19-20a).

I pictured the chaos that would result, as the eyes of my soul saw it—a sunless sky, the solid mountains and everlasting hills all aquiver, a land without an inhabitant, a birdless heaven, productive fields reduced to desert:

> I looked upon the earth,
> And lo, chaos;
> And to the heavens, and their light was gone.
> I looked toward the mountains, and they were aquiver,
> And all the hills were atremble.
> I looked, and lo, there was no man,
> And all the birds of the heaven had fluttered away.
> I looked at the fertile land, and lo, it was wilderness,
> And all its fortified cities were torn down,
> At the presence of Yahweh,
> Because of the heat of his wrath (4. 23-26).

Then I pictured Jerusalem as in the pangs of death at the hands of her destroyers:

> For I hear a cry as of a woman in travail,
> An outcry like one bearing her first child,
> The cry of the daughter of Zion, she gasps for breath,
> And she spreads out her hands.
> "Alas for me,
> My soul faints away
> Before the killers!" (4. 31.)

It was our prophet Hosea, the Ephraimite hero of my boyhood, who had shown me most clearly what was wrong with my people that Yahweh must punish them so severely. My father had often told me the story of this greatest soul of Ephraim. I knew the solemn tragedy of his home which had unlocked for him the mystery of the deep ties that bound Israel to Yahweh. My father, because he had shared Hosea's intense passion for a pure and noble priesthood, had treasured his words and I had often read them. Now I felt the clear guidance of his spirit as in similar vein I strove to teach Judah my conception of religion as exclusive, passionate loyalty

to Yahweh. So in the name of the God to whom the
Judaeans were so faithless, I cried:

> I remember the loyalty of your youth,
> The love at the time of your betrothal;
> How you went after me in the desert,
> In a land unsown.
> Israel was holy to Yahweh,
> The first fruits of his product.
> Do nations exchange their gods?
> Though they are no gods!
> Yet my people have changed their glory
> For what is of no benefit.
> For two evils my people have done:
> They have forsaken me, the spring of living water,
> To dig for themselves cisterns,
> Cracked cisterns, which cannot hold water.
> How can you say, "I have not defiled myself,
> Nor have I gone after the Baals"?
> Although you wash with natron,
> And use much lye,
> Your iniquity stands blood-stained before me (2.
> 2-3a, 11, 13, 23a, 22).

I had been preaching but five years when my nation
was swept by a mighty tide of patriotic and religious
awakening that seemed to promise much for the future.
Our noble and righteous king, Josiah, had inaugurated
the repairing of the Temple. In the process of it Hilkiah, our high priest, came upon a book of the law, a
statute book hitherto unknown to my countrymen, which
stated in solemn words, as if from Moses himself, Yahweh's requirements of his people, and uttered terrible
curses upon all who refused to obey them. For centuries no such laws had been heeded. Hilkiah counseled
with Shaphan, the scribe, and they immediately brought
the newly found code to the king's attention. A dele-

gation appointed by the king, consisting of Hilkiah, Ahikam, son of Shaphan, Achbor, son of Micaiah, Shaphan, the scribe, and Asaiah, the king's servant, consulted Huldah, the prophetess, who lived in the second quarter of Jerusalem, and she counseled action. With such dispatch as stirred the admiration and loyalty of all Jerusalem, the king summoned a great assembly at our capital, composed of representative Judaeans from the entire country, and there the king, the priests, the prophets, and the rank and file of our nation, made a solemn compact to heed the requirements of the newly found law (2 Kings 22-23).

That meant putting into force the radical demands of Deuteronomy, for the new law code was none other than the kernel[5] of that great book. It represented a fresh codification of our ancient laws, but—and this was what made it grip my soul—in the spirit of my great Judaean prophetic heroes, Amos, Isaiah, and Micah and especially of our own Ephraimite prophet Hosea. It was aimed against the Canaanized worship, which, in spite of the antagonism to it of my prophetic predecessors, was still being carried on at Judaean High Places. The new law demanded the utter destruction of these High Places along with all their utensils and symbols of worship. And it likewise demanded the centering of all national worship at Jerusalem in King Solomon's Temple.

With all my heart I was for it. I felt commissioned of Yahweh to make an itinerary on behalf of it, preaching and expounding the meaning of the new law, and interpreting to the perplexed and suspicious people of the various Judaean towns the deeper bearings of the reform.

To me it sounded a call back to the fountains of our faith, back to that classic and normative epoch when, as noble Hosea had said,

> Yahweh found Israel like grapes in the wilderness
>   (Hosea 9. 10),

and she was betrothed unto him. I was convinced that, thus refreshed at the fountains of our national life, we could face with confident, poised, and pioneering minds and hearts the difficult problems of our own transition era. So I called unto my people:

> Stand by the ways and look,
> And ask for the ancient paths,
> Where the good way is; and walk in it,
> And find repose for your soul (6. 16).

Ah, with what enthusiasm I preached and interpreted these great ideals which lay at the heart of Yahweh's covenant bond with Israel! How eagerly I advocated obedience to the new law!

My itinerary brought me to my home town of Anathoth. But in his own town a prophet is without honor, and men whom I had known as a lad now refused to hear me, saying:

> You shall not prophesy in the name of Yahweh,
> Lest you die at our hands (11. 21).

They counted me their enemy, for was I not advocating and backing the reform which would result in the destruction of their local shrine? They even secretly plotted to kill me, a plot of which I at first had no inkling until Yahweh revealed to me the grave peril in which I stood.

> Yahweh made known to me, and I perceived it:
> Then Yahweh let me see their evil deeds.
> While I was like a docile lamb,
> Led to slaughter;
> Nor did I know that
> They had hatched up schemes against me, saying,
> "Let us fell the tree in its young vigor,
> And let us cut him off from the land of the living,
> So his name will no longer be remembered" (11. 18-19).

I escaped from their treacherous schemes, but the hard, bitter antagonism of these men whom I had known from my boyhood gave me a vivid realization of the difficulties with which such a law would have to grapple.

Gradually disillusionment came.[6] I began to see how utterly incapable a law was, even a great one, nobly conceived and effectively enforced, of reaching the heart of our nation. The Deuteronomic reformers were at best superficial healers. They did not penetrate to the depths of the sore. They were shallow optimists, content with surface work. Of them I said:

> They heal superficially
> The wound of the daughter of my people,
> Saying, "It is sound, it is sound,"
> When there is no soundness (8. 11).

Even in those communities where the reform was most effective, it did not reach the heart of our nation to lead our people to repentance and righteous living. It did not make them realize they were Yahweh's people, with his pattern of life written deep in the constitution of their lives. It merely increased the superficial prestige of Jerusalem's Temple. So I began to give utterance to my disappointment and disillusionment:

I have given attention and listened.
They speak not what is right:
No one is repentant about his evil,
Saying, "What have I done?"
Everyone turns to his own course,
Like a horse rushing along in the battle (8. 6).

This new law should have touched into new sensitive-
ness and response the Godward instinct of Judah, im-
planted by Yahweh in the innermost nature of his people,
just as birds of passage respond to the migratory urge of
their being. But this it had not done, for

Even the stork in the heavens
Knows her appointed seasons;
Yes, the turtle dove, and the swift, and swallow
Keep the time of their coming;
But my people do not know Yahweh's way of life.[7]

I saw how even the priesthood misused the law and
manipulated it to their own advantage. It was externally
imposed. And even when the letter of the law was
obeyed, the spirit was not there. Thus a noble document had fallen painfully short of its aim and was fast
becoming impotent. To those quite content with the
superficial prestige the reform had brought to the
Temple, I cried:

How can you say
"We are wise,
And the law of Yahweh is with us"?
But lo, the fact is,
The lying pen of the scribes
Has made it into a lie[8] (8. 8).

From that hour, while not opposing it, I ceased to be
an advocate of the new law. I did not regret my earlier
idealistic allegiance to it, for it had taught me one of the
deepest lessons of my life, which henceforward became

a central tenet in my teaching. You cannot reach men's hearts by law. You cannot compel loyalty to Yahweh by statute. I began now to sense in germ a truth which but gradually grew to clearness—only in recent days have I fully grasped it—that the only law which can transform is the law written deep in the tablets of the human heart.

From this time on the delicacies and difficulties of my being a sincere and fearless spokesman for Yahweh increased apace. The conceptions which I now held ran directly counter to the views popularly cherished by my people, and I keenly felt their cold enmity, even treachery. I knew that I was utterly loyal to Yahweh, yet my lot, compared with that of the superficial, careless ungodly within the nation, was so unfair. It raised for me the whole question of the rectitude of Yahweh's dealings with men. One day I entered into a veritable grapple with Yahweh over it in prayer. I poured out my questioning soul:

> Righteous art thou, O Yahweh,
> When I make complaint against thee;
> None the less I would litigate with thee;
> Why does the course of action of the wicked prosper?
> Why are all who deal very treacherously free from care?
> Thou dost plant them, yes, they take root;
> They reproduce, yes, they bear fruit:
> Intimate art thou in their mouth,
> But far from their dominant affections (12. 1-2).

Yahweh answered me with a challenge. It taught me that he was testing me by these difficult experiences, preparing me by them for the far sterner days yet to come, when even my own family would be my enemies:

If you have run with men on foot, and they exhaust you,
How can you compete in a heated race with horses?
And if you have no repose in a safe region,
Then how will you fare in the wild thicket of the Jordan?
For even your brothers, and your father's house,
Even they deal treacherously with you (12. 5-6a).

How often in these later days that summons from Yahweh to greater heroism of soul has sounded like a trumpet call in my ears!

Never could I speak pleasing words to my people. Sometimes I felt rebellious toward Yahweh because he had made me his prophet:

For as often as I speak, I cry out;
I call out "Violence!" and "Havoc!"
For the word of Yahweh has become for me
The cause of scorn and scoffing all the day (20. 8).

At times I determined to stop my teaching and preaching,

But when I would say, "I will not remember him,
Nor speak any more in his name,"
Then it was in my heart
Like a burning fire
Shut up in my bones,
And I have exhausted myself holding in,
And I could not endure it (20. 9).

By nature I was deeply sympathetic, and loved companionship. The sound of happy-hearted merriment, the joyous wedding celebrations, with the carefree laugh of the bride and the proud voice of the groom, were naturally a delight to me (16. 9). But from all this I was now cut off. Before Yahweh I brooded:

> I did not sit in the circle of those at play,
> But I exulted in gladness of heart.
> Before thy hand I sat alone,
> For indignation filled me.
> Why is my pain perpetual,
> And my wound incurable?   (15. 17-18a.)

I longed for a wife and children, but Yahweh had revealed to me that I must renounce the hope of marriage, for doom awaited my people—fathers and mothers, sons and daughters alike (16. 3-4).   His revelation had come to me:

> You shall not take unto yourself a wife,
> Nor shall you have sons
> Or daughters, in this place (16. 1).

Through my entire life and my whole demeanor before men I was to preach the solemn certainty of Judah's destruction.   For I was the prophet of my people's dying agony.

The nations of the Westland were in turmoil in those days.   For the first half of my prophetic ministry the Scythian raids had terrorized the whole region.   In the twenty-seventh year of the reign of King Josiah, under the combined attack of the Chaldaeans and the Medes, mighty Nineveh, famous capital of Assyria, and my people's most hated enemy, fell, and the Chaldaeans came into mastery of the Westland.   Three years later Pharaoh Necho of Egypt started north and east on the old military road toward Harran, the new seat of the remnant of the Assyrian Empire, in order to aid his Assyrian ally to withstand the Chaldaeans.   For some reason which we could not fathom, but possibly because flushed with the new prestige which the Deuteronomic reform had brought to him and his capital, so that he had come to consider himself a world power, our King Josiah courageously resisted Pharaoh Necho at Megiddo, but there met his death at the hand of the Egyptian monarch. It was a sad day for my people when his servants brought our beloved king's dead body in a chariot from Megiddo to Jerusalem, where he was mourned with universal and sincere grief, and buried in his own tomb in solemn ceremony. An uprising of the common people in Judah, who largely shared King Josiah's antagonism to Egypt, then placed his younger son, Jehoahaz, upon the throne (2 Kings 23. 29-30). Even while the multitude in public assembly were wailing King Josiah's death,[9] I chanted a dirge song for the new king;

> Do not weep for the dead,
> Lament not for him;
> Weep passionately for him who is to go away;
> For he shall not return again,
> Nor see the land of his birth (22. 10).

Jehoahaz had been king but three months when my intuition became reality. Pharaoh Necho, returning from his fruitless attempt to oust the Chaldaeans from Harran, came down through Palestine, dethroned Jehoahaz, then imprisoned him temporarily at Hamath, and later took him to Egypt. Necho then elevated to the throne of my people Josiah's elder son, Eliakim, giving him the throne name, Jehoiakim (2 Kings 23. 31-34).

The coronation of King Jehoiakim was the occasion that brought into the Temple courts vast throngs of Judaeans from all the cities and towns of Judah.[10] Their minds were under the spell of the mood of relief, for in spite of Pharaoh Necho's domination of Judah our sanctuary still stood inviolate, the nation was yet intact, and a native king of royal blood was head over our people. I counted it my opportunity to reach the ear of the nation. I directed my message against the superficial sense of security of my countrymen with their superstitious trust in the protection of the Temple which the Deuteronomic reform had strengthened. The new prestige and prominence it was enjoying had given rise to a quite unjustified feeling of political and religious complacency. The simple-minded Judaean pilgrims were awed by the Temple area with its magnificent equipment and symbols. They were led to feel that here no destruction could overtake them. If they could but come under its shadow, they would be safe from all harm. Standing in the gate of the Temple where a great throng had gathered, I proclaimed to them in Yahweh's name:

> Trust not in deceptive words, saying to yourselves, "The Temple of Yahweh, the Temple of Yahweh, the Temple of Yahweh, is this place." Will you steal, will you murder, and commit adultery, and swear a false oath, and burn incense to the Baal, and go after other gods whom you do not know, then come and stand in my presence in this house which is called by my name and say, "We have been delivered!"—in order that you may do all these abominations? Has this house, which is called by my name, become a cave of robbers in your eyes? So now because you have done all these deeds, and I spoke to you, but you did not hear, and I called you, but you did not answer, I will do to the house which is called by my name, in which you are trusting, and to the place which I gave to you and your fathers, just as I did to Shiloh, and I will fling *you* away from my presence even as I cast out all your brothers, all the offspring of Ephraim (7. 4, 9-11, 13-15).

When these last words were being uttered I was aware that an ominous silence had come over the throng, and when I touched upon the destruction of the Temple and of the Judaean state, the priests and the prophets were furious and violently seized me. Word of the commotion in the Temple court reached the princes in the palace, and they hastened up to the Temple to see what it was all about. Then the priests and the prophets solemnly and passionately appealed to the princes and to the people in general, saying:

> A verdict of death for this man; for he has prophesied against this city, as you have heard with your ears! (26. 11.)

Then I made my defense, telling them that I was not venturing *my opinion* about what would happen to Jerusalem and the Temple, but that I was declaring Yahweh's word, and that the only thing that could change his purpose thus to bring judgment upon his people was repentance on their part. I ended my plea as follows:

> But as for me, lo, I am in your power; do to me as seems to you good and right. Only know for certain that if you should put me to death, then you would bring innocent blood upon yourselves and upon this city, and upon you who are dwelling in it, for truly Yahweh sent me to you, to speak all these words in your ears (26. 14-15).

For a few moments it looked pretty dark for me. But the princes and people generally showed cooler judgment than the priests and the prophets. Said they:

> This man does not deserve the verdict of death; for he has spoken to us in the name of Yahweh our God (26. 16).

Then some of the old men recalled words similar to mine which the prophet Micah, one of my prophetic predecessors, had uttered about Jerusalem and the Temple. His words had been heeded by King Hezekiah, his message had been obeyed, and Jerusalem had been saved

(Micah 3. 12). So they warned the people against putting me to death saying:

We would be bringing great evil upon ourselves (26. 19b).

Their recall of Micah's preaching turned the tide. Thus did the fearless, courageous words of Yahweh's prophetic spokesman of a former generation become for me not only a comforting reassurance, but veritably the means of saving my life. That day across the chasm of a century I felt the warm hand clasp of Judah's noble preacher of democracy.

From now on I was an object of suspicion. To many of the leaders I was a dangerous character. My ideas were bitterly, even ruthlessly opposed. They tried to catch me up in some utterance that might justify my execution. I was thus thrown back upon myself, upon the honest scrutiny of my own innermost heart and mind. And in such hours of fearless self-examination and of the probing of my hidden motives, I came to be conscious of the unseen presence of Another greater than I, likewise searching me to the core of my being:

> Treacherous is the heart,
> Yes, incurably sick is it.
> Who knows it?—thus I questioned (17. 9).

And I seemed to hear Yahweh say in answer to my searchings:

> I, Yahweh, am exploring the heart
> And examining the dominant desires,
> In order to give to a man in accordance with his ways,
> And in proportion to the fruitage of his deeds (17. 10).

At times I was a coward and swerved from my duty, but at such moments an inner voice summoned me to the winning of soul values that have been purged, tried, and tested in the fires of persecution. One such revelation from Yahweh I shall never forget. In yet more desperate hours it has brought me great solace and I have thoroughly proved that it was, in all reality, Yahweh's word to me. Yahweh thus spoke in me:

If you will turn back to me,
Then I will allow you to return.
And you shall stand before me;
And if you bring forth what is precious from the worthless,
You will be like my mouth.
They shall turn back to you,
But you shall not turn back to them (15. 19).

In that part of my experience that might seem to me to be worthless, even vile, I was to search for something precious. And if I found this and remained true to my highest sense of duty, the time would come when I would be a pure medium of Yahweh's will, his spokesman, like unto his mouth, and Judah would listen.

I was living, during these days, with thoughts of the certain and irrevocable destruction of my people. I could see nothing hopeful ahead for Judah. One day, led by an impulse from Yahweh, I bought a pottery vessel, and taking along with me as witnesses a number of the elders of Jerusalem, I went out through the Potsherd Gate into the Valley of Ben-Hinnom. There I proclaimed the utter destruction of the city, and in the presence of the witnesses, I dashed the pottery to the ground where it broke into a thousand pieces. Then I cried:

Just as this potter's vessel is shivered to pieces so that it cannot be mended, so will I break this people and this city (19. 11ab).

Then returning to the court of the Temple I told
what I had done and interpreted its meaning: Yahweh's
judgment upon his people, the utter and irrevocable destruction of the Judaean nation. When Pashhur, the
chief priest of the Temple, heard me proclaiming this
destruction, in burning anger he ordered me beaten with
rods, then put me in the stocks, for he interpreted my
symbolic action as working a magic spell on Jerusalem!
When he released me on the following day I predicted to
him the ignominious fate that he himself and his friends
would suffer in Babylon, where they would die as captives of the Chaldaeans (20. 1-6).

While I was yet brooding over the destruction which
awaited my people, I felt a powerful impulse to go down
to the potter's shop and watch him fashion his vessels on
the wheel (18. 1ff.). Often before when I was a lad, and
had been in the capital, I went down to his shop, for I
reveled in the beautiful forms of the vessels he so loved
to shape and was fascinated as I watched them taking
form under his skilful, sensitive fingers. He knew me
well and welcomed me. That day I watched him while
he fashioned a vessel, but as he was molding it the vessel
was spoiled in the potter's hand. I saw what was happening and fully expected him to throw it out, take some
new clay and start again. But this he did not do. The
wheel kept on turning and swiftly his purpose changed;
and I watched the marred vessel being shaped into
another vessel, different in form from the earlier one he
had started, but beautiful, useful, and free from flaw.
Like a flash it came upon me that the impulse to watch
the potter had been from Yahweh! He had sent me
there! And from that very hour there began a new note

246

of hope in my message. I did not cease to preach the destruction of Judah. But Yahweh had taught me that destruction was not his final word. Judah was the clay, and Yahweh was the Potter, the Potter of infinite resourcefulness. The clay, though it had been marred, was yet good, the wheel kept on turning, and the Potter still loved his task! Judah was still in the Potter's hands! From that hour I became more than a proclaimer of doom. I began to look for and to build for a future of hope.

In the fourth year of King Jehoiakim's reign Egypt's flare of leadership in the Westland was given a fateful blow by the crushing defeat inflicted upon Pharaoh Necho's army at Carchemish by the mighty Chaldaean Nebuchadrezzar, whereupon the dominion of the Westland passed into the vigorous hands of the Chaldaeans. That was one of the most decisive battles that occurred during my lifetime and it stirred up tremendous interest among my people. Much as the most influential party in my nation hated Egyptian domination, they preferred it to that of the Chaldaeans. An impulse from Yahweh led me to count this an appropriate time to try once more to reach the heart of Judah by summarizing what or twenty-one strenuous years I had been teaching and preaching. By this time I had Baruch, loyal comrade and efficient scribe, at my side. He seemed to me then to be veritably a gift from God, and for twenty years has been my intimate associate, sharing bravely my lot. I dictated to him summaries of my preaching across the years, and he wrote them down upon a scroll. I counted it the most momentous step I had yet taken, and when the roll was completed, I awaited a suitable time to reach the conscience of my countrymen. That was afforded by a national fast proclaimed for December of the fifth year of Jehoiakim's reign, after the tidings of Carchemish had reached Jerusalem, thus awakening apprehensions of another invasion, this time of the Chaldaeans. For memories of Sennacherib's invasion a century earlier were still fresh in Judah. It seemed to me that if my people would ever listen, they would listen now. In consequence of my recent clash with Pashhur I was hindered from entering the Temple in person (36. 5). So I sent Baruch to read the scroll to the throngs, which he did in the hearing of the people, from the chamber of Gemariah, son of Shaphan, the court scribe, which was in the upper court just at the entrance of the new gate of the Temple (36. 8-10).

Micaiah, grandson of Shaphan, who was present, hurried down to the palace to tell the princes, the ministers of state, and counselors of the king who were in conclave, what he had heard. They sent for Baruch and made him read it once more in their hearing. As they heard the direct condemnation of leaders which it contained, particularly of King Jehoiakim, their faces blanched with alarm, and they asked Baruch:

Pray, tell us, how did you write all these words?

And Baruch answered them:

Jeremiah called to me all these words from his mouth and I kept writing them down with ink upon the scroll (36. 18).

To guard us from the vengeance of King Jehoiakim the princes urged that both Baruch and myself should go into hiding. They took the roll, however, and deposited it in the chamber of Elishama, the scribe, while they reported the matter to the king. He ordered the roll brought to his winter house by Jehudi, who then read it before the king and his courtiers, as the king sat shivering before his winter fire burning in the brazier. King Jehoiakim put on an air of utter contempt for my words. Every three or four columns[11] that Jehudi read, the king cut up with his penknife and flung into the fire until the whole scroll was burned up. Three of his counselors, Gemariah, Shaphan's son, among them, tried to prevent the king from thus burning it, but he gave no heed to their protests. He ordered a delegation of his princes to arrest Baruch and me, but they could not find us! Following a second impulse from Yahweh I took another scroll and dictated afresh the content of the first scroll and added many words of a like nature (36. 32).

I could not respect King Jehoiakim. With forced labor, and utter indifference to the payment of his workmen, he had built a luxurious palace after Egyptian models, and had led my people further and further away from the dignity and simplicity that had characterized the reign of his just and righteous father (22. 13-19).

Nebuchadrezzar invaded our country in King Jehoiakim's ninth year. Our king perforce accepted his overlordship, and for three years thereafter paid him tribute. Then his consuming ambition, combined with rash politics, led him to revolt. Nebuchadrezzar punished him by encouraging the bedouin bands of Chaldaeans, Aramaeans, Moabites, and Ammonites to maraud his territory, until at length the Chaldaean king himself would be ready to strike down our Judaean state (2 Kings 24. 1-2). Jehoiachin had succeeded to the throne of my people at King Jehoiakim's death, and had been king but three months when Nebuchadrezzar laid siege to Jerusalem. It was a time of terror to my people. Our eighteen-year-old monarch, along with the queen mother and his court, surrendered to Nebuchadrezzar and pleaded for clemency. They were taken as prisoners, the Temple and palace were looted of their treasures, and most of the priests, nobles, soldiers, and skilled artisans were taken into exile in Babylonia. Mattaniah, the third son of Josiah, was placed over Jerusalem as the puppet of the Chaldaeans, and was given the throne name, Zedekiah. Those were searching hours in the experience of my people (2 Kings 24. 10-17).

The Judaeans who were left in Jerusalem had a quite unjustified feeling of superiority over their kinsmen and neighbors who had been carried into exile. I kept hearing them say, concerning their countrymen now in Babylonia:

> They are far distant from the land of Yahweh;
> The land has been given to *us* for a possession (Ezekiel 11. 15).

In Yahweh's name I set myself to correct this exaggerated estimate of their own importance. One day in a vision I saw two baskets of figs in front of the Temple, one of very good figs, the other of very bad ones, so bad that they could not be eaten. Yahweh showed me that the bad figs represented Zedekiah, his princes, and the remnant left in Jerusalem. But the good figs represented their countrymen who were in exile (24. 1-10). This I preached very frankly to the Judaeans in the capital. To me the hope of the future lay with the flower of our nation now far way from the homeland in pagan Babylonia. But among the exiles were a number of prophets such as Ahab, the son of Kolaiah, and Zedekiah, the son of Maaseiah, and Shemaiah, the Nehelamite, who had been keeping the exiles all stirred up with hopes of an immediate restoration. So I wrote the Babylonian exiles a letter counseling them to give up any hope of a speedy return to Palestine (29. 4ff.). I was convinced that some two generations would elapse before they could come back. I urged them to build homes there and rear their families. They should not resist the Chaldaeans but should submit to them. Submission to Babylon, under the circumstances, meant submission to God, and their frank acceptance of the truly spiritual rather than political mission of Judah. Within the empire of the Chaldaeans, even dependent upon its protection, my people would be given the opportunity to lay the foundations for a spiritual restoration. So I told them to increase in numbers and in strength, and to pray for Babylon, in whose welfare theirs was bound up. I counseled them in such words as I had never before known how to utter. There in pagan Babylon, uprooted from their homeland, removed from the jurisdiction of their own institutions, far away from the Temple, its feasts and its sacrifices, they should pray to Yahweh. With the destruction I had so long preached already begun, I now realized that, emancipated from all institutional trappings, civil and religious, religion could still exist in their individual hearts. I told them how Yahweh was saying to them these wonderful words:

And you shall call upon me, and I will answer you, and you shall pray to me and I will listen to you. And you shall seek me and find me, when you search for me with all your heart. And I will let myself be found by you,

251

and I will restore your captivity, and I will gather you from all the nations and from all the places to which I banished you—it is the oracle of Yahweh—and I will bring you back to the place from where I took you into exile (29. 12-15).

The prophets who were with the exiles and who were encouraging them to expect a speedy return to the homeland were angered by the counsel in my letter. One of them, Shemaiah, sent a letter to Zephaniah, the priest in charge of the Temple at Jerusalem, rebuking him for not exercising his authority to imprison me. He wrote:

Yahweh has made you priest—to be overseer of the house of Yahweh, over every mad man who plays the prophet, and you should put him in the stocks and in the pillory! So now why have you not rebuked Jeremiah of Anathoth who is playing the prophet among you? (29. 26-27.)

Zephaniah read his letter to me, without comment, and I uttered Yahweh's stinging rebuke to be sent back to Shemaiah (29. 30-32).

In the fourth year of King Zedekiah's reign a movement began to show itself on the part of the Palestinian states, Edom, Moab, Ammon, and our nation, to throw off the Chaldaean yoke (27. 2-3). I was sharply opposed to it. Yahweh had led me to see that the distinctive mission of his people was not political but spiritual. Judah's only hope for security to carry out this spiritual mission lay in submission to the Chaldaeans. If we Judaeans should attempt resistance to their control, we would know in still more terrible experience the power of Chaldaean arms. I was solidly opposed to the prophetic party in this, which kept fomenting and abutting the revolt. In order to teach my people that the sole way to that measure of security needed to work out their spiritual mission was in submission to Babylon, I made a wooden yoke, fastened its bars together by thongs, and wore it upon my neck, and I preached the message directly to King Zedekiah.[12]

But the king was under the influence of that group of nationalistic prophets, diviners, soothsayers, and sorcerers, who kept constantly assuring him and the leaders of Judah that the Chaldaeans could not master Judah, and that soon the brass vessels recently taken from the Temple by the Chaldaeans would be back in Yahweh's house.

One day I was in the Temple when one of these shallow optimists among the prophets, Hananiah, son of Azur, whose home was at Gibeon, ten miles northwest of Jerusalem, confronted me in the presence of the priests and people generally, and had the effrontery to speak to me in Yahweh's name. Said he:

> Thus Yahweh says: I have broken in pieces the yoke of the king of Babylon. Within two years I will bring back to this palace the vessels of Yahweh's house, which Nebuchadrezzar, king of Babylon, took from this place and carried to Babylon; and I will bring again to this place Jeconiah (Jehoiachin) and the captivity of Judah that went to Babylon, for I will break the yoke of the king of Babylon (28. 2-4).

There I stood, listening to his presumptuous utterance, and wearing the wooden yoke across my shoulders, thus silently preaching a message directly contrary to his words! Priests and people who were in the Temple had by this time gathered about us in great numbers, for they knew the sharp difference of opinion between us on this question. In calm words, but weighing every syllable, I said:

Verily, let Yahweh do so! Let Yahweh carry out your words which you have prophesied. Nevertheless, pray hear this word which I am about to speak in your ears and in the ears of all the people: The prophets who preceded me and you from olden times prophesied against many lands and against great kingdoms, concerning war and famine. The prophet who prophesies of security, when his word comes to pass, they shall know that truly Yahweh has sent him to them (28. 6ab, 7-9).

Hananiah's face was hot with indignation. Almost beside himself he stepped forward, and grabbing the yoke from my shoulders, broke it in pieces over his knee. Then turning to the people who were breathlessly looking on, he said:

Thus says Yahweh: Like that will I break the yoke of Nebuchadrezzar, king of Babylon, within but two years, from off the neck of all nations (28. 11).

I had nothing further to say, so simply went on my way. But shortly after this I was led by Yahweh to make a yoke of iron, and as I wore it across my shoulders one day I confronted Hananiah and said to him:

You have broken the bars of wood; but I will make instead of them bars of iron. For thus has Yahweh said: I have put a yoke of iron upon the neck of all these nations that they may serve Nebuchadrezzar, king of Babylon (28. 14).

The revolt, however, did not then materialize. Psammetichus II succeeded Pharaoh Necho on the throne of Egypt the following year. He was kept busy attempting to recover Nubia, which, since the Ethiopian kingdom was founded, had been lost to Egypt.[13] My countrymen knew that without Egyptian help no revolt against the Chaldaeans could be successfully carried through.

But when five years later Pharaoh Hophra succeeded his father, the old Egyptian program to recover Asiatic dominions again became evident, and now, with expectation of Egyptian aid, the hotheaded, reckless Judaean leaders who were for revolt against the Chaldaeans, forced the hand of our weak, irresolute king, and he rebelled against his overlord. In the ninth year of King Zedekiah's reign, this revolt broke out, and in the tenth month of that same year, Nebuchadrezzar came with swiftness and dispatch against Jerusalem (2 Kings 25. 1). That was a day which will never be erased from the memory of my people, when again the Chaldaeans were at Jerusalem's gates.

King Zedekiah sent a priestly delegation to me, consisting of Pashhur and Zephaniah, with this message:

Pray, seek Yahweh on our behalf; for Nebuchadrezzar, king of Babylon, has engaged in battle against us. Perhaps Yahweh will deal with us in accordance with all his wonderful works and make him retreat from us (21. 2).

I sent them back to the king to tell him the certainty of Jerusalem's capture, and the misery that awaited the people because of pestilence and Chaldaean cruelty. I sent a message likewise to the people:

Thus has Yahweh said: Lo, I set before you the way of life and the way of death. He who remains in this city shall die by the sword, and by famine, and by pestilence; but he who goes out, and goes over to the Chaldaeans who are besieging you shall live, and shall have his life for his booty (21. 8-9).

As the siege went on I continued to preach surrender to the Chaldaeans. The princes now accused me of treason and of cutting the nerve of the Judaean defense by my ideas (38. 4). Their opportunity to arrest me soon came. The appearance of Pharaoh Hophra's Egyptian troops coming to the aid of Jerusalem caused the withdrawal of the Chaldaean troops and the lifting of the siege of the capital. I knew it was but a temporary relief and sent word to that effect to King Zedekiah (37. 6-10). But I decided to take the opportunity given by the withdrawal of the Chaldaean army to visit my native village of Anathoth, on an errand which had to do with my family inheritance. I started to leave the capital by the gate on the north wall of the city which leads to the territory of Benjamin, but was challenged by a sentinel at the gate, who, laying hold upon me, charged:

You are deserting to the Chaldaeans! (37. 13.)

I indignantly replied:

That is false. I am not deserting to the Chaldaeans (37. 14).

However, he would not listen to my defense but took me to the princes. They, having been given authority by King Zedekiah, who was powerless in their hands, seized me, beat me, and imprisoned me in the house of Jonathan the scribe, where they hurled me into a miry dungeon (37. 15; 38. 6). Enough news of what was happening seeped into that awful hole to let me learn, as I had anticipated, that the Chaldaean army was soon back at our capital, renewing the siege.

Never can I forget the kindness of the Negro slave, Ebed Melech, who got me out of that terrible dungeon. After I had been there many days he dared to plead directly with King Zedekiah for me, describing my desperate condition and awakening the sympathy of the king.

He gave Ebed Melech thirty slaves to rescue me. With rope improvised out of old rags tied together they gently drew me from the dungeon (38. 7-13). A messenger took me at once,[14] in the strictest secrecy, into the king's presence. It was pitiful to me to see the terror that was written all over his weak features as he tremblingly asked:

Is there a word from Yahweh?

My answer to him was true but comfortless:

There is! you shall be given up into the hand of the king of Babylon (37. 17).

I went on to reveal to him Yahweh's will in the crisis:

If you will surely go out to the princes of the king of Babylon, your soul shall live, and this city shall not be burned with fire (38. 17).
Listen, pray, to the voice of Yahweh according to which I am speaking to you: then it shall go well with you, and your soul shall live (38. 20).

But our king lacked the courage and the stamina to do what he knew was right (38. 19). He swore me to secrecy that he had consulted me, and then committed me to the court surrounding the palace where prisoners were guarded.[15]

One day while I was confined in this guard court I had an intuition that my cousin, Hanamel, my uncle Shallum's son, would come to see me to offer for sale our family inheritance at Anathoth (32. 6-15).[16] When Hanamel appeared with exactly that errand, I knew his presence was in line with Yahweh's will. I felt in his request an opportunity to give tangible embodiment to my faith that there was yet a hopeful future for Judah in our homeland. So I bought the property in Anathoth, paying seventeen shekels in silver for it.[17] I signed the deed, sealed it, and paid the money in the presence of witnesses, all according to the law and custom of my people. Then I handed the sealed purchase deed and the open one to Baruch, my faithful scribe, and solemnly directed him to put them in a pottery vessel where for many days they would be safe. Thus I gave effective expression to Yahweh's assurance that

> Yet again shall houses and fields and vineyards be bought in this land (32. 15).

The Chaldaean siege, which lasted two and one half years (2 Kings 25. 1-2), gradually reduced us to desperate straits. As long as there was bread to be had in Jerusalem I received my daily ration of a single loaf (37. 21). But on the ninth day of the fourth month famine stalked through our city, for the common people had no bread. Then our king and the soldiers fled ignominiously by night by way of the royal garden by the gate between the two walls, and made for the Jordan valley. But they were pursued by the Chaldaeans and overtaken in the steppes of Jericho. Our king was seized and taken to Nebuchadrezzar at Riblah, a city in the district of Hamath, in the Orontes valley, about one hundred miles north of Dan, his army headquarters. He killed our king's sons before his eyes, and put him in chains to carry him to Babylon. Then the Chaldaeans burned the Temple, palace, and the houses of the common people and demolished the walls of the city. Leaving a few thousand poor peasants to till the soil, Nebuchadrezzar carried the bulk of the population as prisoners to Babylon (2 Kings 25. 4-12).

Gedaliah, grandson of Shaphan, the scribe, a brave and good man, and a member of one of the noblest Judaean families, was placed at the head of the devastated Judaean province, and the seat of his authority was transferred from Jerusalem to Mizpah (2 Kings 25. 23). The Chaldaeans carried me as far as Ramah, just a few miles north of Jerusalem. Here Nebuzaradan, captain of the forces in charge of the captives, interpreting my attitude as being pro-Chaldaean, and, accordingly, considering me a Chaldaean asset whether in Babylon or at Mizpah, gave me my choice—either to be well cared for in Babylon, or to support Gedaliah at Mizpah. My duty was clear as daylight to me. So back to the impoverished and destitute remnant of my people I went to help Gedaliah build into them courage and energy, and to aid in establishing the foundation of a hopeful future (40. 1-6).

But vigorous forces soon combined against Gedaliah, and in an uprising led by Ishmael, a prince who was in league with the Ammonites, he was brutally murdered (2 Kings 25. 25). The other leaders then in despair, headed by Johanan, son of Kareah, asked my counsel for the future. They said to me:

> Pray, let our supplication be presented before you, and intercede on our behalf with Yahweh, your God, that Yahweh, your God, may show us the way wherein we should walk, and the thing that we should do (42. 2a-3).

After ten days of brooding and prayer, I called them to me and counseled them to remain in Judah and to build for the future (42. 7). But their wills were already set. Putting my counsel aside, they went to Egypt, taking Baruch and me forcibly with them (43. 6). And here I am as I tell my story, Baruch, my faithful comrade, setting it down in writing as I speak it.

My heart is sad for my people. Here they are in Egypt,

again worshiping the goddess Astarte, Queen of Heaven, and, as in former days they did in Palestine, they are still burning incense to her (44. 15-19).

> Can the Ethiopian change his skin,
> Or the leopard his spots?
> Then may you also do good
> Who are accustomed to do evil (13. 23).

Once I was young, now I am old. In the nature of the case I cannot live much longer. And sometimes when I feel the sharp antagonism to my words that still exists I fear I may experience a violent death.

But in my heart there burns a flame of inextinguishable hope. It is based on the deepest thing I know. It is the richest fruitage of my stormy years of heart searching and of preaching. It is my last will and testament to my people. Yahweh has revealed to me that a time will come when he will make a new covenant with my people, based not upon engraved or inscribed national laws, but the inner response of the individual human heart to him. Religion then will be universally experienced by my people, as a deep, vital, personal relationship between Yahweh and the individual soul, a relationship such as has become through these stormy years the very anchorage of my own life. For Yahweh said to me:

> I will put my law in their inward parts, and upon their heart will I write it. And I will be their God, and they shall be my people. And they shall not teach any more, each his neighbor, and each his brother, saying, "Know Yahweh." For they shall all know me, from the least of them unto the greatest of them. For I will forgive their iniquity, and their sin will I remember no more (31. 33-34).

NOTES

CHAPTER I: NOTES ON AMOS OF TEKOA

1. Cf. J. Morgenstern: "Amos Studies I," p. 84, note 88, meaning either "weak" or, perhaps better, "young," immature, not yet able to realize the enormity of his offense.

2. So A. Weiser: *Die Prophetie des Amos,* p. 43 who, following Volz, reads for *berō'sh, bera'ash.*

3. I follow the chronology given in the most thorough and valuable recent study of the question in Joachim Begrich: *Die Chronologie der Könige von Israel und Juda,* as assembled on p. 155. He dates Jeroboam II's reign as 787-747. He dates the reign of Uzziah of Judah as 785-747, with Jotham his regent from 758-747.

4. In agreement with almost unanimous critical judgment, I consider the oracles against Tyre, Edom, and Judah as later supplements to Amos's original message.

5. This is to be identified with the Bit-Adini on both shores of the Euphrates between Bâlis and Biredschick, cf. E. Schrader: *Die Keilinschriften und das Alte Testament,*[2] p. 327; cf. 2 Kings 19. 12; Isaiah 37. 12; Ezekiel 27. 23.

6. Amos 2. 6-8; 5. 10-12; 8. 4-6.

7. The ivories of Samaria found by Fitzgerald are illuminating at this point: cf. PEFQS (1933), 7-26, plates I-III.

8. This rendering attempts to bring out the paronomasia of the speech of Amos: *haggilgāl gālô yighleh ûbhêth ēl yihyeh le'āwen.* "Gilgal will surely go into captivity and Bethel will become idolatry."

9. I follow here, in part, the suggestive views of J. Morgenstern in his "Amos Studies I" (1936), especially pp. 123-129; cf. Zechariah 14. 5 and Josephus: *Antiquities,* IX, 10, p. 299 (W. Whiston ed.); cf. 2 Chronicles 26. 16-21.

THE PROPHETS TELL THEIR OWN STORY

CHAPTER II: NOTES ON HOSEA OF EPHRAIM

1. Hosea 1. 2, cf. W. Riedel: *Alttest. Untersuchungen* I, 1902, 1-18, as advanced by Allwohn: *Die Ehe des Propheten Hosea,* p. 35, which designates her as a Baal devotee; see also pp. 46-53.

2. For rendering of last line cf. H. S. Nyberg: *Studien zum Hoseabuche,* pp. 21ff.

3. Cf. the keen sensitive insight of Gunkel, in "Hosea," in RGG² II, 2022.

4. Cf. Deuteronomy 23. 18.

5. Cf. H. Gunkel: "Hosea," in RGG² II, 2022.

6. I follow W. Robertson Smith in his judgment that *ᵒōdh,* in 3. 1, means not "again" but "still," and modifies the primary verb in the sentence, "love"; cf. his *Prophets of Israel,* p. 410.

7. Cf. G. B. Gray: *Sacrifice in the Old Testament,* p. 223.

8. Roundly about £400,000, so J. Skinner: *Kings* (New Century Bible), p. 363; cf. 2 Kings 15. 19-20; and G. A. Barton: *Archaeology and the Bible,*⁶ p. 463, line 50. The date is 738 B. C.

9. Reading *kî qirbām kattannûr libbām bō'ēr bām;* cf. M. Heilprin: *Historical Poetry of the Ancient Hebrews,* II, 145, who follows Schorr in thus restoring the text of 7. 6a.

10. I follow S. Mowinckel in part at this point. Cf. *Psalmstudien* II: *Das Thronbesteigungsfest Jahwäs und der Ursprung der Eschatologie,* esp. p. 6.

11. Beginning at this point, I follow in the main A. Alt's suggestive and illuminating analysis of the references in Hosea's words to the Syrian-Ephraimite war in "Hosea 5. 8-6. 6," in N K Z 1919, 537-568.

12. Cf. Genesis 49. 22-26; Deuteronomy 33. 13-17.

13. So A. T. Olmstead: *History of Palestine and Syria,* p. 454,

NOTES

cf. 2 Kings 17. 4; cf. also J. H. Breasted: *History of Egypt,* p. 549, who identifies So with Sewa, "either an otherwise unknown Delta dynast or ruler of Musri, a kingdom of North Arabia."

CHAPTER III: NOTES ON ISAIAH OF JERUSALEM

1. Cf. J. Morgenstern in "Amos Studies I," p. 139, in reference to 2 Chronicles 26. 16-23.

2. Cf. the suggestive, imaginative discussion of A. B. Davidson: *The Called of God,* pp. 189-191, who believes the momentous death of Uzziah gave the psychological origin of the vision.

3. I follow here, in the main, the suggestive interpretation of Isaiah 5. 1-7 offered by W. C. Graham: "Notes on the Interpretation of Isaiah 5. 1-14," in AJSL, Vol. 45 (1929), pp. 167-178.

4. So G. W. Wade: *Isaiah,* p. 31, who thus renders Isaiah's paronomasia with the play upon *mishpāṭ* (rule) and *miçpāḥ* (misrule); and *çᵉdhāqāh* (redress, i. e., righteousness), and *çᵉʿāqāh* (distress, i.e., the cry of the distressed); better still is B. Duhm's brilliant rendering:
   "Und er hoffte auf gut Regiment, und siehe da: ein Blutregiment,
   Auf Rechtsprechung, und siehe da: Rechtsbrechung!"; cf. p. 33.

5. B. Duhm considers this a possibility, p. 69. I base it primarily on vs. 8 (Heb. vs. 7), "A word has Yahweh sent unto Jacob" (*bᵉyaᵃqōbh*), Isaiah's specific knowledge of what people in Samaria were saying, and the inherent likelihood of it, in view of Amos's example.

6. There is in Isaiah's words a brilliant play upon the hiphil (trust, believe) and the niphal (be confirmed or established) stems of the verbal root, *'āman* = confirm, support.

7. I construe *çôr* = "bind-up, preserve," as an infinitive absolute from *çārar; tᵉʿûdhāh* means "testifying revela-

tion," i.e., the testifying of the prophet himself as to what Yahweh had revealed to him; I point *hāthôm*, likewise an infinitive absolute, corresponding to *çôr*.

8. D. D. Luckenbill: *Ancient Records of Assyria and Babylonia* I, 815: Hanno of Gaza fled to Egypt; G. A. Barton: *Archaeology and the Bible*[6], p. 464, lines 19-21.

9. Literally, "plantings of Naaman," a by-name of Adonis.

10. For the complete account of this campaign, cf. D. D. Luckenbill: op. cit., I, 777; G. A. Barton: *Archaeology and the Bible*[6], p. 464f.

11. So T. H. Robinson in Oesterley and Robinson: *History of Israel,* I, p. 377.

12. Luckenbill, II, 4; Barton, *Archaeology and the Bible*[6], p. 465.

13. Cf. 2 Kings 17. 6; cf. T. H. Robinson in Oesterley and Robinson: *History of Israel,* I, pp. 380-3.

14. Cf. Luckenbill, II, 5; G. A. Barton: *Archaeology and the Bible*[6], p. 466.

15. Cf. Luckenbill, II, 18; called Pir'u. Bocchoris (718-712 B. C.) was the sole king of the 24th dynasty.

16. Luckenbill, II, 30; Barton: *Archaeology and the Bible*[6], p. 467. The date is 711 B. C.

17. He had been ousted by Sargon in 709 B. C., cf. D. D. Luckenbill, II, 31, 35; he regained the throne of Babylon in 705 B. C., cf. D. D. Luckenbill, II, 257, 259.

18. Zoan = Tanis, between the two most easterly mouths of the Nile; Hanes, Egyptian Hnes, is *Heracleopolis magna,* and is still called Ahnas, cf. John Skinner: *Isaiah,* ad. loc.

19. That is, seal a treaty by a customary libation, so K. Marti.

20. Reading the hophal, with H. Schmidt: *Die grossen Propheten*[2], p. 87, *rahabh hammoshbāth.* Rahab is the monster of chaos and here the name is cryptically applied to Egypt. The "monster," in the prophet's thought, lies dead on the ground!

NOTES

21. Luckenbill, II, 259-263.

22. Cf. D. D. Luckenbill: *Annals of Sennacherib*, p. 7.

23. W. F. Albright calls this "one of the most vivid descriptions of the advance of an hostile army ever given." My translation is based on his reconstruction of the text. Cf. Appendix IV—"The Assyrian March on Jerusalem," in AASOR IV, (1924), 134-140.

24. Cf. Luckenbill, II, 309.   The date is 701 B. C.

25. Cf. D. D. Luckenbill: *The Annals of Sennacherib*, from the Oriental Institute Prism Inscription (H2), col. II, line 51—col. III, line 74, for an account of this campaign.

26. Now identified with Tell Duweir; cf. A. T. Olmstead: *History of Assyria*, fig. 127 (opposite page 308), for a picture of the siege of Lachish.

27. Luckenbill: *Annals of Sennacherib*, p. 156, no. xxv.

28. About £280,000 sterling, so A. Lods (p. 34); cf. 2 Kings 18. 14, which reads 300 talents of silver.

29. Cf. 2 Kings 19. 9, where he is called king of Ethiopia, to which position he attained thirteen years afterward, so J. H. Breasted: *History of Egypt*[2], p. 552.

30. Cf. Herodotus II, 141, as interpreted by G. A. Smith: *Historical Geography of the Holy Land*, pp. 158ff.   The Biblical legend that grew up around this is given in 2 Kings 19. 35.

31. B. Duhm: *Isaiah*[3], p. 14, rightly accepts Isaiah 32 and 2. 1-4 as coming from Isaiah and as being his swan song.

32. Cf. S. R. Driver in *Deuteronomy*, p. 74; G. B. Gray: *Isaiah*, p. 44.   The Assyrian phrase *ina aḥrat umi* is not late, nor is the Hebrew phrase itself, "in the latter days," late.   I believe these two expressions of the Messianic hope were inspired by Isaiah's brooding over the remarkable "inviolability" of Jerusalem.

33. Cf. Isaiah 2. 2-4; Bishop Francis J. McConnell suggestively calls this "spiritual gravitation."

CHAPTER IV: NOTES ON MICAH OF MORESHETH-GATH

1. The LXX designates it as *kleronomias Geth,* "inheritance of Gath"; cf. also the Vulgate, *hereditas Geth,* and the Peshitto, *jartûtha de-Gath.* Gath itself is identified by H. Guthe and W. F. Albright with Tell el Menshîyeh near the village of 'Araq el-Menshîyeh about 6½ miles west of Beit Jibrin, and about 7 1/5 miles slightly southwest of Tell ej-Judeideh, so Albright in AASOR II, 4, 8-11.

2. The most likely site with which Moresheth-Gath is identified is Tell ej-Judeideh, as argued with great conclusiveness by Joachim Jeremias in "Moreseth-Gath, die Heimat des Propheten Micha," in *Palästinajahrbuch,* 1923, 42-53. This tell is the highest point of the train of hills, on the southern spurs of which are *khirbet es-'id,* the succeeding settlement in the post-exilic times, and *khirbet el-basal,* that of Roman-Byzantine times. At *khirbet es-'id* Jeremias found a necropolis which he identifies with the burial place of Micah referred to by Pseudo-Epiphanius.

3. Spelled Baetogabri by Claudius Ptolemy of the second century A. D. in his *Geographia,* ed. C. Müller, I, pars secunda, 15. 5. Nestle (ZDPV, I, 222-5) believes the word is Aramaic and means "House of Men," or "Strong Men." It was later called Eleutheropolis, "free city." How it was designated in Micah's day we do not know. It was about two miles south of Tell ej-Judeideh.

4. That Micah knew some of the major elements of Amos's message seems reasonable when we compare Micah 2. 6 with Amos 2. 12; 5. 11; and 7. 10f.; and Micah 3. 1-4 with Amos 5. 12, 15; and Micah 6. 9-16 with Amos 3. 10 and 8. 5.

5. That Micah had actually heard Isaiah we can only infer from (1) the inherent likelihood that Micah had often been in Jerusalem, (2) from the witness of Jeremiah 26. 17-19, which implies that he had been there, and (3) from his familiarity with the thoughts of Isaiah as seems clear

266

NOTES

from a comparison of Micah 2. 1-5 with Isaiah 5. 8-10;
and Micah 3. 3. with Isaiah 3. 15.

6. Cf. W. C. Graham: "The Interpretation of Micah 1. 10-
16," p. 252, who rightly views *bāmôthê* (so *kethîbh* reading) *'ereç* as meaning the High Places of the land of Palestine.

7. I believe with J. Lindblom, p. 166, note 2, that the message to Samaria was not delivered in person but was sent
in the form of a bulletin or fly-leaf.

8. Cf. 2 Kings 17. 5-6; G. A. Barton: *Archaeology and the
Bible*[3], p. 369.

9. Until recently scholars have interpreted Micah 1. 10-16
as having to do with cities that lay in the path of the destructive Assyrians, and more particularly with the Assyrian invasion of Philistine territory in 711 B. C., mentioned in Isaiah 20. 1. So still J. Lindblom: "Micha,
literarisch untersucht," pp. 39-51. W. C. Graham,
however, in a penetrating analysis of the passage, "The
Interpretation of Micah 1. 10-16," in AJSL 47 (1931),
pp. 237-258, has conclusively shown that there is no
ground for maintaining that the places here mentioned
lie upon the route of this or any other Assyrian advance,
and that the correct view of the passage is obtained
through a cultural approach. The key to his argument
is the meaning of the term *yôshebheth*, which occurs
in vss. 11 (twice), 12, 13, 15, and is translated in A.S.V.
"inhabitant," mg. "inhabitress," and in *An American
Translation*, as "the inhabitant." The term is the qal
active participle in the feminine construct of the root
rāshabh, meaning "to sit." Graham construes it as an ab-
stract form designating a title or office; cf. G.-K. sec.
122r, and as, in Micah's mouth, a sarcastic or contemptuous term designating the mother goddess of the local
fertility cult in each case, which I have rendered "mistress." The following reconstruction of the text and its
interpretation is greatly indebted to this study. The
present writer, however, would date the passage after
720 B. C., when the fall of Samaria had made its profound
impression upon Judah, but considerably before the

267

events of 711 B. C. Thus the particular type of prophetic symbolic action which seems to be suggested in 1. 8 would precede in point of time rather than follow the somewhat similar prophetic action performed by the prophet Isaiah as described in Isaiah 20. My translation of the passage follows for the most part the reconstructed text resulting from the keen suggestions of Graham.

10. Cf. J. L. Starkey: "Excavations at Tell el-Duweir 1933-34" in PEFQS, 1934, 170-171, and Plate V, fig. 2, for an isometric view of the Temple which dates from the Late Bronze Age, c. 1400 B. C., and which was itself built on the site of a yet earlier sanctuary, cf. J. L. Starkey: "Excavations at Tell el-Duweir 1934-35," in PEFQS, 1935, p. 200; cf. also W. C. Graham and H. G. May: *Culture and Conscience,* p. 113f.

11. Cf. D. D. Luckenbill: *Ancient Records of Assyria and Babylonia,* II, sec. 30 and sec. 195.

12. I view 1. 5b as authentic but out of place in its present context, which deals exclusively with Samaria. Manifestly a fit setting for it is a kind of *apologia* for his deliverance of this crucial and influential message at the capital.

13. D. D. Luckenbill: *The Annals of Sennacherib,* p. 156, epigraph: Sennacherib at Lachish, lines 1-4.

14. This is a likely inference from the situation.

15. Cf. G. A. Barton: *Archaeology and the Bible*[6], p. 476.

16. For the priestly torah, cf. Deuteronomy 33. 10; Psalms 15. 24; Malachi 2. 7; for the prophetic oracle, cf. Haggai 2. 11 and Zechariah 7. 3, which represent no innovation in procedure but mirror ancient (i.e., pre-exilic) as well as post-exilic practice.

CHAPTER V: NOTES ON ZEPHANIAH OF JERUSALEM

1. The dates of Manasseh's reign are 696-642 B. C., embracing approximately 55 years. If Zephaniah were approximately 30 years of age when he began his prophetic

ministry, it would mean that he was born not earlier
than 660 B. C., for his prophetic activity is dated by the
Scythian invasion of Palestine, which E. H. Minns
(C.A.H. III, 189) dates 630-625 B. C.; S. A. Cook (C. A. H.
III, 394) dates it 635-625 B. C.

2. Cf. Zephaniah 1. 1; G. B. Gray in *Studies in Hebrew
Proper Names*, p. 262, note 1, calls attention to the fact
that four out of the five names of this genealogy are com-
pounded with *Yah*, compounds which prevail in royal
rather than in other circles; and he favors the suggestion
that the "Hezekiah" here referred to, is the king of
Judah. This accounts for the tracing of the prophet's
genealogy back to the fourth generation, contrary to custom, cf. A. Lods, *The Prophets and the Rise of Judaism*,
p. 131.

3. Cf. R. W. Rogers: *Cuneiform Parallels to the O. T.*,
Prism B, col. V, 1. 13, where, as H. R. Hall notes (*The
Ancient History of the Near East*, p. 497, dating this 677
B. C.), Manasseh is designated only as *shar (alu) Iaudi*,
"king of the *city* of Judah," thus showing that from the
Assyrian angle, his authority was viewed as extending
no farther than the walls of Jerusalem. Cf. also D. D.
Luckenbill: *Ancient Records of Assyria and Babylonia*,
II, sec. 690.

4. In 668 B. C. and 667 B. C., respectively; cf. J. H. Breasted:
Ancient Records of Egypt, IV, secs. 892, 917. Its destruction took place in 661 B. C., secs. 902, 920.

5. Cf. A. T. Olmstead: *History of Palestine and Syria*, p.
482. Cf. also for the Jewish tradition that Isaiah, during
the reign of Manasseh, was sawn in two with a wooden
saw, A. Dillmann: *Ascensio Isaiae* 5. 1-14; cf. also Hebrews 11. 37.

6. I read with the Massoretic text, *malkhām*, i. e., "their
(god) Malk" (=Molech=Moloch). The reading is not
milkhōm, which would mean the Ammonite deity Mil-
com (1 Kings 11. 5, 33 and 2 Kings 23. 13), but it is the old
Canaanite king deity, Malk or Milk, who usually ap-
pears as Molech with the vowels of *bôsheth*" (shame),

and, in the LXX, as Moloch. I render it "Moloch," which at once calls to mind the exact emphasis of his cult (child sacrifice), which under Manasseh had flared up afresh. Cf. Wolf Baudissin in *Realencyklopädie,* Vol. 13, p. 278.

7. Cf. W. O. E. Oesterley: *The Sacred Dance,* p. 47; François Lenormant: *La Magie chez les Chaldéens,* pp. ix and 47ff.; T. Canaan: *Aberglaube und Volksmedizin im Lande der Bibel,* pp. 19-21. Cf. also the practice of the priests of Dagon in his temple at Ashdod, 1 Samuel 5. 4-5; and of the Judaean keepers of the threshold in the Jerusalem Temple, 2 Kings 23. 4; 1 Chronicles 9. 22; 2 Chronicles 23. 4.

8. Cf. A. R. Gordon in *Peake's Commentary,* p. 570; cf. also W. R. Smith: *The Prophets of Israel*2, p. 364.

9. Cf. the fine interpretation in Chas. V. Pilcher: *Three Hebrew Prophets,* p. 169.

10. The remainder of Zephaniah, 3. 14-20 is from the hand of a later writer who is filled with the contrast between the era in which he lives and the Golden Age yet to come.

CHAPTER VI: NOTES ON NAHUM OF ELKOSH

1. So Epiphanius in Migne: *Patrologia Graeca,* Vol. 43; cf. also G. Nestle: "Where is the birthplace of the Prophet Nahum to be Sought?" in PEFQS (1879), pp. 136-8, who tends to identify it with Kessijeh, a little s.w. of Beit Jibrin. U. Cassuto in *Giornale della Società Asiatica Italiana* (1914), pp. 291ff., however, identifies it with Umm Lagish, half way between Beit Jibrin and Gaza; cf. R. H. Pfeiffer: *Harvard Theological Review* 27 (1934), p. 282, which locality exactly fits the evidence from Epiphanius.

2. Cf. 2 Chronicles 33. 11-13, viewed as historical by A. T. Olmstead in *History of Palestine and Syria,* p. 486, and in *History of Assyria,* p. 384.

3. Cf. A. T. Olmstead: *History of Assyria,* pp. 629ff.; A. Lods: *The Prophets and the Rise of Judaism,* p. 42f.

NOTES

4. From this point on, the chief source is British Museum tablet B.M. 21,901 published in C. J. Gadd: *The Fall of Nineveh,* 1923.

5. So best argued by Sigmund Mowinckel in *Psalmenstudien* II and III, (1922-3). Cf. also the excellent brief summary of his views by Paul Humbert: "Le problème du livre de Nahoum," in RHPR, 1932, p. 13; for the Temple prophets, cf. M. Haller: "Nahum," in RGG² IV, 406-7; cf. also Jeremiah 20. 1ff.; 28. 5; 29. 26; and, for the prophetic oracle, cf. Psalm 81. 6ff.; 95. 7b-10; and 2 Chronicles 20. 14-17.

6. This is also sometimes the case with the liturgical poetry of Mediaeval Judaism; cf. S. Mowinckel in RHPR, 1932, p. 3.

7. The meaning is, the count of the days before Nineveh's destruction has been achieved.

8. The pillagers are the Chaldaeans and Medes; the pillaged are the Assyrians. Cf. *The Babylonian Chronicle* (Gadd), line 45.

9. I am indebted here to Paul Humbert: "Essai d'analyse de Nahoum 1. 2–2. 3," in ZAW 44 (1926), esp. pp. 272-276.

10. Cf. the suggestive and illuminating interpretation in Paul Humbert: "La vision de Nahoum 2. 4-11," in Archiv für Orientforschung V (1928), p. 19; cf. also the similar dramatic. actualization in the Babylonian cult as given by E. Ebeling: *Tod und Leben nach den Vorstellungen der Babylonier* (1931), p. 41, who emphasizes the pantomime and the more or less detailed dialogue between the leading cultic figure and the choir; and cf. K. Sethe: *Dramatische Texte zu altaegyptischen Mysterienspiele* (1928), for the similar dramatic representation and realization in the Egyptian cult.

11. Cf. A. Billerbeck and A. Jeremias: "Der Untergang Nineveh's und die Weissagungsschrift des Nahum von Elkosch," in *Beiträge zur Assyriologie,* III (1895), pp. 87-188, who show how the description of the fall of Nineveh

reveals detailed knowledge of military technique employed.

12. For the vision style, cf. H. Gunkel: "Die Propheten als Schriftsteller und Dichter," in Einleitung (3) to Hans Schmidt: *Die grossen Propheten*,[2] pp. xlii-xlvii especially; for imitation of vision style, xlv.

13. Cf. Paul Humbert: "La Vision de Nahoum 2. 4-11," p. 17; and Billerbeck and Jeremias, op. cit., p. 101.

14. Cf. C. J. Gadd: *The Fall of Nineveh*, line 41 (sec. 1177 in Luckenbill), and Diodorus Siculus: Book II, chap. 26. 9; 27. 2 (G. Booth translation, Vol. I, p. 122f.), who gives the picture vividly but confuses the Tigris with the Euphrates.

15. So W. Max Müller, in "Put," in HDB IV, pp. 176-7, who identifies it with Punt, Put being the Semitic form with the assimilation of the n. See excellent map opposite column 1208 in *Encyclopaedia Biblica* II.

16. So Diodorus II. 27 (Booth, Vol. I, p. 123).

17. So Diodorus II. 27.

CHAPTER VII: NOTES ON HABAKKUK OF JERUSALEM

1. Cf. E. Sellin: *Das Zwölfprophetenbuch* II[2], p. 383, in reference to Habakkuk 1. 4 and 2. 4.

2. Habakkuk 2. 2; 3. 2; 3. 16.

3. Cf. the correct view of the personality of Habakkuk given by O. Eissfeldt, who says, "Habakkuk was also a real visionary, and it is certainly no accident, when the superscription of his book gives him expressly the title Nabhi (prophet)," *Einleitung in das Alte Testament* (1934), p. 471. Eissfeldt believes that Isaiah 21. 1-10 gives us a glimpse of the type of the experience characteristic of him.

4. Cf. the suggestive view of the cult prophet offered by S. Mowinckel: *Psalmenstudien* III (1923), pp. 14-29, "Der

Nabi als Kultdiener," and *Psalmenstudien* II (1922), p. 117, where he emphasizes the oracle of the cult prophet as having a fixed place in the liturgy of the New Year's festival.

5. Cf. C. J. Gadd: *The Fall of Nineveh,* also D. D. Luckenbill: *Ancient Records of Assyria and Babylonia* II, secs. 1167-1186.

6. Cf. the narrative given best by the Chronicler in 2 Chronicles 35. 20-25, which is rightly viewed as trustworthy by J. Lewy in "Forschungen zur alten Geschichte Vorderasiens," p. 22.

7. D. D. Luckenbill: op. cit., secs. 1183-1184.

8. Cf. C. L. Woolley: *Carchemish,* part 2, pp. 123-6, who describes the archaeological evidence of the capture and destruction of Carchemish in 605 B. C. In a large house, designated D, belonging to a wealthy Hittite and which had been destroyed by fire, were found a large number of objects of Egyptian origin or which showed Egyptian influence, including, in room 5, clay seal impressions bearing the cartouche of Necho. The burnt ruins had left in them evidences of a desperate struggle, with hundreds of arrow heads in bronze and iron, javelin heads, sword, and shield.

9. Cf. J. H. Breasted: *History of Egypt,* p. 583f.

10. Cf. Herodotus II, 159.

11. I follow here the careful and illuminating analysis of J. Lewy: "Forschungen zur alten Geschichte Vorderasiens" in MVAG, (1924), p. 41, esp. note 3, who distinguished this campaign of 602-1 B. C. Cf. also the LXX of 2 Chronicles, which inserts 2 Kings 24. 1-4 between 2 Chronicles 36. 5 and 6.

12. According to 2 Kings 24. 14, the figure is given as 10,000, not including the blacksmiths and locksmiths. In 2 Kings 24. 16 the figure is placed at 8,000. According to the most detailed statistics, Jeremiah 25. 28-30, these exiles numbered 4,600 men.

13. The view of Habakkuk as a prophetic liturgy is maintained by E. Balla: "Habakkuk," in *Rel. u. Gesch. d. Gegenwart*[2] II, 1556-57; E. Sellin: *Einleitung in das alte Testament*[5] (1929), p. 120; in his *Das Zwölfprophetenbuch* II (2nd and 3rd editions, pp. 381ff.); and in his *Israelitisch-jüdische Religionsgeschichte* (1933), p. 83, where he dates it after the captivity of 597 B. C., cf. 1. 10f.; W. Staerk in ZAW 51 (1933), pp. 1ff.; H. Gunkel and J. Begrich in *Einleitung in die Psalmen,* pp. 407-415; S. Mowinckel, *Psalmenstudien* III (1923), pp. 24-29. See also Charles Venn Pilcher: *Three Hebrew Prophets,* for Nahum and Habakkuk; and H. Gunkel: "The Close of Micah," in his *What Remains of the Old Testament.*

14. This eschatological meaning of 1. 5-11, as over against the "immanent historical," is illuminatingly substantiated by W. Staerk in, "Zu Habakuk 1. 5-11. Geschichte oder Mythos," in ZAW 51 (1933), pp. 1-28.

15. His retreat might have been a mountaintop; cf. Balaam, Numbers 22. 40; Moses, Exodus 33. 21; Elijah, 1 Kings 19. 11, or a tower, or a place on the roof of his house.

16. Cf. Stephen Langdon: *Building Inscriptions of the Neo-Babylonian Empire,* Part I, p. 5. For first building enterprises cf. ibid., No. 9, col. 1, 41-51, the wall called Imgur-Bel; No. 4, col. 1, 14-30; No. 5, col. 1, 16-24, called Ebarra; No. 12, col. 1, 28-37; No. 17, col. 2, 8-36, called E-temin-anki; Stephen Langdon dates his rebuilding of the Temple at Sippar in 597-6 B. C., and the East Wall, the zikkurat E-temin-anki, the city wall, Esagila, Ezida in Borsippa, Temples in Larsa, Ur Dilbat, Bas, and Erech, the southern palace, and two graves and walls between Opis and Sippar as before 595 B. C., ibid., chapter I, esp. p. 8.

17. These dragons of chaos, disorder, and evil are here given eschatological significance; cf. J. Hempel: "Drache," in RGG[2] I, 1996-1999; cf. also H. Gunkel: *Schöpfung und Chaos,* pp. 46ff., 64ff.

18. Stephen Langdon: op. cit., p. 5.

274

NOTES

19. I agree with E. Sellin and B. Duhm (although not accepting Duhm's date), that, contrary to the opinion of most interpreters, this chapter is authentic, and that a real visionary experience of Habakkuk underlies it.

20. Cf. the illuminating words of C. V. Pilcher: *Three Hebrew Prophets*, p. 137f.; cf. also the illuminating passage with its parallel concepts in Psalm 77. 17-20; cf. also the conception of the chaotic floods over which Yahweh is master in Psalm 93. 3; and cf. the priestly account of creation, Genesis 1.

21. Cf. A. B. Davidson: *Habakkuk* (Cambridge Bible), on 3. 17-19.

CHAPTER VIII: NOTES ON JEREMIAH OF ANATHOTH

1. Ca. 645 B. C., cf. Jeremiah 1. 2. The dates of the reign of Josiah are spring 639/8 to summer of 609, so J. Begrich. Jeremiah was quite probably under twenty when his call came, cf. J. Skinner: *Prophecy and Religion,* p. 24, note 1, on *na'ar*. If at 626 he was nineteen, he was born c. 645 B. C., which was the fifty-first year of the reign of Manasseh, whose dates are spring of 696/5 to spring of 642/1.

2. Cf. K. Gross: "Hoseas Einfluss auf Jeremias Anschauungen, in N K Z 42 (1931), 241-55; 327-43. Jeremiah, in his ethnological connections, was not a Judaean but an Israelite, as Anathoth belonged in the old tribal limits of Benjamin, cf. Jeremiah 1. 1; 32. 8; 37. 12.

3. Cf. the suggestive, imaginative words of H. Schmidt: *Die grossen Propheten*[2], p. 206. Just such a tree the author saw outside the door of the American colony in Jerusalem on March 6, 1930, in its brilliant flowering beauty.

4. Jeremiah here makes use of a play upon words: the twig of *shāqēdh* (wakeful tree) suggests that Yahweh is *shōqēdh,* continuously "awake."

5. Deuteronomy 12–26, 28. T. H. Robinson inclines to the view that the original document included also the horta-

tory introduction, 4. 44–11, cf. *An Introduction to the O. T.,* p. 45f. J. Skinner: *Prophecy and Religion,* p. 91, confines it to the legislative kernel of chapters 12-26.

6. Cf. the discriminating words of T. H. Robinson, in Oesterley and Robinson: *An O. T. Introduction,* p. 308f.

7. The term *mishpat* (judgment, custom) here means the "manner" of life Yahweh requires, the law of their being as Yahweh's worshipers; cf. J. Skinner: *Prophecy and Religion,* p. 139 (note).

8. Thus Duhm suggestively renders vs. 8b, and for interpretation, cf. T. H. Robinson, op. cit., p. 308f.

9. Cf. J. Skinner: op. cit., p. 235.

10. So B. Duhm plausibly suggests, cf. J. Skinner: op. cit., p. 169.

11. Cf. Jeremiah 36. 23, as translated by A. R. Gordon, in *The Old Testament, An American Translation.*

12. Cf. Jeremiah 27. 1, reading, with 3 MSS and Syriac, Zedekiah, instead of Jehoiakim, and dating it (cf. Jeremiah 28. 1) in the fourth year of Zedekiah, c. 594 B. C., cf. A. S. Peake, *Jeremiah,* Vol. 2, pp. 39ff.

13. 593 B. C., cf. J. H. Breasted: *History of Egypt,* p. 585.

14. A. S. Peake: *Jeremiah,* Vol. 2, p. 170, places this on the same day. I put it immediately upon release from the dungeon, 37. 17.

15. This is the meaning of "the court of the guard," cf. S. R. Driver: *Jeremiah,* p. 367.

16. Cf. also for his right and duty in such a case, Leviticus 25. 25, and Ruth 4. 3f.

17. About eleven dollars, but relatively of much greater value then; cf., J. E. McFadyen: *Jeremiah in Modern Speech,* p. 210.

CHRONOLOGICAL TABLE

ALL DATES ARE B. C.

Jeroboam II, king of Israel	787-747
Uzziah, king of Judah	785-747
Ministry of Amos of Tekoa	760
Jotham of Judah, regent 758-747, king	747-743
Ministry of Hosea of Ephraim	747-722
Ministry of Isaiah of Jerusalem	747-701
Zechariah, king of Israel (6 months)	747-746
Shallum, king of Israel (1 month)	746
Menahem, king of Israel	746-737
Tiglath-pileser (Pul) of Assyria	745-727
Ahaz, king of Judah	742-725
Tiglath-pileser's 1st campaign into West	740
Menahem, king of Israel, pays him tribute	738
Pekahiah, king of Israel	736-735
Pekah, king of Israel	734-733
Plot of Syria and Ephraim vs. Judah	734
Tiglath-pileser's third campaign into West	733-732
Tiglath-pileser captures and loots Gaza	733
Tiglath-pileser overruns and reduces Israel	733
He displaces Pekah by Hoshea	733
Hoshea, king of Israel	732-724
Fall of Damascus to Tiglath-pileser	732
Ahaz pays tribute to Tiglath-pileser	732
Shalmaneser V of Assyria	727-722
Hezekiah, king of Judah	725-697
Ministry of Micah of Moresheth-Gath	725-694
So (Sibu) of Egypt arouses Hoshea to revolt	725
Shalmaneser V besieges Samaria	724-721
Sargon of Assyria	722-705
Fall of Samaria to Sargon of Assyria	721
Merodach-baladan (the Chaldaean), king of Babylon	721
Sargon puts down rebellion of Hamath	720
Battle of Raphia (Sargon vs. So and Hanno)	718
Bocchoris of Ethiopia pays Sargon tribute	718-712
Revolt of Azuri of Ashdod vs. Assyria	714-711
Shabaka takes initiative vs. Assyria	712-700
Sargon's tartan puts down Ashdod's revolt	711
Sargon ousts Merodach-baladan from Babylon	709

Sennacherib of Assyria	705-681
Merodach-baladan regains throne of Babylon	705
Merodach-baladan sends delegation to Jerusalem	705
Sennacherib ousts Merodach-baladan from Babylon	703
Sennacherib's expedition into Judah	701
Manasseh, king of Judah	696-642
Taharkah, Pharaoh of Egypt	688-663
Esarhaddon of Assyria	681-668
Manasseh pays him tribute at Tyre	677
Esarhaddon invades Egypt and captures Memphis	668
Ashurbanipal of Assyria	668-626
Ashurbanipal drives Tanutamon from Memphis	663
Psammetichus I of Egypt	663-609
Ashurbanipal sacks Thebes (No Amon)	661
Shamash-shum-ukin rebels vs. Assyria	652
Jeremiah born	c.645
Psammetichus I throws off Assyrian yoke	645
Josiah, king of Judah	639-609
The Scythian invasion	630-625
Ministry of Zephaniah of Jerusalem	630
Ashur-etil-ilani of Assyria	626-622
Ministry of Jeremiah of Anathoth	626-586
Nabopolassar founds the Chaldaean Empire	625
Cyaxares the Mede besieges Nineveh	625
Sin-shar-ishkun of Assyria	622-612
Josiah's rebellion and the Deuteronomic reform	621
Nabopolassar defeats Assyrians at Qablinu	616
Psammetichus I allies himself with Assyrians	616
Nabopolassar defeats Assyrians	615
Cyaxares in alliance with Nabopolassar vs. Assyria	615-612
Fall of Nineveh to Chaldaeans and Medes	612
Ministry of Nahum of Elkosh	612
Ashur-uballit sets up Assyrian throne at Harran	612
Nabopolassar the Chaldaean captures Harran	611
Necho, Pharaoh of Egypt	609-593
Necho advances to help Assyrians at Harran	609
Josiah killed at Megiddo	609

277

CHRONOLOGICAL TABLE

BIBLIOGRAPHY

KEY TO ABBREVIATIONS

AASOR   Annual of the American Schools of Oriental Research, New Haven, Conn.

AJSL   American Journal of Semitic Languages and Literatures, Chicago.

ABC   Abingdon Bible Commentary, N. Y., Abingdon, 1929.

BA   Beiträge zur Assyriologie und vergleichenden semitischen Sprachwissenschaft, Leipzig.

BASOR   Bulletin of the American Schools of Oriental Research, New Haven, Conn.

ERE   Encyclopaedia of Religion and Ethics, N. Y., Scribner's.

HDB   Hastings Dictionary of the Bible, N. Y., Scribner's.

ICC   International Critical Commentary, N. Y., Scribner's.

JBL   Journal of Biblical Literature, Philadelphia, Pa.

NKZ   Neue kirchliche Zeitschrift, Leipzig, Deichert.

OLZ   Orientalische Literaturzeitung, Leipzig.

PC   A. S. Peake's Commentary on the Bible, N. Y., Nelson.

PEFQS   Palestine Exploration Fund Quarterly Statement, London.

PJB   Palästinajahrbuch, Berlin.

RGG[2]   Die Religion in Geschichte und Gegenwart,[2] Tübingen.

TSK   Theologische Studien und Kritiken, Stuttgart and Gotha.

ZDMG   Zeitschrift der deutschen morgenländischen Gesellschaft, Leipzig.

ZDPV   Zeitschrift des deutschen Palästina-Vereins, Leipzig.

ZAW   Zeitschrift für die alttestamentliche Wissenschaft, Giessen.

Hebrew and Greek Texts of the Prophetic Books

Kittel, R.: *Biblia Hebraica,* Third edition edited by A. Alt, O. Eissfeldt, and (for Masoretic text) P. Kahle, Stuttgart, Privilegierte Württembergische Bibelanstalt, 1929-1933.

Ralphs, Alfred: *Septuaginta,* Vol. 2, *Libri poetici et prophetici,* Stuttgart, Privilegierte Württembergische Bibelanstalt.

Old Testament Introductions to the Prophetic Books

Eissfeldt, O.: *Einleitung in das alte Testament,* Tübingen, Mohr, 1934.

Oesterley, W. O. E., and Robinson, T. H.: *An Introduction to the Books of the O. T.,* N. Y., Macmillan, 1934.

History and Geography of the Ancient Near East

Barton, G. A.: *Archaeology and the Bible[7],* Philadelphia, American S. S. Union, 1937.

Begrich, Joachim: *Die Chronologie der Könige von Israel und Juda,* Tübingen, Mohr, 1929.

Breasted, J. H.: *Ancient Records of Egypt,* Vol. 4, Chicago, U. of C., 1906.

Breasted, J. H.: *A History of Egypt,*[2] N. Y., Scribner's, 1909.

Goodspeed, G. S.: *A History of the Babylonians and Assyrians,* N. Y., Scribner's, 1915.

Hall, H. R.: *The Ancient History of the Near East.*

Luckenbill, D. D.: *Ancient Records of Assyria and Babylonia,* 2 Vols., 1913, Chicago, U. of C., 1927.

Maspero, G.: *The Passing of the Empires* (850 B. C. to 330 B. C.), London, SPCK, 1900.

Olmstead, A. T.: *History of Assyria,* N. Y., Scribner's, 1923.

Olmstead, A. T.: *History of Palestine and Syria,* N. Y., Scribner's, 1931.

Robinson, H. W.: *The History of Israel,* N. Y., Scribner's, 1938.

Robinson, T. H.: *The Decline and Fall of the Hebrew Kingdoms,* Oxford, Clarendon, 1926.

Robinson, T. H.: *A History of Israel,* Vol. I, Oxford, Clarendon, 1932.

Rogers, R. W.: *Cuneiform Parallels to the O. T.,* N. Y., Eaton and Mains, 1912.

Rogers, R. W.: *A History of Babylonia and Assyria*[3], Vol. II, N. Y., Eaton, 1900.

Schrader, E.: *Keilinschriftliche Bibliothek,* Vols. I and II, Berlin, Reuther, 1889-90.

Smith, G. A., and Bartholomew, J. G.: *Atlas of the Historical Geography of the Holy Land,* London, Hodder, 1931.

Smith, G. A.: *The Historical Geography of the Holy Land,*[25] London, Hodder, 1931.

Smith, Sidney, in *Cambridge Ancient History* III, pp. 1-131.

Thompson, R. Campbell: "Assyria" in CAH II (1924), 227-251.

Old Testament Religion

Cook, S. A.: *The Old Testament: A Reinterpretation,* London, SPCK, 1936.

BIBLIOGRAPHY

Cook, S. A.: *The "Truth" of the Bible*, N. Y., Macmillan, 1938.

Comins, H. L.: *The Jewish Prophets*, Cincinnati, Union of Am. Heb. Congregations, 1936.

Knudson, A. C.: *The Religious Teachings of the O. T.*, N. Y., Abingdon, 1918.

Leslie, E. A.: *Old Testament Religion in the Light of Its Canaanite Background*, N. Y., Abingdon, 1936.

Lods, A.: *Israel From Its Beginnings to the Middle of the Eighth Century*, N. Y., Knopf, 1932.

Oesterley, W. O. E., and Robinson, T. H.: *Hebrew Religion*[2], N. Y., Macmillan, 1927.

Pedersen, J.: *Israel, Its Life and Culture*, London, Oxford Uni. Press, 1926.

Robinson, H. W. (editor): *Record and Revelation*, Oxford, Clarendon, 1938.

Sellin, E.: *Israelitisch-jüdische Religionsgeschichte*, Leipzig, Quelle u. Meyer, 1933.

Sellin, E.: *Theologie des alten Testaments*[2], Leipzig, Quelle u. Meyer, 1936.

Smith, W. R.: *Lectures on the Religion of the Semites*, annotated and supplemented by S. A. Cook, London, Black, 1927.

Welch, A. C.: *The Religion of Israel Under the Kingdom*, Edinburgh, Clark, 1912.

Old Testament Prophets

Cornill, C. H.: *The Prophets of Israel*, N. Y., Putnam's, 1899.

Davidson, A. B.: *Old Testament Prophecy*, Edinburgh, Clark, 1903.

Driver, S. R.: *The Minor Prophets* II (Nah., Hab., Zeph., Hagg., Zech., Mal.) in the New Century Bible, Edinburgh, Jack.

Duhm, B.: *Israels Propheten*,[2] Tübingen, Mohr, 1922.

Eiselen, F. C.: *The Prophetic Books of the O. T.*, 2 Vols., N. Y., Abingdon, 1923.

Gordon, A. R.: *The Prophets of the O. T.*, N. Y., Hodder, 1916.

Graham, W. C.: *The Prophets and Israel's Culture*, Chicago, U. of C., 1934.

Horton, R. F.: *The Minor Prophets* I (Hos., Joel, Am., Obad., Jonah, Mic.) in The New Century Bible, Edinburgh, Jack.

Knudson, A. C.: *Beacon Lights of Prophecy,* N. Y., Abingdon, 1924.

Lods, A.: *The Prophets and the Rise of Judaism,* N. Y., Dutton, 1937.

Orchard, W. E.: *The Oracles of God,* London, Clarke, 1922.

Porteous, N. W.: "The Religion of Israel (2) Prophecy," in H. W. Robinson's *Record and Revelation* (see under O. T. Religion), pp. 216-249.

Robinson, H. W.: "The Psychology and Metaphysic of 'Thus saith Yahweh,'" in ZAW41 (1923), 1-15.

Robinson, T. H.: "The Ecstatic Element in O. T. Prophecy," in *Expositor* 21 (1921), 217-38.

Robinson, T. H.: *Prophecy and the Prophets in Ancient Israel,* N. Y., Scribner's, 1923.

Robinson, T. H.: *Das zwölf kleinen Propheten* (Hosea to Micah), in O. Eissfeldt's *Handbuch zum alten Testament,* Tübingen, Mohr, 1938.

Sellin, E.: *Das Zwölfprophetenbuch* II [2] and [3] (Nahum to Malachi), in E. Sellin's *Kommentar zum alten Testament,* Leipzig, Dichert, 1930.

Smith, G. A.: *The Book of the Twelve Prophets,*[2] 2 Vols., London, Hodder, 1928.

Smith, J. M. P.: *The Prophets and Their Times,* Chicago, U. of C., 1925.

Smith, W. R.: *The Prophets of Israel,*[2] London, Black, 1895.

Thomas, D. E.: "The Psychological Approach to Prophecy," in *American Journal of Theology* 18 (1914), 241-256.

Wellhausen, J.: *Die kleinen Propheten, übersetz mit Noten,* in *Skizzen und Vorarbeiten,* Heft 5, Berlin, Reimer, 1892.

Wolfe, R. E.: "The Editing of the Book of the Twelve," in ZAW 53 (1935), 90-130.

Amos of Tekoa

Baumann, E.: *Der Aufbau der Amosreden,* Beiheft VII ZAW, Giessen, Ricker, 1903.

BIBLIOGRAPHY

Budde, K.: *Zur Geschichte des Buches Amos,* Beiheft XXVII ZAW, Giessen, Töpelmann, 1914.

Budde, K.: "Zur Text und Auslegung des Buches Amos," in JBL 1924, 46-131; 1925, 63-122.

Cripps, R. S.: *A Critical and Exegetical Commentary on the Book of Amos,* London, Macmillan, 1930.

Crowfoot, J. W.: "The Ivories from Samaria," in PEFQS 1933, 7-26, plates I-III.

Driver, S. R.: *Joel and Amos* (Cambridge Bible), Cambridge, University Press, 1915.

Edghill, E. A.: *The Book of Amos* (Westminster Commentary), London, Methuen, 1914.

Ferguson, Henry: "The Verb *shaphaṭ,*" in JBL, 1888, 130-36.

Gressmann, H.: *Die älteste Geschichtsschreibung und Prophetie Israels,* in *Die Schriften des alten Testaments,* Abteilung 2, Band 1, Göttingen, Vandenhoeck u. Ruprecht, 1921.

Gwynn, R. M.: *The Book of Amos,* Cambridge, Uni. Press, 1927.

Josephus: *Antiquities* IX, 10, W. Whiston (editor), p. 299.

Löhr, Max: *Untersuchungen zum Buch Amos,* Beiheft IV ZAW, Giessen, Ricker, 1901.

Morgenstern, J.: "Amos Studies I," in *Hebrew Union College Annual,* 1937.

Robinson, T. H.: *The Book of Amos.* Hebrew text edited with critical and grammatical notes, London, SPCK, 1923.

Schrader, E.: *Die Keilinschriften und das alte Testament,* second edition, Giessen, Ricker, 1883; third edition by H. Zimmern and H. Winckler, Berlin, Reuther, 1903.

Smith, J. M. P.: *A Commentary on the Books of Amos, Hosea, and Micah,* N. Y., Macmillan, 1914.

Weiser, A.: *Die Prophetie des Amos,* in Beiheft 53 ZAW, 1929.

Welch, A. C.: *Prophet and Priest in Old Israel,* London, SCM, 1936.

Williams, A. L.: *The Minor Prophets Unfolded,* Vol. 2 (Joel and Amos), London, SPCK, 1918.

Zimmern, A.: "Die Beschwörungstäfel Surpu," in *Beiträge*

zur Kenntnis der Babylonischer Religion, Leipzig, Hinrichs, 1901.

Hosea of Ephraim

Allwohn, A.: *Die Ehe des Propheten Hosea in psychoanalytischer Beleuchtung,* Giessen, Töpelmann, 1926.

Alt, A.: "Hosea 5. 8–6. 6, in NKZ 30 (1919), 537-68.

Brown, Sydney L.: *The Book of Hosea* (Westminster Commentary), London, Methuen, 1932.

Cheyne, T. K.: *Hosea* (The Cambridge Bible), Cambridge, Uni. Press, 1889.

Cook, S. A.: *The Old Testament: A Reinterpretation.*

Crafter, T. W.: *The Book of Hosea,* Cambridge, Uni. Press, 1923.

vonGall, A. F.: *Altisraelitsche Kultstätten,* in Beiheft III ZAW, Giessen, Ricker, 1898.

Gray, G. B.: *Sacrifice in the O. T.,* Oxford, Clarendon, 1925.

Gunkel, H.: "Hosea," in RGG[2] II (1928), 2020-2023.

Heilprin, M.: *The Historical Poetry of the Ancient Hebrews,* 2 Vols., N. Y., Appleton, 1879-80.

Hölscher, G.: *Die Propheten,* Leipzig, Hinrichs, 1914.

Mowinckel, S.: *Psalmenstudien* II (*Das Thronbesteigungsfest Jahwäs und der Ursprung der Eschatologie*), Kristiania, Dybwad, 1922.

Nyberg, H.: *Studien zum Hoseabuche,* Upsala, Lundequist, 1935.

Peters, N.: *Osee und die Geschichte,* Paderborn, Bonifaciusdruckerei, 1924.

Schmidt, H.: "Die Ehe des Hosea," in ZAW 42 (1924), 245-72.

Scott, Melville: *The Message of Hosea,* London, SPCK, 1921.

Sellin, E.: "Die geschichtliche Orientierung der Prophetie des Hosea," in NKZ 36 (1925), 607-58, 807.

Skinner, J.: *I and II Kings* (New Century Bible).

Smith, W. R.: *The Prophets of Israel.*[2]

Theophratus: *Enquiry into Plants,* Sir Arthur Hort, Translator, Book 6, sec. 7. 3, in Vol. II, p. 47 (for Adonis gardens), N. Y., Putnam's, 1916.

Isaiah of Jerusalem

Albright, W. F.: "The Assyrian March on Jerusalem," in AASOR IV (1924), Appendix IV, 134-140.

Balla, E.: "Jesaja und Jesajabuch," in RGG² III, 93-103.

Barton, G. A.: "Demons and Spirits" (6, on seraphim), in ERE Vol. 4, p. 595.

Boutflower, Chas.: *The Book of Isaiah in the Light of the Assyrian Monuments,* London, SPCK, 1930.

Budde, K.: *Jesaja's Erleben; eine gemeinverständliche Auslegung der Denkschrift des Propheten* (Kap. 6. 1-9. 6), Gotha, Klotz, 1928.

Burney, C. F.: *Notes on the Hebrew Text of the Books of Kings,* Oxford, Clarendon, 1903.

Cheyne, T. K.: *The Prophecies of Isaiah,* N. Y., Whitaker, 1884.

Cheyne, T. K.: *The Book of the Prophet Isaiah* (Polychrome Edition), N. Y., Dodd, Mead and Co., 1898.

Davidson, A. B.: *The Called of God,* Edinburgh, 1902.

Driver, S. R.: *Deuteronomy* (ICC), N. Y., Scribner's, 1895.

Duhm, B.: *Das Buch Jesaia übersetz und erklärt,* in W. Nowack's *Göttinger Handkommentar zum alten Testament,* Göttingen, Vandenhoeck u. Ruprecht, 1914.

Gordon, A. R.: *The Faith of Isaiah,* London, Clarke, 1919.

Graham, W. C.: "Notes on the Interpretation of Isaiah 5. 1-14," in AJSL 45(1929), 167-78.

Gray, G. B.: *Isaiah I-XXVII* (ICC), N. Y., Scribner's, 1912.

Herodotus: *History* II, 141; III, 120, ed. by A. D. Godley, N. Y., Heinemann, 1926.

Kellner, M. L.: *The Prophecies of Isaiah: an outline study of Isaiah's writings in the chronological order in connection with the contemporary Assyrio-Babylonian records,* Cambridge, Mass., Graves and Henry, 1895.

Luckenbill, D. D.: *The Annals of Sennacherib,* Chicago, U. of C., 1924.

Marti, K.: *Jesaja,* in K. Marti's *Kurzer Hand Commentar zum Alten Testament,* Tübingen, Mohr, 1900.

Mitchell, H. G.: *Isaiah: A Study of Chapters 1-11,* N. Y., 1897.

Olmstead, A. T.: *Western Asia in the Days of Sargon of Assyria,* Lancaster, Pa., New Era Printing Co., 1906.

Plutarch: *Of Isis and Osiris,* 15-16, in *Morals,* ed. by W. Goodwin; Boston, Little, Brown & Co., 1874.

Procksch, O.: *Jesaia* I, in E. Sellin's *Kommentar zum A. T.,* Leipzig, Deichert, 1930.

Rost, Paul: *Die Keilinschrifttexte Tiglat-pilesers III,* Leipzig, E. Pfeiffer, 1893.

Schmidt, H.: *Die grossen Propheten.*[2]

Skinner, John: *Isaiah I-XXXIX* (Cambridge Bible), 1910.

Smith, G. A.: *The Book of Isaiah,* new revised ed., Vol. I, N. Y., Doran, 1927.

Smith, Sidney, *The First Campaign of Sennacherib, King of Assyria, B.C. 705-681,* London, Luzac & Co., 1921.

Thomson, C. H., and Skinner, John: *Isaiah* I-XXXIX, Cambridge, Uni. Press, 1910-14.

Wade, G. W.: *Isaiah* (Westminster Commentary), N. Y., Gorham, 1912.

Micah of Moresheth-Gath

Albright, W. F.: "Contributions to the Historical Geography of Palestine," in AASORII(1923), 4, 8-11.

Budde, K.: "Das Rätsel von Micah 1," in ZAW 37(1917), 77-108.

Budde, K.: "Micha 2 und 3," in ZAW 38(1920), 2-22.

Cheyne, T. K.: *Micah* (Cambridge Bible), Cambridge, Uni. Press, 1895.

Duhm, B.: "Anmerkungen zu den zwölf Propheten," in ZAW 31(1911), 81-93.

Graham, W. C., and May, H. G.: *Culture and Conscience,* Chicago, U. of C., 1936.

Graham,W. C.: "The Interpretation of Micah 1. 10-16," in AJSL 47(1931), 237-258.

Gressmann, H.: *Altorientalische Texte* (Vol. I) *zum A. T.,*[2] Berlin, Gruyter, 1926.

Jeremias, Joachim: "Moreseth-Gath, die Heimat des Propheten Micha," in PJB 19(1923), 42-53.

Lindblom, J.: "Micha literarisch untersucht," in *Acta Academiae aboensis, Humaniora,* VI, 2, Helsingfors, 1929.

Lucian: *De Dea Syria,* translated in H. A. Strong and J. Garstang: *The Syrian Goddess,* London, Constable, 1913.

BIBLIOGRAPHY

Nestle, G.: "Wo ist der Geburtsort des Propheten Nahum?," in ZDPV I, 222-5.

Ptolemy, Claudius: *Geographia*, I, Part 2, ed. C. Müller, Paris, A. F. Didot, 1883-1901.

Smith, J. M. P.: *Micah, Zephaniah, Nahum* (ICC), N. Y., Scribner's, 1911.

Starkey, J. L.: "Excavations at Tell el-Duweir, 1933-34," in PEFQS 1934, 164-175, plate V, fig. 2; 1934-35, in PEFQS 1935, 198-207; and 1935-6, in PEFQS 1936, 178-189.

Starkey, J. L.: "Lachish as Illustrating Bible History," in PEFQS 1937, 171-179, especially for Lachish as "a stronghold of heathen practices."

Zephaniah of Jerusalem

Baudissin, W.: "Moloch," in *Realencyklopädie*, Vol. 13, 269-303, esp. p. 278.

Canaan, T.: *Aberglaube und Volksmedezin im Lande der Bibel*, Hamburg, Friederichsen, 1914.

Charles, R. H.: "The Martyrdom of Isaiah," 5. 1-14, in his *Apocrypha and Pseudepigrapha*, Vol. II, Oxford, Clarendon, 1913.

Cook, S. A.: "The Rise and Fall of Judah" (Chapter 18), 388-408, in *Cambridge Ancient History*, III.

Cornill, C. H.: "Die Prophetie Zephanjas," in TSK 89 (1916), 297-332.

Cramer, Carl F.: *Scythische Denkmäler in Palästina*, Kiel and Hamburg, Bohn, 1777.

Davidson, A. B.: *Zephaniah* (Cambridge Bible), Cambridge, Uni. Press, 1920.

Ferguson, Henry: "The Historical Testimony of the Prophet Zephaniah," in JBL 1883, 42-59.

Gordon, A. R.: "Zephaniah," in PC, 569-571.

Graham, W. C.: "Zephaniah," in ABC, 809-814.

Gray, G. B.: *Studies in Hebrew Proper Names*, London, Black, 1896.

Herodotus: I, 103-106, Trans. by A. D. Godley (Loeb Class. Lib.), Vol. I (Books I and II), N. Y., Heinemann, 1926.

Oesterley, W. O. E.: *The Sacred Dance*, Cambridge, 1923.

Pilcher, C. V.: *Three Hebrew Prophets and the Passing of Empires*, London, Religious Tract Soc., 1931.

287

vonPrashek, Justin V.: *Geschichte der Meder und Perser,* Vol. I, Gotha, 1906.

Schwally, F.: "Das Buch Sefanjâ, eine historisch-kritische Untersuchung," in ZAW 10(1890), 165-240.

Smith, J. M. P.: *Zephaniah,* see under Micah.

Stonehouse, G. G.: *Zephaniah* (Westminster Commentary), London, Methuen, 1929.

Volz, P.: "Zephanja und Zephanjabuch," in RGG² V, 2105f.

Nahum of Elkosh

Arnold, W. R.: "The Composition of Nahum 1. 2-2. 3," in ZAW 21 (1901), 225-65.

Billerbeck, A., and Jeremias, A.: "Der Untergang Nineveh's und die Weissagungsschrift des Nahum von Elkosch," in BA 3(1895), 86-188.

Davidson, A. B.: *Nahum* (Cambridge Bible), Cambridge, Uni. Press, 1896.

Diodorus the Sicilian, edited by Carl Müller, Paris, Didot, 1842; translated by G. Booth, *The Historical Library of Diodorus the Sicilian,* in 15 books, London, McDowall, 1814.

Ebeling, Erich: *Tod und Leben nach den Vorstellungen der Babylonier,* Berlin, Gruyter, 1931.

Eissfeldt, O.: "The Literature of Israel (3) Modern Criticism," in H. W. Robinson (ed.), *Record and Revelation,* 74-109.

Epiphanius, in J. P. Migne: *Patrologia Graeca,* Vol. 43, born near Eleutheropolis and to whom is ascribed *De Vitis Prophetarum.*

Eusebius, in A. Schoene, editor: *Eusebi Chronicorum,* Liber Prior, Berlin, Weidmannos, 1875.

Gadd, C. J.: *The Fall of Nineveh: the newly discovered Babylonian Chronicle, No. 21,901, in the British Museum,* London, Oxford Uni. Press, 1923.

Gadd, C. J.: "The Fall of Nineveh," from the *Proceedings of the British Academy,* Vol. X, pp. 473-478, 1923.

Gunkel, H.: "Nahum I," in ZAW 13(1893), 223-44.

Gunkel, H.: "Jesaia 33, eine prophetische Liturgie," in ZAW 42(1924), 177-208.

BIBLIOGRAPHY

Gunkel, H.: "Die Propheten als Schriftsteller und Dichter," in Einleitung (3) to H. Schmidt: *Die grossen Propheten*,[2] xlii-xlvii.

Haller, M.: "Nahum," in RGG[2] IV, 406-7.

Humbert, Paul: "Essai d'analyse de Nahoum 1. 2–2. 3," in ZAW 40 (1926), 266-280.

Humbert, Paul: Le Problème du livre de Nahoum," in *Revue d'histoire et de philosophie religieuses,* Strasbourg, 1932, 1-15.

Humbert, Paul: "La Vision de Nahoum 2. 4-11," in *Archiv für Orientforschung* 5(1928), 14-19.

Johnson, A. R.: "The Rôle of the King in the Jerusalem Cultus," Chapter 3, pp. 71-111, in S. H. Hooke: *The Labyrinth*, N. Y., Macmillan, 1935.

Josephus: *Contra Apionem* I, 19; concerning the history of Babylon by the Chaldaean Berosus, priest of the temple of Bel at Babylon, c. 330-250 B. C.

Josephus: *Antiquities,* Vol. VI (Book 9, 11, sections 239-41), trans. by Ralph Marcus, Cambridge, Uni. Press, 1937.

Kleinert, Paul: "Nahum und der Fall Nineves," in TSK 83 (1910), 501-34.

Lewy, Julius: "Forschungen zur alten Geschichte Vorderasiens," in *Mitteilungen der Vorderasiatisch-aegyptischen Gesellschaft,* Leipzig, Hinrichs, 1925.

Mowinckel, S.: *Psalmenstudien* II (*Das Thronbesteigungsfest Jahwäs*), and III (*Kultprophetie und prophetische Psalmen*), Kristiania, Dybwad, 1922-23.

Müller, W. Max: "Put," in HDB IV, 176-7.

Nestle, G.: "Where is the Birthplace of the Prophet Nahum to be Sought?," in PEFQS 1879, pp. 136-8.

Pfeiffer, R. H.: *Harvard Theological Review* 27(1934), p. 282.

Schmidt, H.: *Die Thronfahrt Jahwes am Fest der Jahreswende im alten Israel,* Tübingen, Mohr, 1927.

Sethe, K.: *Dramatische Texte zu altägyptischen Mysterienspielen,* I, Leipzig, Hinrichs, 1928.

Smith, J. M. P.: *Nahum,* see under Micah.

Smith, Sidney: *Babylonian Historical Texts relating to the capture and downfall of Babylon,* London, Methuen, 1924.

Snaith, N. M.: "The Religion of Israel (3) Worship," in H. W. Robinson (ed.): *Record and Revelation*, 250-274.

Steindorf, Georg: "Die keilinschriftliche Wiedergäbe ägyptischer Eigennamen," in BA, Vol. I(1890), 593-616.

Stonehouse, G. G.: *Nahum* (Westminster Commentary), 1929.

Weill, J.: "Nahum 2. 9-12 et Josèphe (Ant. IX, 11, secs. 239-241)," in *Revue Études Juives* 76 (1923), 96ff.

Welch, A. C.: *The Code of Deuteronomy; a new theory of its origin*, London, Clarke, 1924.

Habakkuk of Jerusalem

Balla, E.: "Habakuk," in RGG² II, 1156-7.

Budde, K.: "Habakuk," in ZDMG 84 (1930), 139-47.

Budde, K.: "Zum Text von Habakuk Kap. 1 u. 2," in OLZ 34(1931), 409-11.

Cannon, W. W.: "The Integrity of Habakkuk, cc. 1.2," in ZAW 43(1925), 62-90.

Davidson, A. B.: *Habakkuk* (Cambridge Bible), Cambridge, Uni. Press, 1896.

Driver, S. R.: "A Problem of Faith," in his *The Ideals of the Prophets*, 34-43, Edinburgh, Clark, 1915.

Gadd, C. H.: "The Fall of Nineveh," in D. D. Luckenbill: *Ancient Records of Assyria and Babylonia*, II, 1167-86.

Gunkel, H.: "Mythen und Mythologie in Israel," in RGG² IV, 629f.

Gunkel, H.: *Schöpfung und Chaos in Urzeit und Endzeit*, Göttingen, Vandenhoeck und Ruprecht, 1895.

Gunkel, H.: "The Close of Micah," in *What Remains of The O. T.* (for a prophetic liturgy), London, Allen and Unwin, 1928.

Gunkel, H., and Begrich, J.: *Einleitung in die Psalmen*, Göttingen, Vandenhoeck und Ruprecht, 1933.

Hempel, J.: "Drache," in RGG² I, 1996-99.

Herodotus: *The History of Herodotus*, trans. by G. Rawlinson, Vol. I, N. Y., Appleton, 1859.

Johnson, A. R.: "The Prophet in Israelite Worship," in *Expository Times* 47 (1936), 312-19.

Langdon, Stephen: *Building Inscriptions of the Neo-Babylonian Empire*, Paris, Leroux, 1905.

BIBLIOGRAPHY

Langdon, Stephen: *Die Neubabylonischen Königsin-schriften,* Leipzig, Hinrichs, 1912.

Lenormant, François: *Chaldean Magic: Its Origin and Development,* London, Bagster, 1878.

Lewy, J.: "Forschungen zur alten Geschichte Vordera-siens," see under Nahum.

Mowinckel, S.: *Psalmenstudien* III (*Kultprophetie und prophetische Psalmen*), 24-29 (1923).

Pilcher, C. V.: *Three Hebrew Prophets.*

Sellin, E.: *Einleitung in das alte Testament,*[5] Leipzig, Quelle und Meyer, 1929.

Sellin, E.: *Das Zwölfprophetenbuch,* on Habakkuk.

Sellin, E.: *Israelitisch-jüdische Religionsgeschichte,* p. 83.

Sellin, E.: *Theologie des alten Testaments.*[2]

Simpson, D. C.: "1 and 2 Kings," in *Abingdon Bible Commentary,* 412-438.

Stade, B.: "Habakuk," in ZAW 1884, 154-59.

Staerk, W.: "Zu Habakuk 1. 5-11 Geschichte oder Mythos," in ZAW 51 (1923), 1-28.

Stephens, F. J.: "The Babylonian Dragon Myth in Habakkuk 3," in JBL 43(1924), 290-91.

Wade, G. W.: *Habakkuk* (Westminster Commentary), London, Methuen, 1929.

Ward, Wm. Hayes: *Habakkuk* (ICC), N. Y., Scribner's, 1911.

Winckler, Hugo: *Untersuchungen zur altorientalischen Geschichte,* Leipzig, E. Pfeiffer, 1889.

Woolley, C. L.: *Carchemish,* Part II, London, British Museum, 1914-21.

Jeremiah of Anathoth

Albright, W. F.: "Two Great Discoveries Bearing on the Old and New Testaments," in BASOR 58 (1935), 2-3.

Albright, W. F.: "A Supplement to Jeremiah: The Lachish Ostraca," in BASOR 61(1936), 10-16.

Albright, W. F.: "Additional note" (to E. P. Blair, see below), pp. 25-26.

Alt, A.: PJB 22 (1926), 23-4, for identification of Anathoth with Ras el-Karrubeh.

Baumgartner, Walter: *Die Klagegedichte des Jeremia,* Beiheft 32 ZAW, Giessen, Töpelmann, 1917.

Binns, L. E.: *Jeremiah* (Westminster Commentary), London, Methuen, 1919.

Blair, E. P.: "Soundings at 'Anata (Roman Anathoth)," in BASOR 62(1936), 18-25.

Calkins, Raymond: *Jeremiah the Prophet*, N. Y., Macmillan, 1930.

Driver, S. R.: *The Book of the Prophet Jeremiah*, N. Y., Scribner, 1906.

Duhm, B.: *Jeremiah*, in *Kurzer Hand Commentar*, Tübingen, Mohr, 1901.

Erbt, Wilhelm: *Jeremia und seine Zeit*, Göttingen, Vandenhoeck u. Ruprecht, 1902.

Gordon, T. C.: *The Rebel Prophet*, N. Y., Harper, 1932.

Gross, Karl: "Hoseas Einfluss auf Jeremias Anschauungen," in NKZ, 42 (1931), 241-56, 327-43.

Haupert, Raymond S.: "Lachish—Frontier Fortress of Judah," in *The Biblical Archaeologist*, Vol. I (1938), No. 4, 21-32, New Haven, ASOR.

McFadyen, J. E.: *Jeremiah in Modern Speech*, London, Clarke, 1919.

Robinson, T. H.: "Baruch's Roll," in ZAW 42(1924), 209-21.

Peake, A. S.: *Jeremiah*, 2 Vols. (New Century Bible), N. Y., Frowde, 1910-12.

Robinson, T. H., and Oesterley, W. O. E.: *An Introduction to the O. T.* (on Deuteronomy).

Schmidt, H.: *Die grossen Propheten*.[2]

Skinner, John: *Prophecy and Religion*, Cambridge, Uni. Press, 1922.

Smith, G. A.: *Jeremiah*[4] (Baird Lecture), London, Hodder, 1929.

Starkey, J. L.: "Lachish as Illustrating Bible History," in PEFQS 1937, 171-179.

Streane, A. W.: *Jeremiah* (Cambridge Bible), Cambridge, Uni. Press, 1913.

Volz, P.: *Der Prophet Jeremia übersetzt und erklärt*[3], in E. Sellin's *Kommentar zum alten Testament*.

Welch, A. C.: *Jeremiah, His Time and His Work*, London, Oxford Uni. Press, 1928.

INDEX OF BIBLICAL REFERENCES

INDEX OF BIBLICAL REFERENCES

INDEX OF BIBLICAL REFERENCES

INDEX OF BIBLICAL REFERENCES

INDEX OF BIBLICAL REFERENCES

INDEX OF BIBLICAL REFERENCES

INDEX OF SUBJECT MATTER AND AUTHORITIES

(d) indicates that reference is to a deity

INDEX OF SUBJECT MATTER, AUTHORITIES

INDEX OF SUBJECT MATTER, AUTHORITIES

INDEX OF SUBJECT MATTER, AUTHORITIES

INDEX OF SUBJECT MATTER, AUTHORITIES